LEGENDS FROM
DARKWOOD

Chapter 1............003

LEGENDS FROM
DARKWOOD

Chapter 2............037

GENDS FROM
DARKWOOD

Chapter 3............069

LEGENDS FROM
DARKWOOD

T 43814

D1214001

Chapter 4............100

LEGENDS FROM DARKWOOD
THE UNICORN HUNTERS

Artist - John Kantz
Writer- Christopher Reid
Graphic Designer - John Kantz and Guru e-FX
Cover Design - Guru e-FX
Layout - Paul Kilpatrick

Editor in Chief - Jochen Weltjens
President of Sales and Marketing - Lee Duhig
Art Direction - Guru e-FX
VP of Production - Rod Espinosa
Publisher - Joe Dunn
Founder - Ben Dunn

Come visit us online at www.antarctic-press.com

ANTARCTIC PRESS

Legends from Darkwood Pocket Manga Volume 1 by John Kantz and Christopher Reid

Antarctic Press
7272 Wurzbach Suite 204 San Antonio, TX 78240

Collects *Legends from Darkwood* issue 1-4
First published in 2003 by Antarctic Press.

"Give it back! GIVE IT BACK!!"

ISBN: 1-932453-49-0

Printed in China by Sung Fung Offset Binding Co. Ltd.

VOLUME 1

map by Richard Brooks

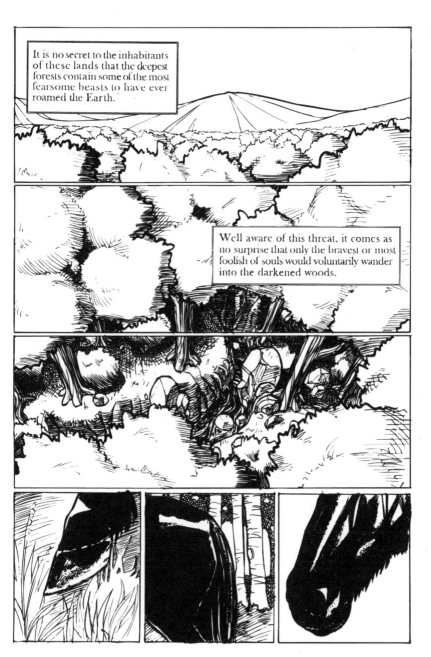

It is no secret to the inhabitants of these lands that the deepest forests contain some of the most fearsome beasts to have ever roamed the Earth.

Well aware of this threat, it comes as no surprise that only the bravest or most foolish of souls would voluntarily wander into the darkened woods.

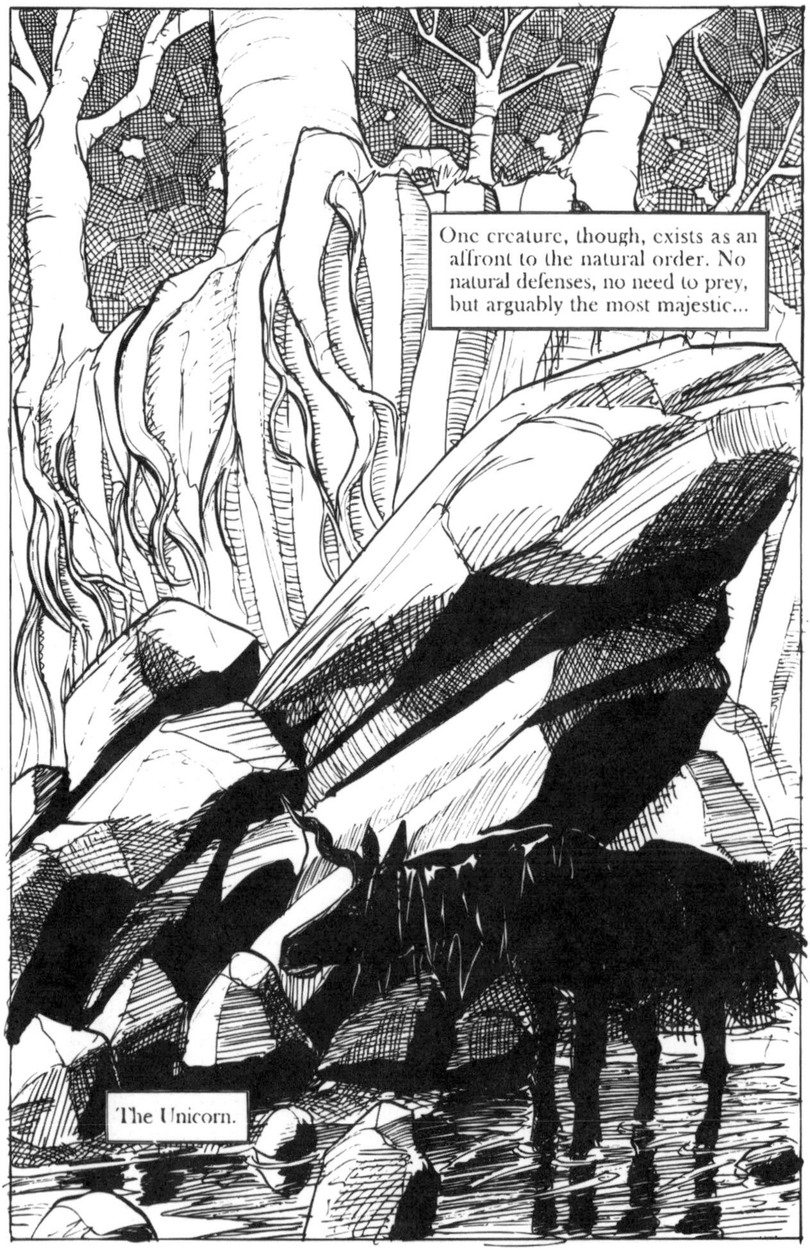
One creature, though, exists as an affront to the natural order. No natural defenses, no need to prey, but arguably the most majestic...
The Unicorn.

TO MOST THEY STILL LIVE ONLY IN LEGEND. UNLIKE THE GOBLINS AND ORCS, THEY KEEP TO THEMSELVES IN THE DEEPEST WOODS.

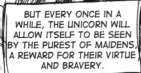

THE BLACK UNICORN! THE KING...

BUT EVERY ONCE IN A WHILE, THE UNICORN WILL ALLOW ITSELF TO BE SEEN BY THE PUREST OF MAIDENS, A REWARD FOR THEIR VIRTUE AND BRAVERY.

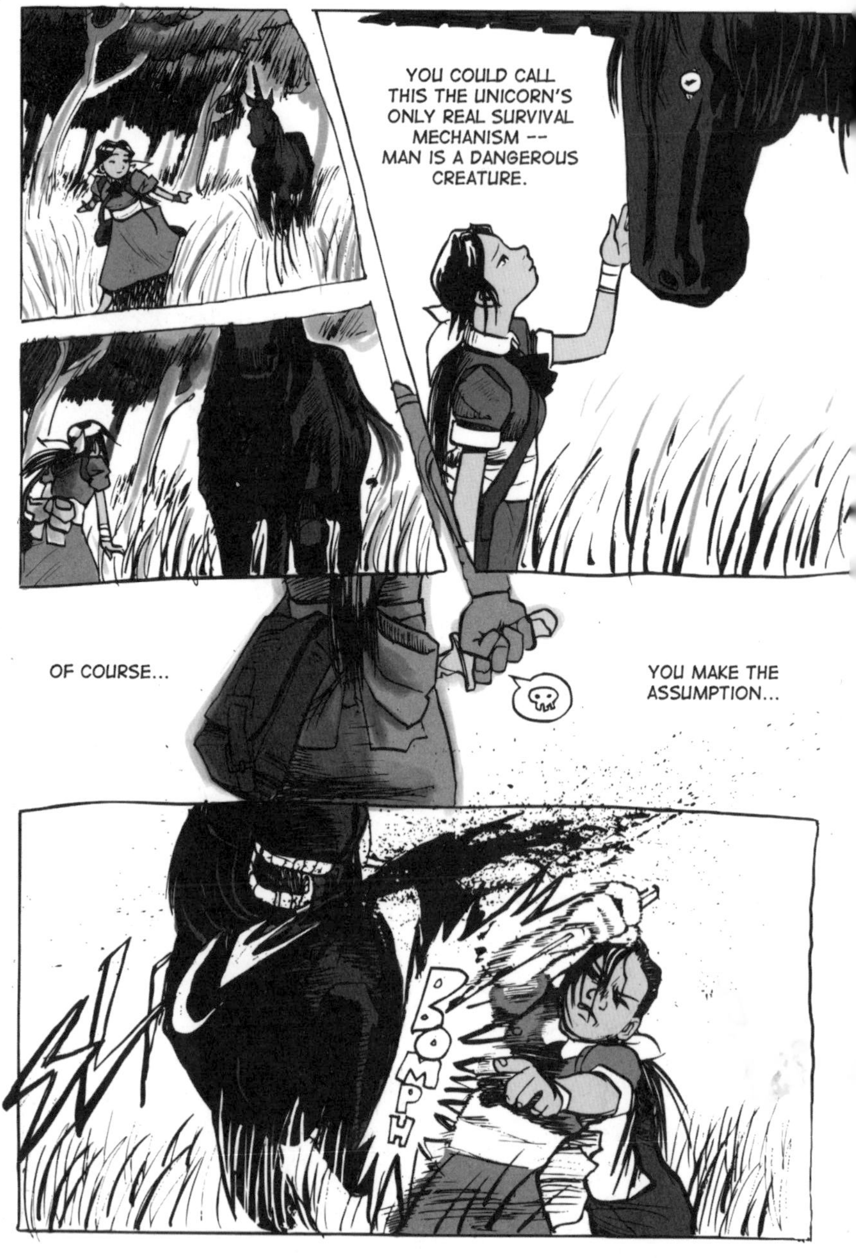
YOU COULD CALL THIS THE UNICORN'S ONLY REAL SURVIVAL MECHANISM -- MAN IS A DANGEROUS CREATURE.
OF COURSE...
YOU MAKE THE ASSUMPTION...
BOOMPH

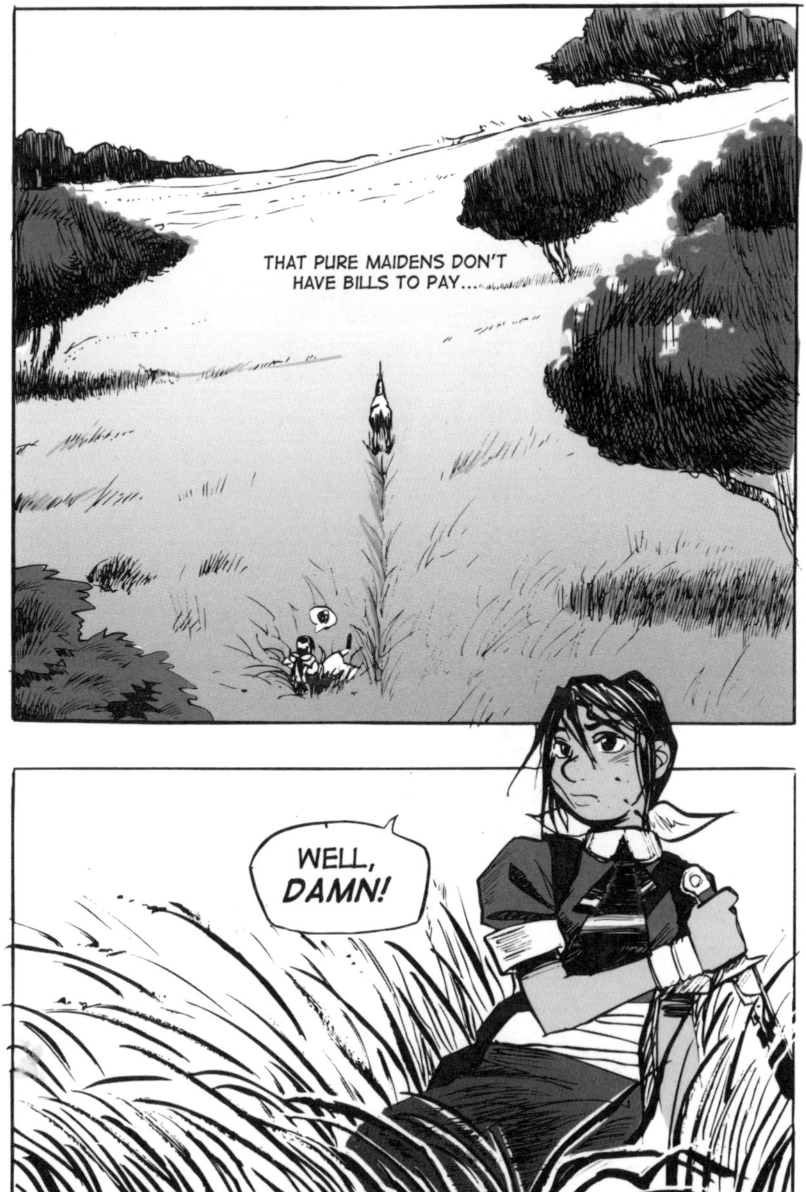
THAT PURE MAIDENS DON'T HAVE BILLS TO PAY...
WELL, DAMN!

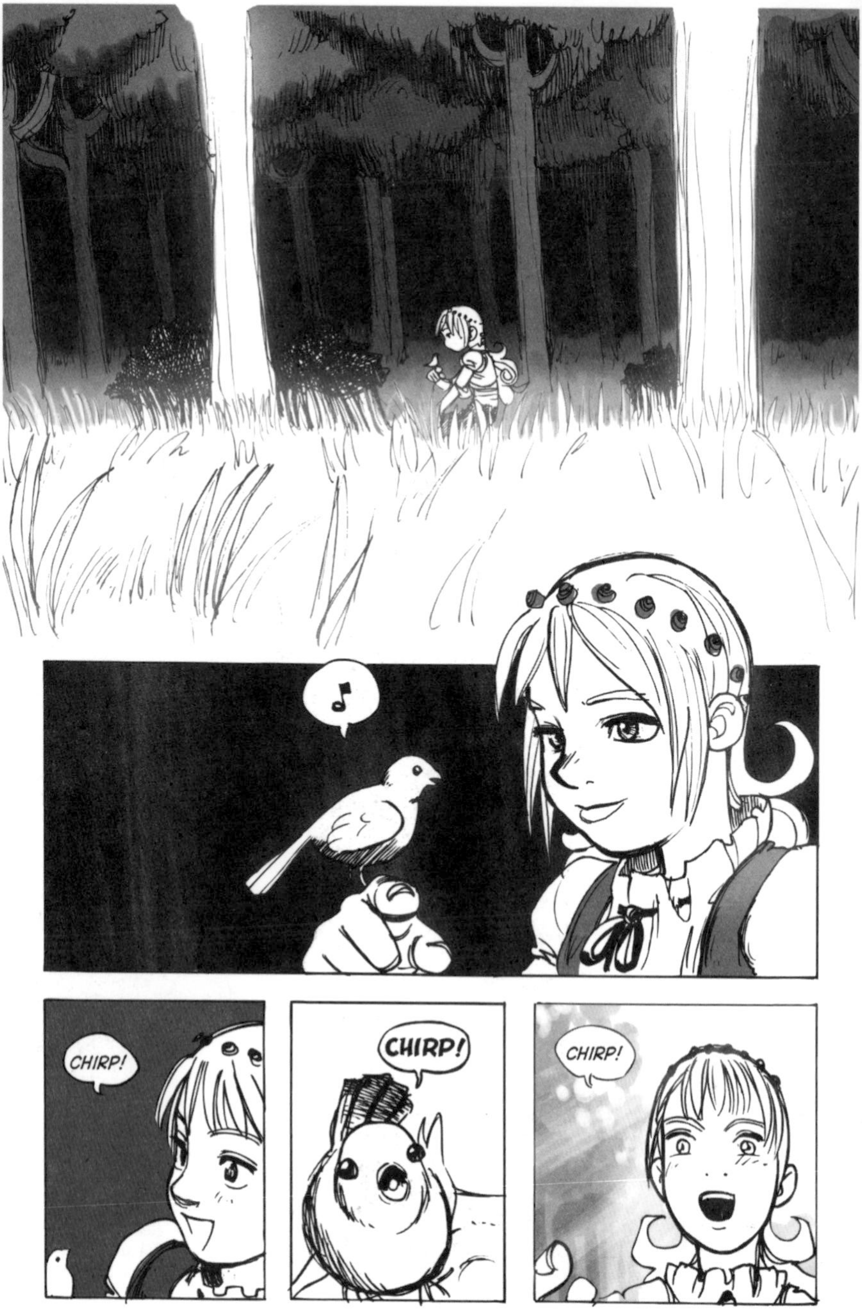
♪
CHIRP!
CHIRP!
CHIRP!

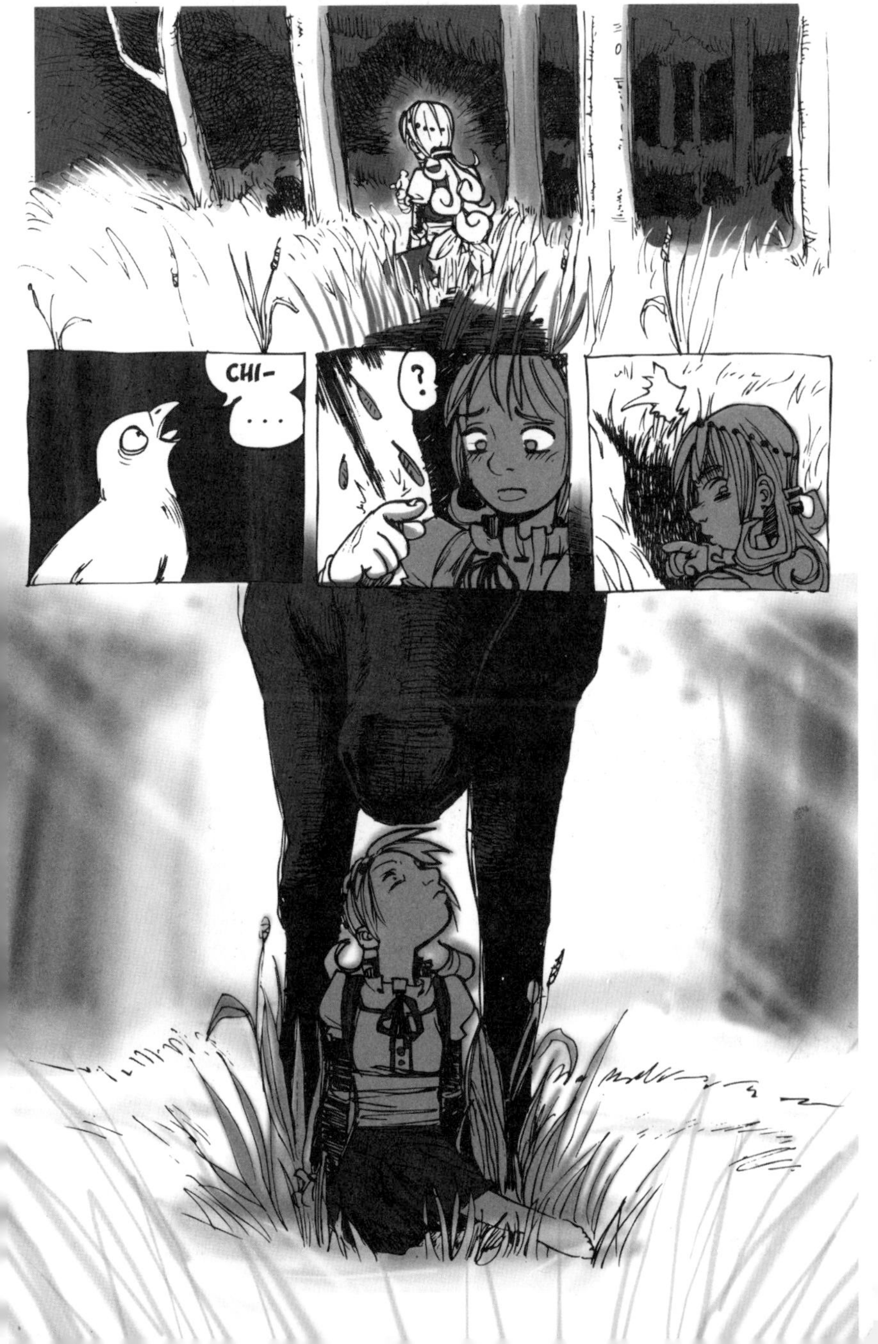
CHI-
...
?

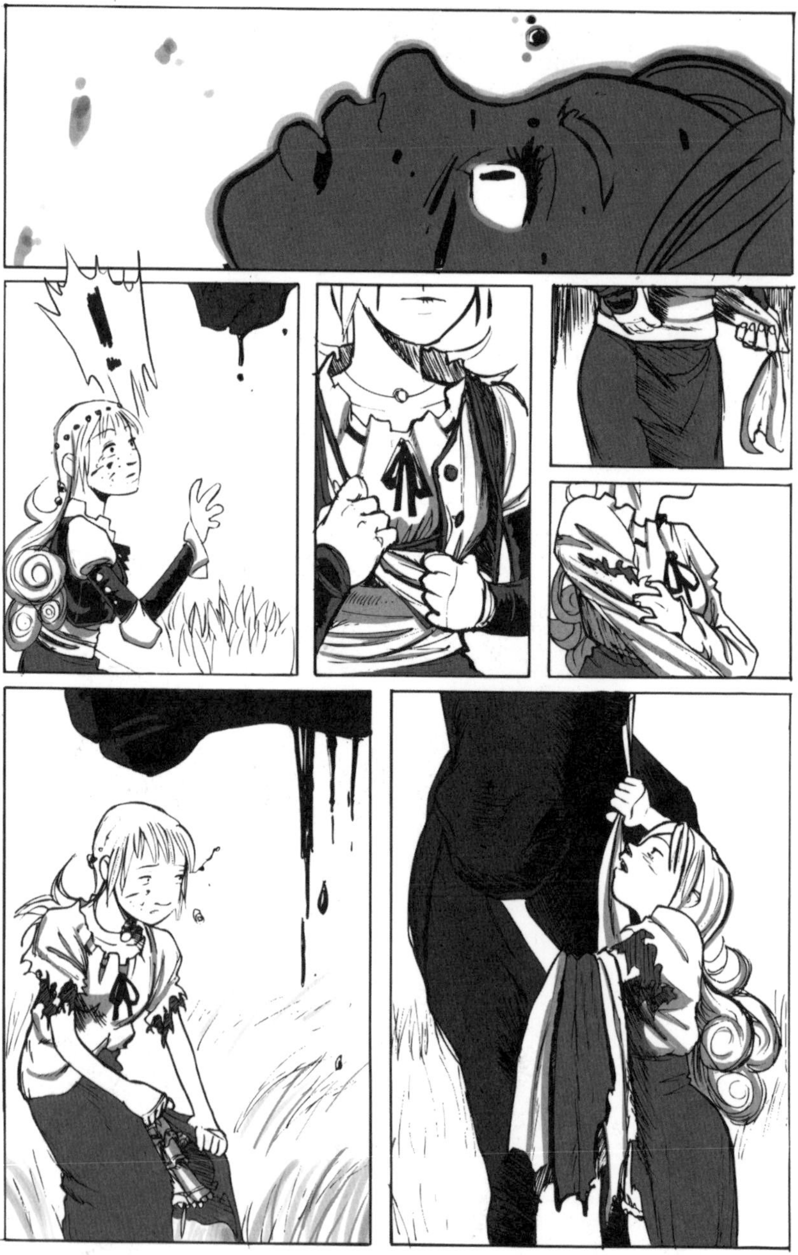
!

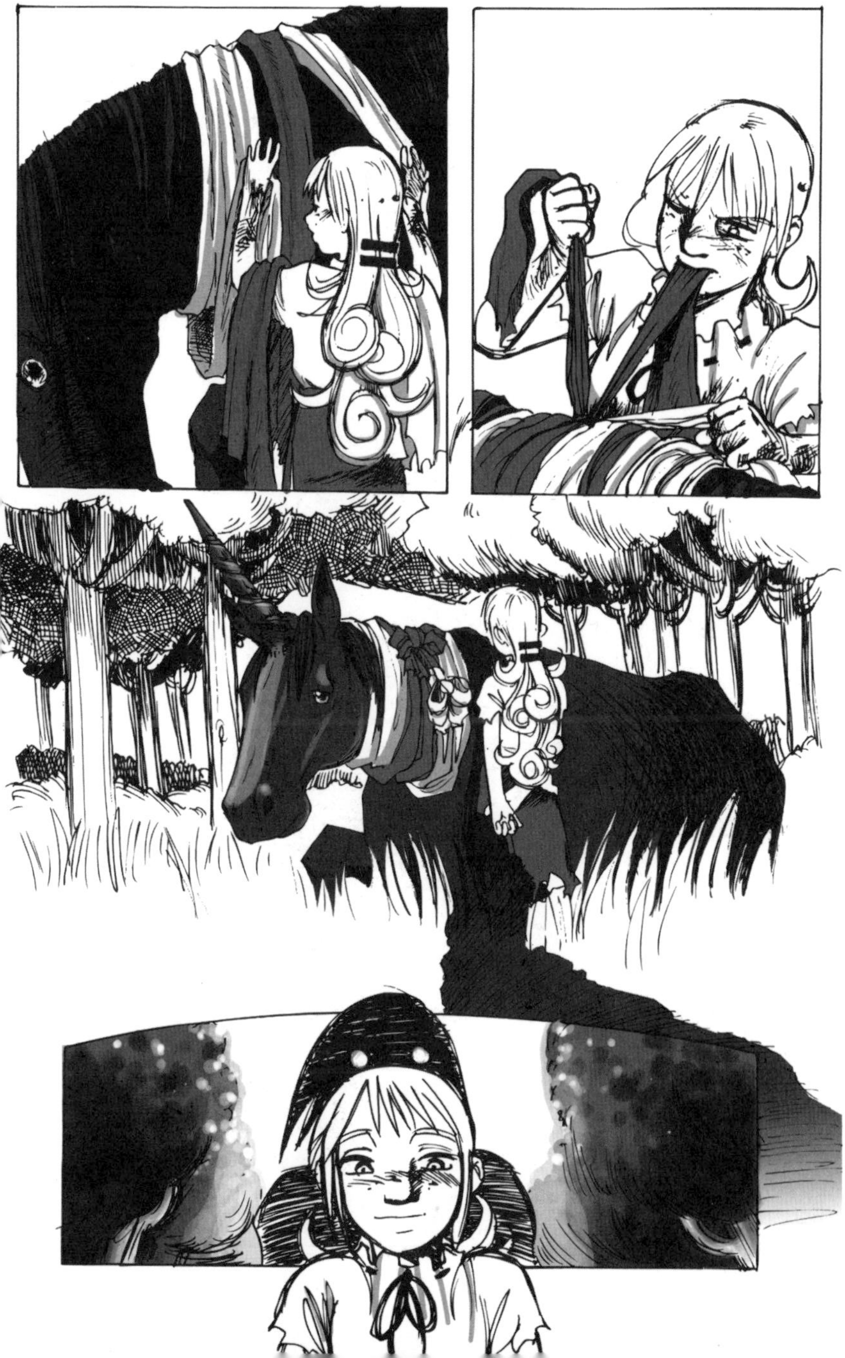

legends from DARKWOOD

THE UNICORN HUNTERS:

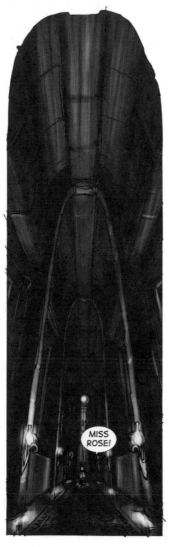

killing|**Christopher Reid**　　　eating|**Johno Kantz**

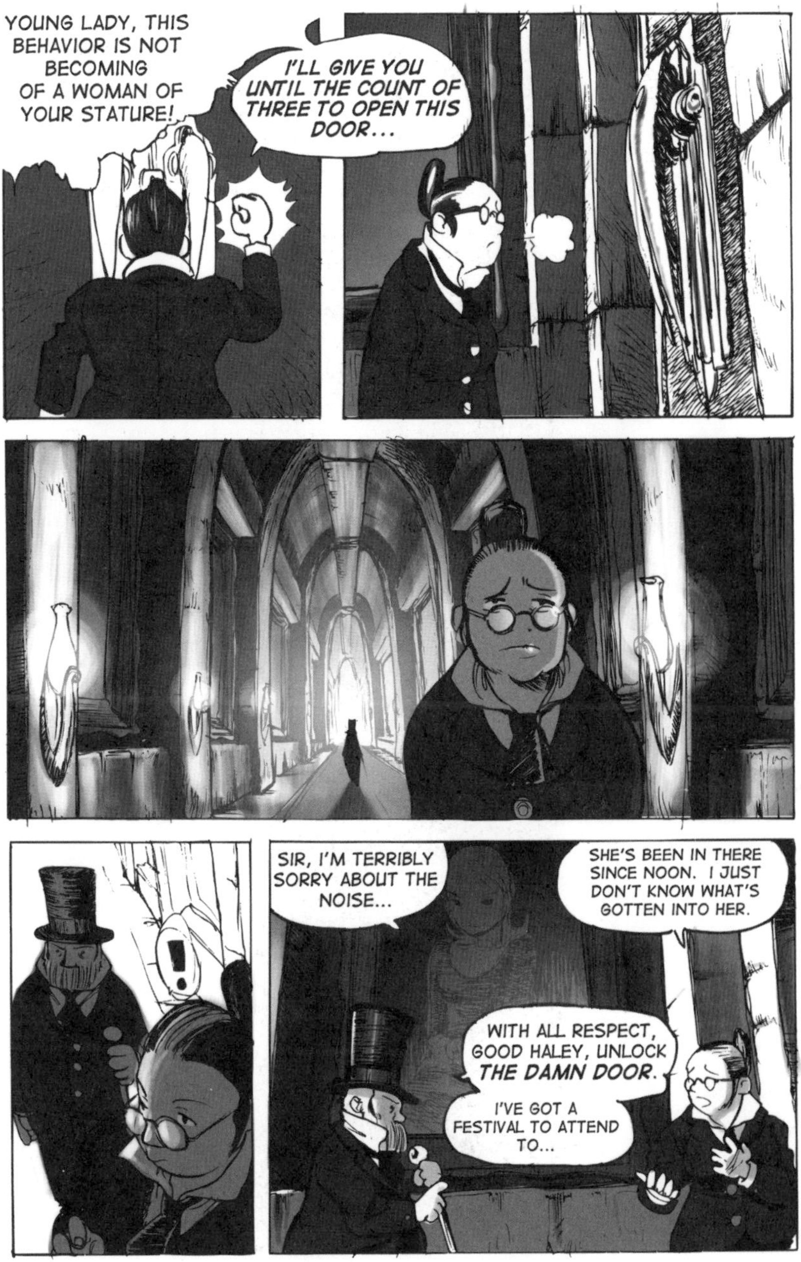
YOUNG LADY, THIS BEHAVIOR IS NOT BECOMING OF A WOMAN OF YOUR STATURE!
I'LL GIVE YOU UNTIL THE COUNT OF THREE TO OPEN THIS DOOR...
!
SIR, I'M TERRIBLY SORRY ABOUT THE NOISE...
SHE'S BEEN IN THERE SINCE NOON. I JUST DON'T KNOW WHAT'S GOTTEN INTO HER.
WITH ALL RESPECT, GOOD HALEY, UNLOCK *THE DAMN DOOR*.
I'VE GOT A FESTIVAL TO ATTEND TO...

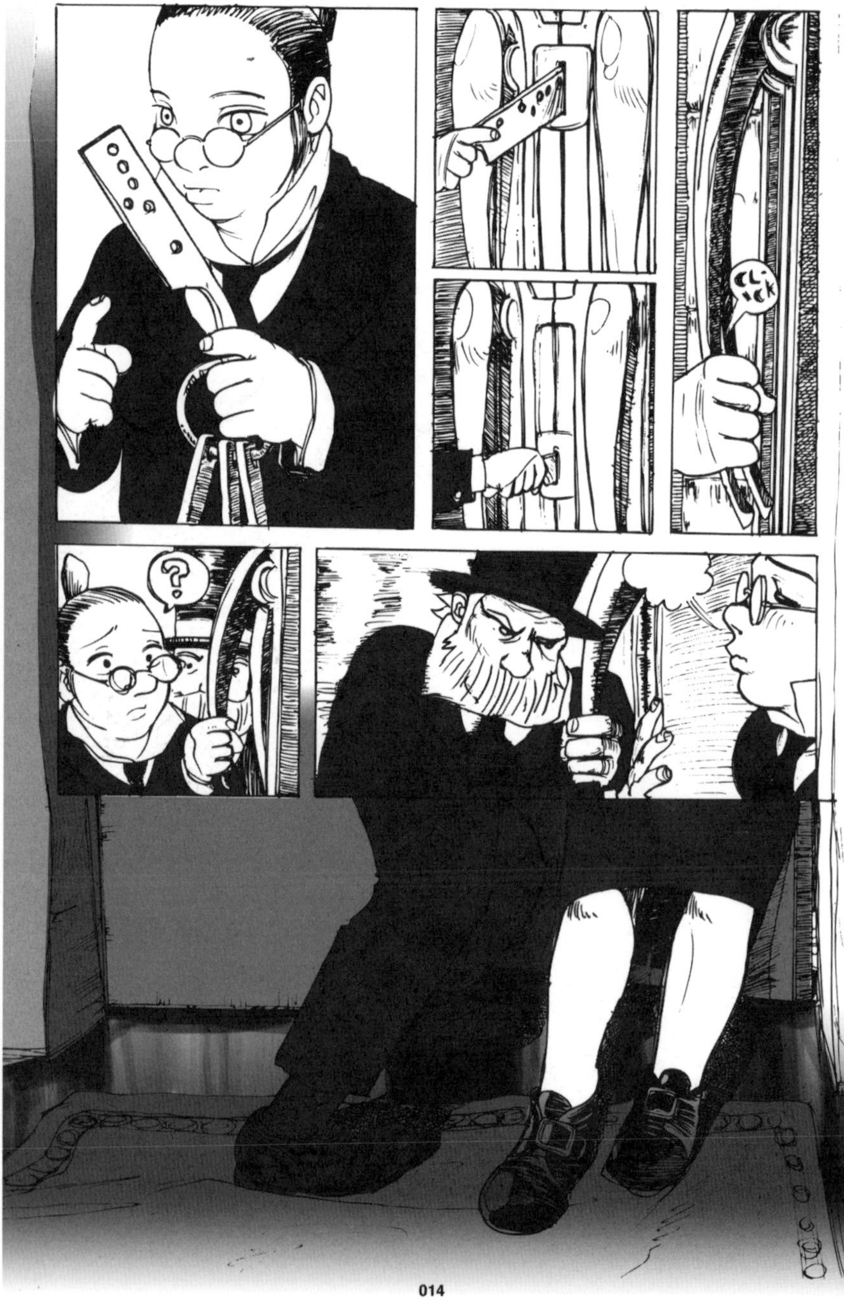
CL-ICK
?

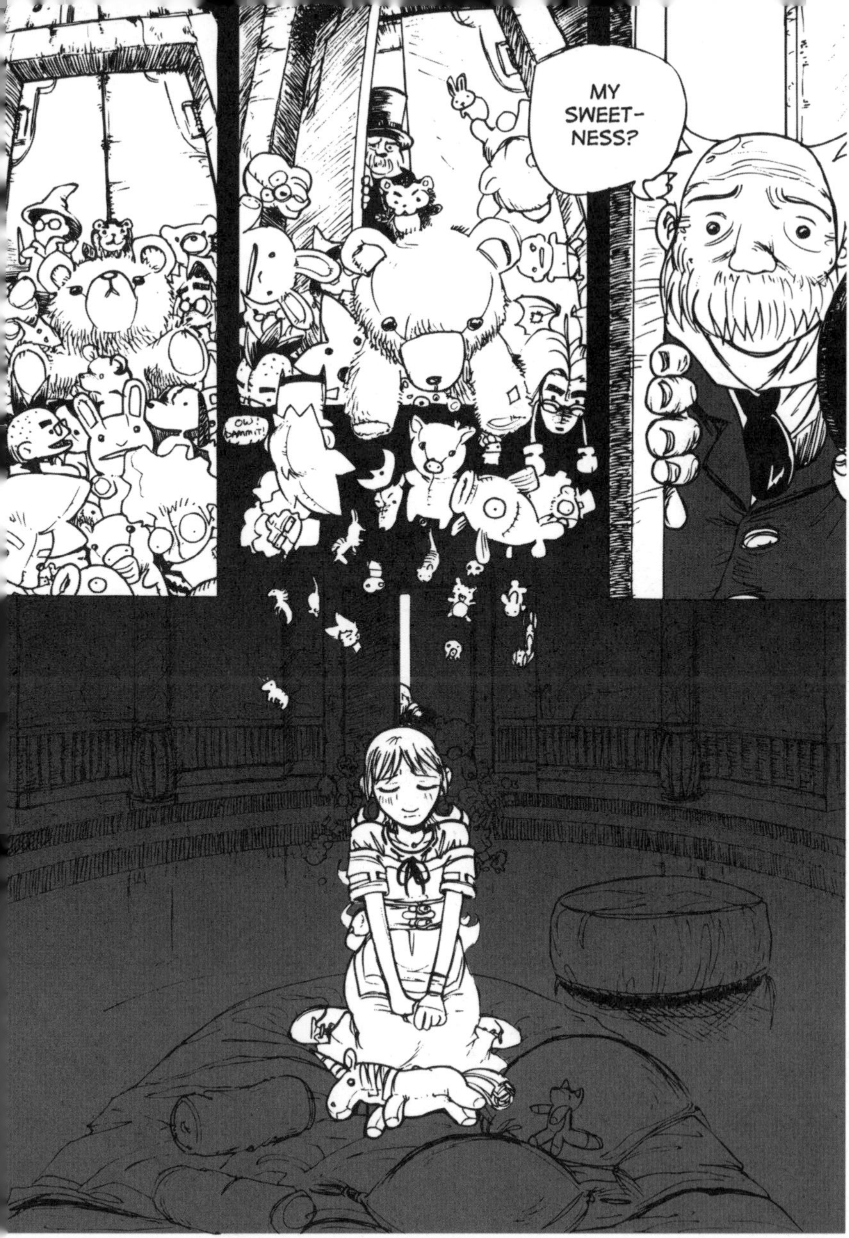
MY SWEET-NESS?
OW! DAMMIT!

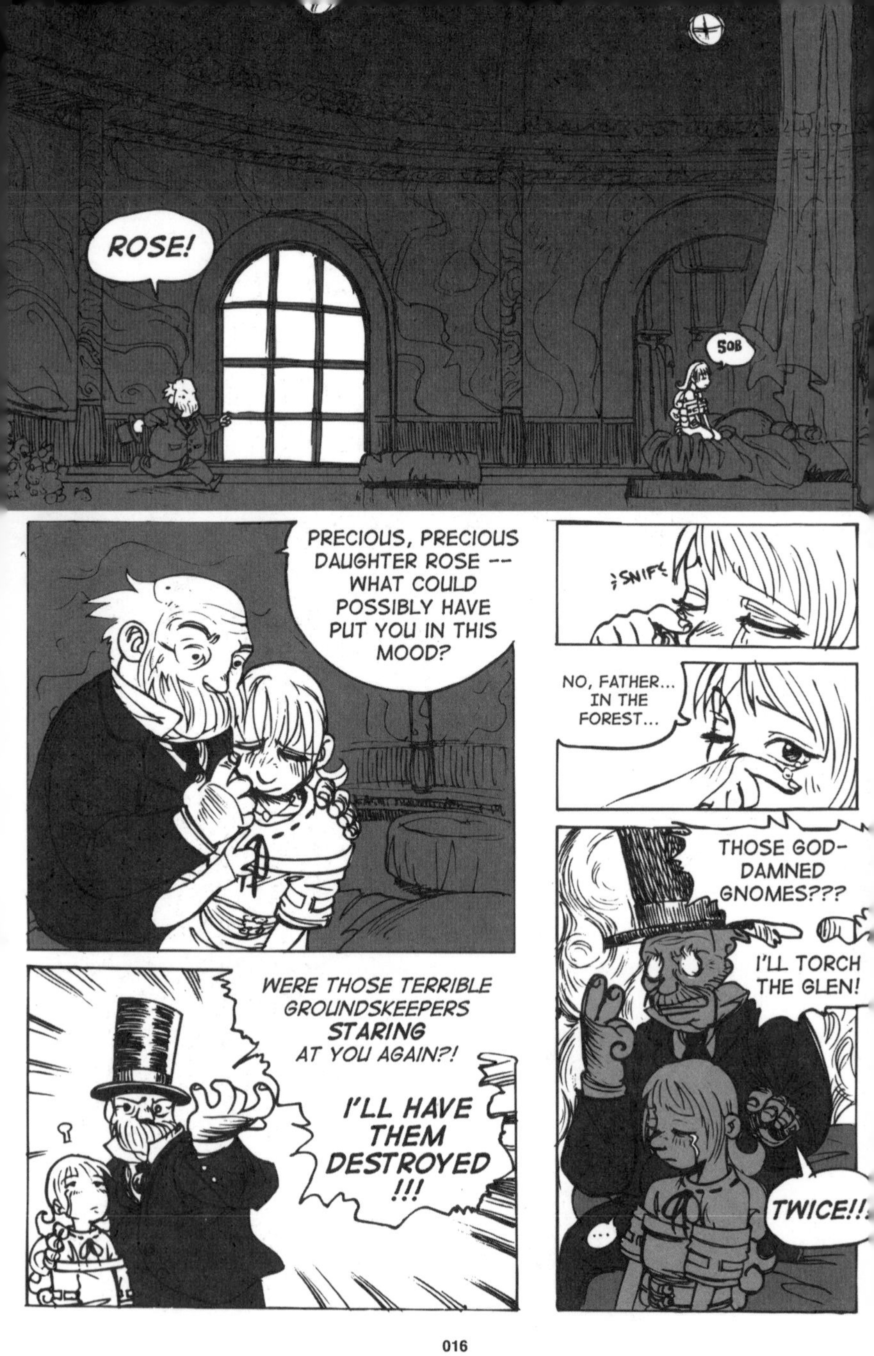
ROSE!
SOB
PRECIOUS, PRECIOUS DAUGHTER ROSE -- WHAT COULD POSSIBLY HAVE PUT YOU IN THIS MOOD?
SNIFF
NO, FATHER... IN THE FOREST...
WERE THOSE TERRIBLE GROUNDSKEEPERS STARING AT YOU AGAIN?!
I'LL HAVE THEM DESTROYED !!!
THOSE GOD-DAMNED GNOMES???
I'LL TORCH THE GLEN!
TWICE!!!
...

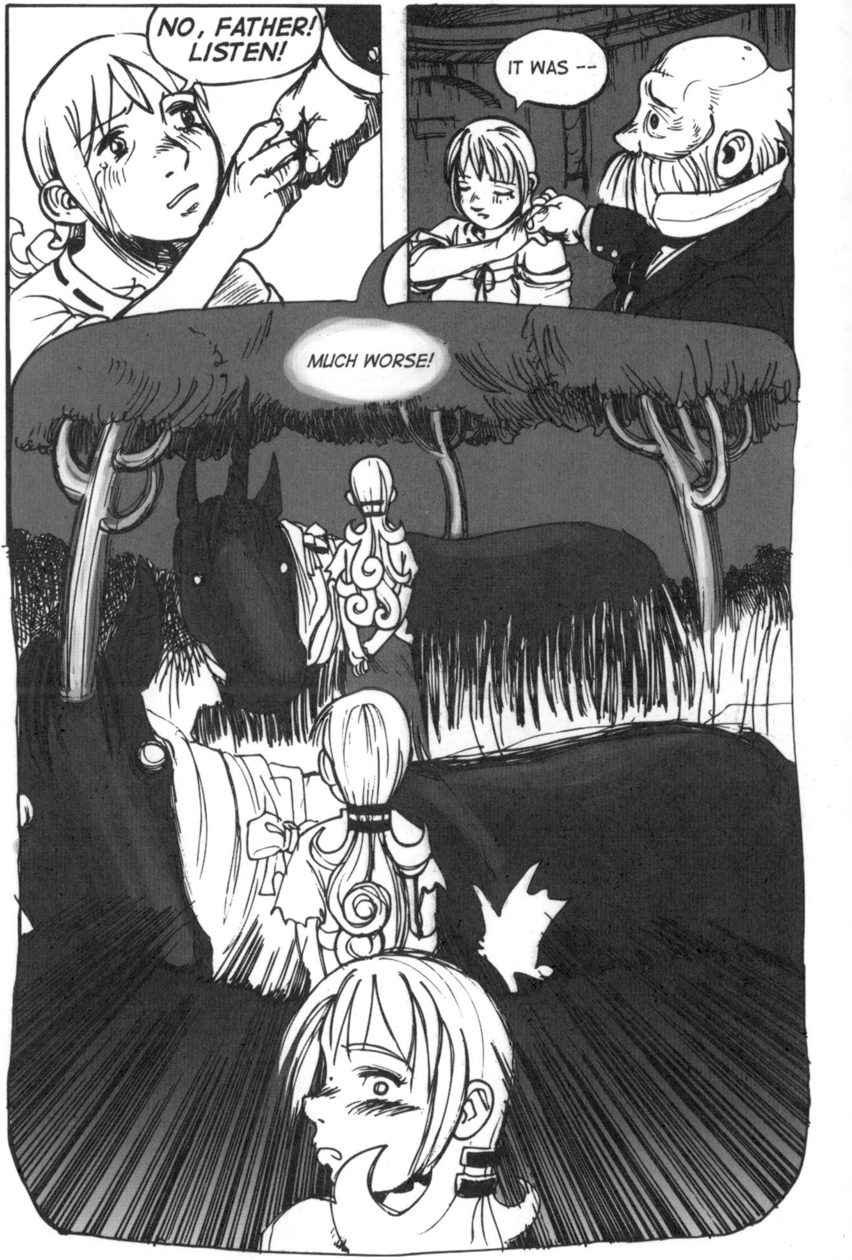
NO, FATHER! LISTEN!
IT WAS --
MUCH WORSE!

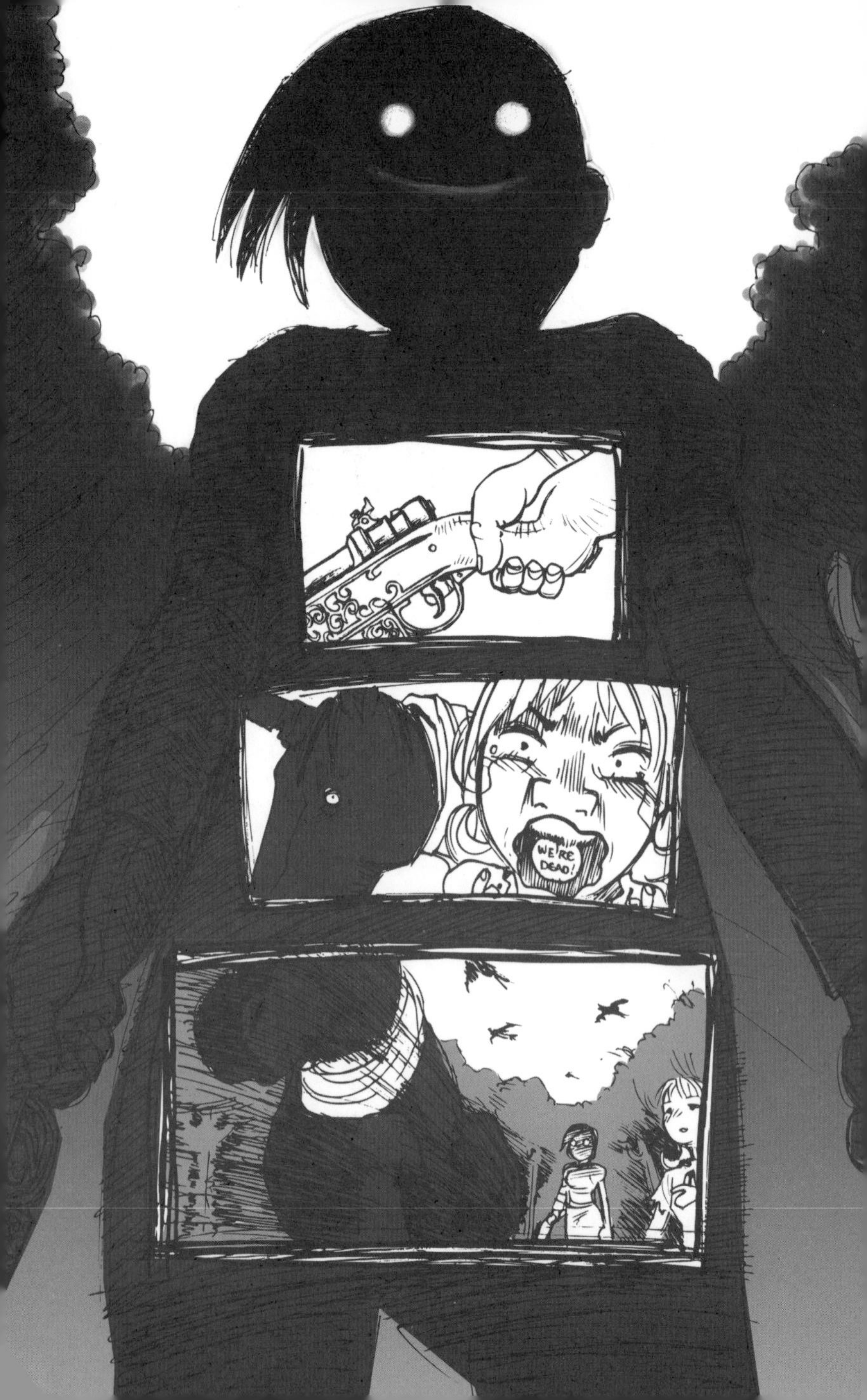
WE'RE DEAD!

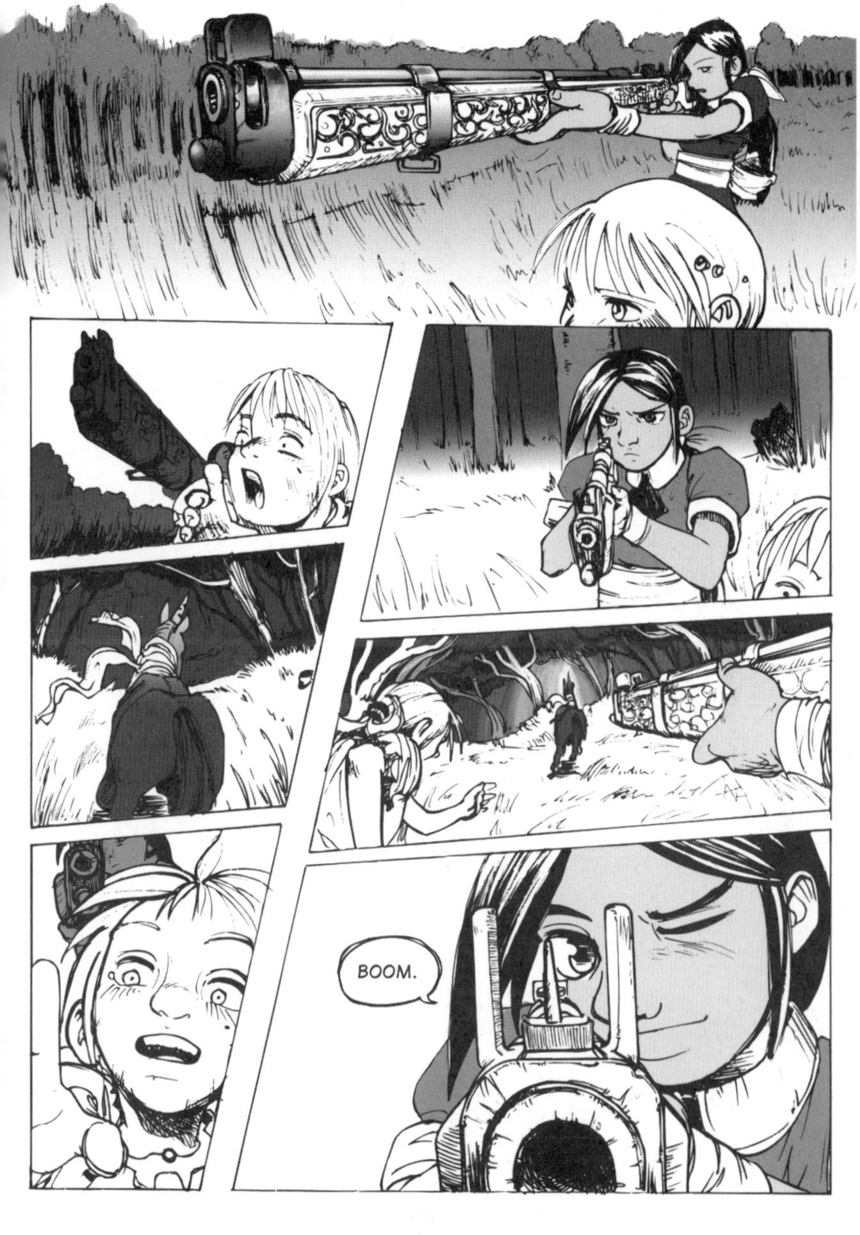
BOOM.

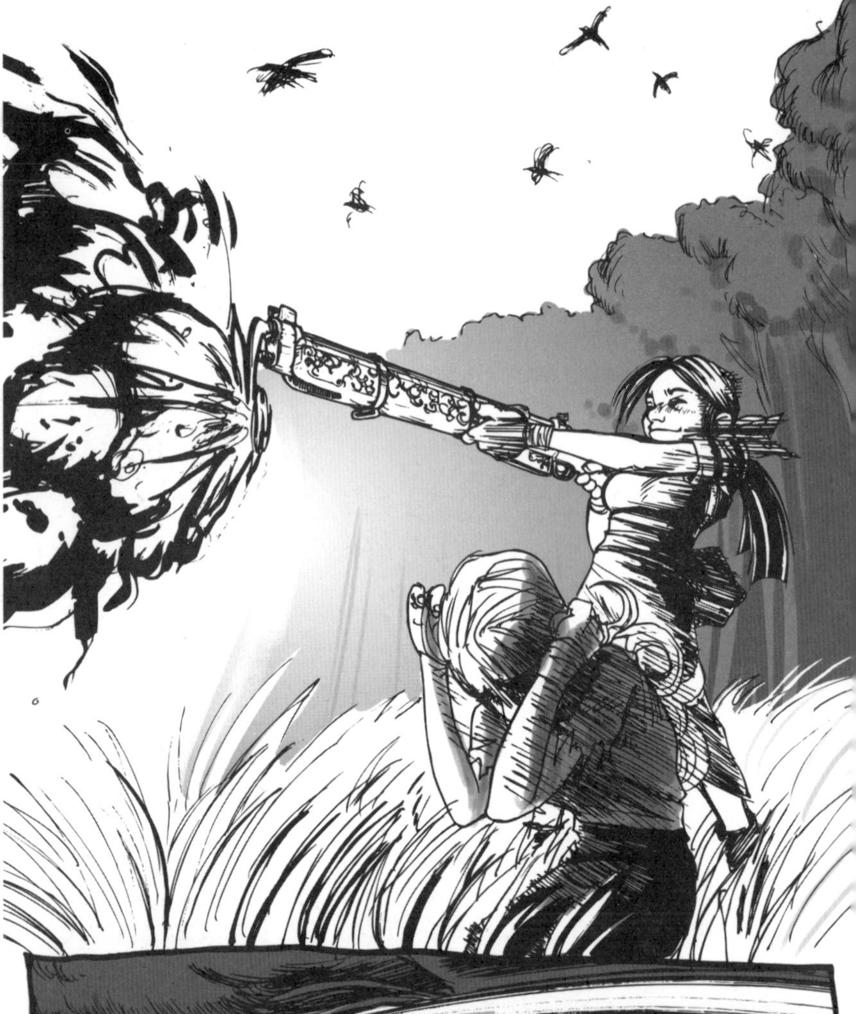
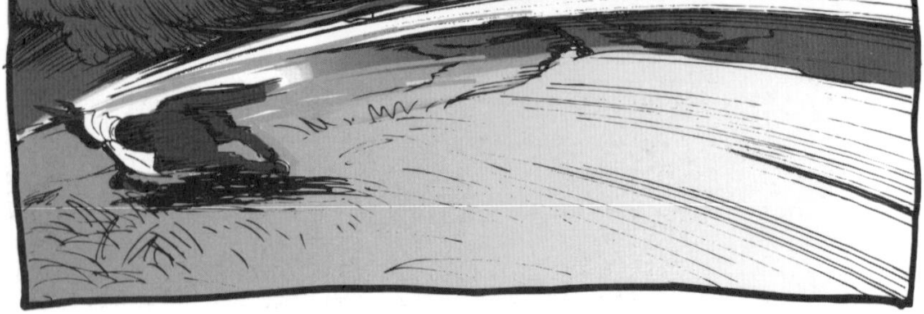

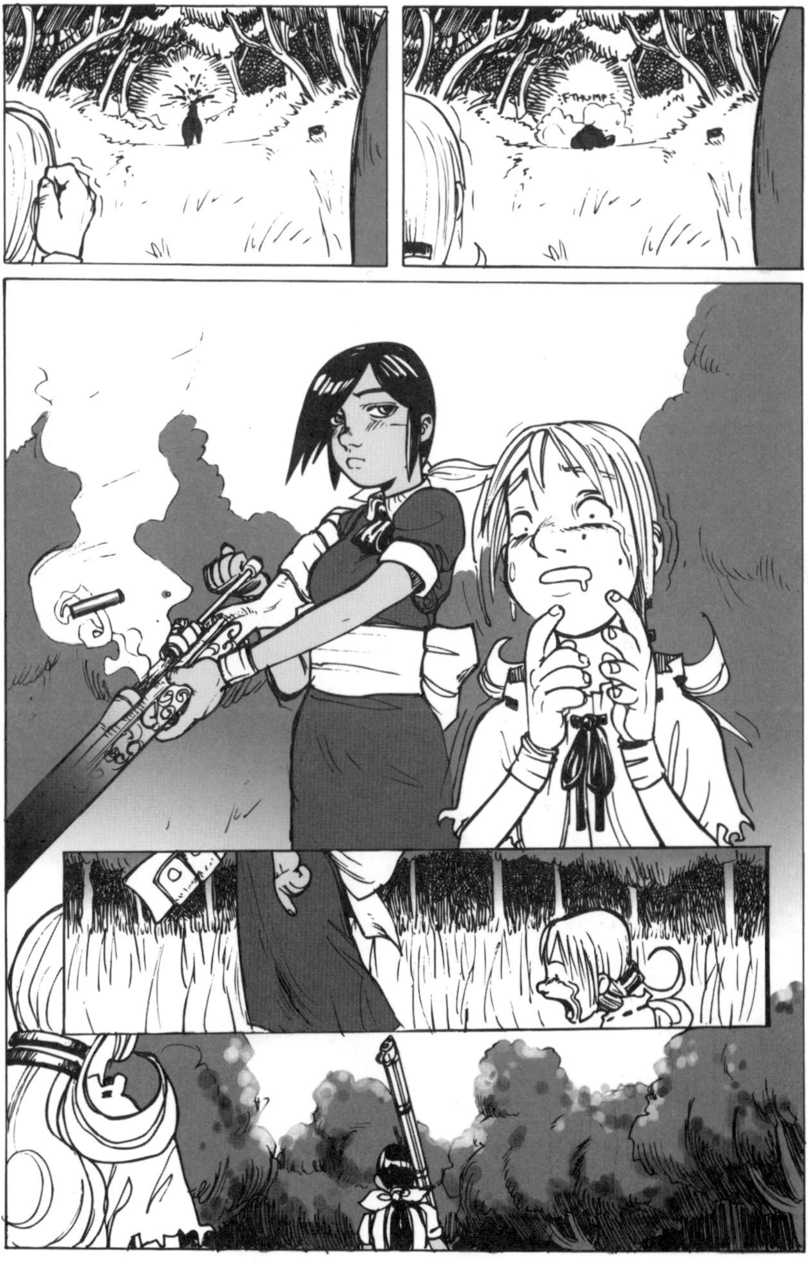
FTHUMP

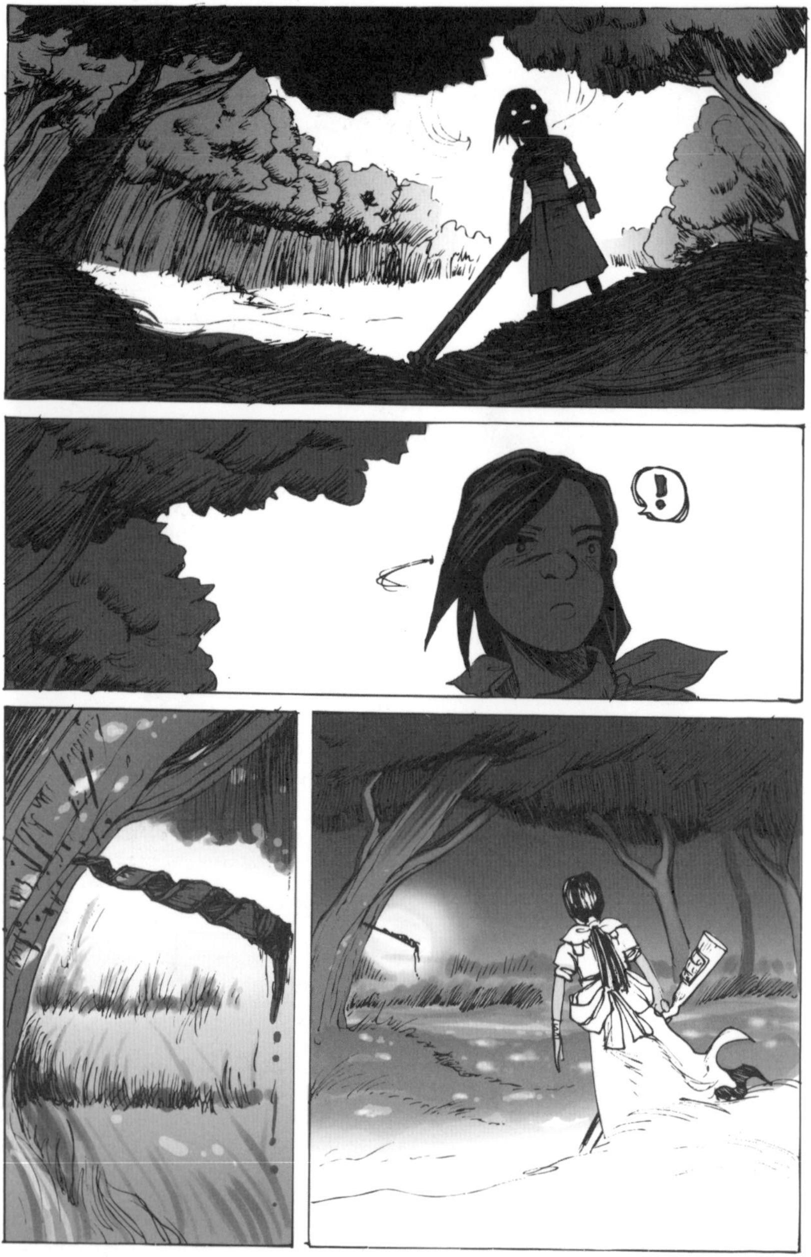
!

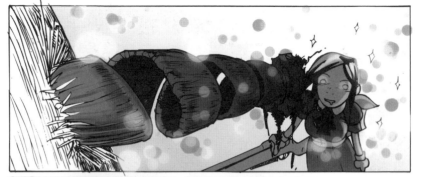

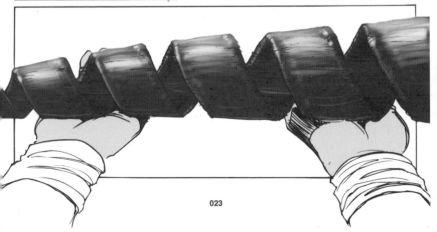

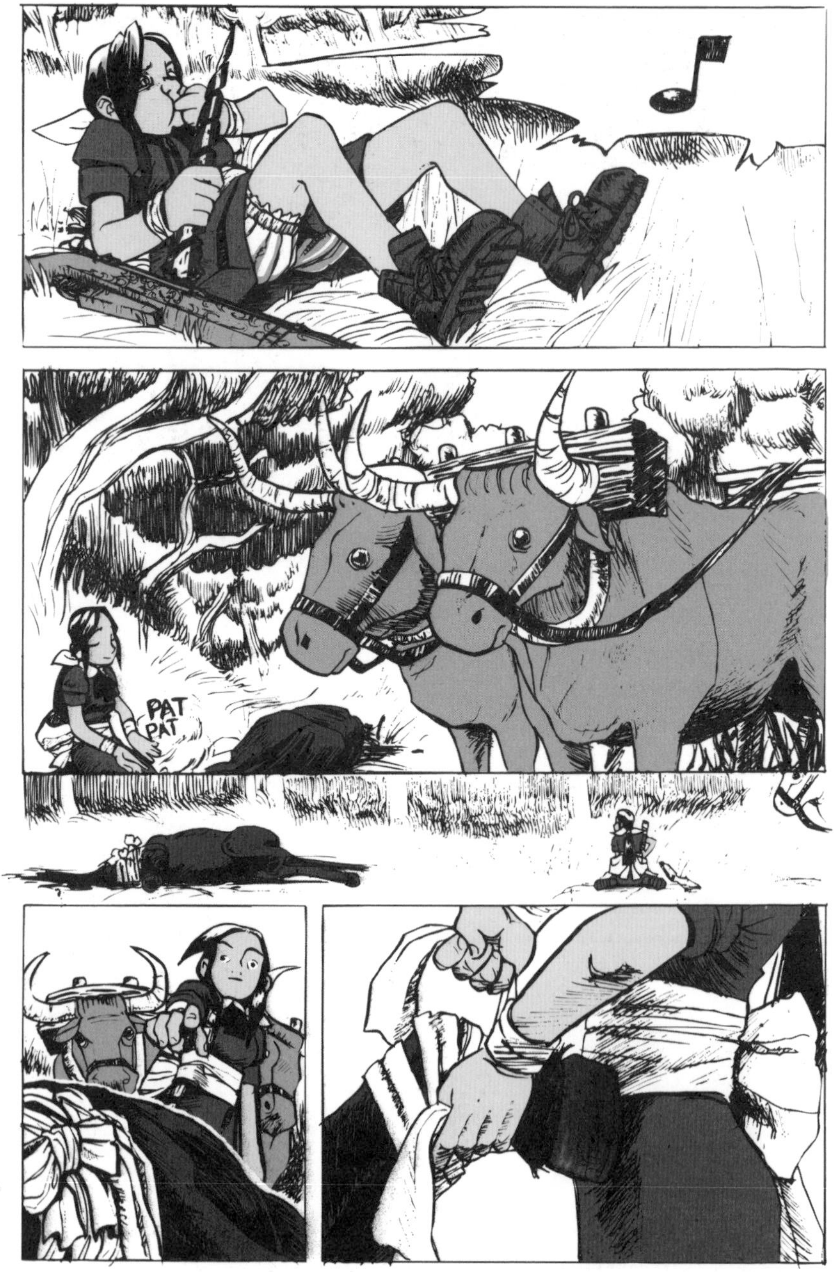
PAT
PAT

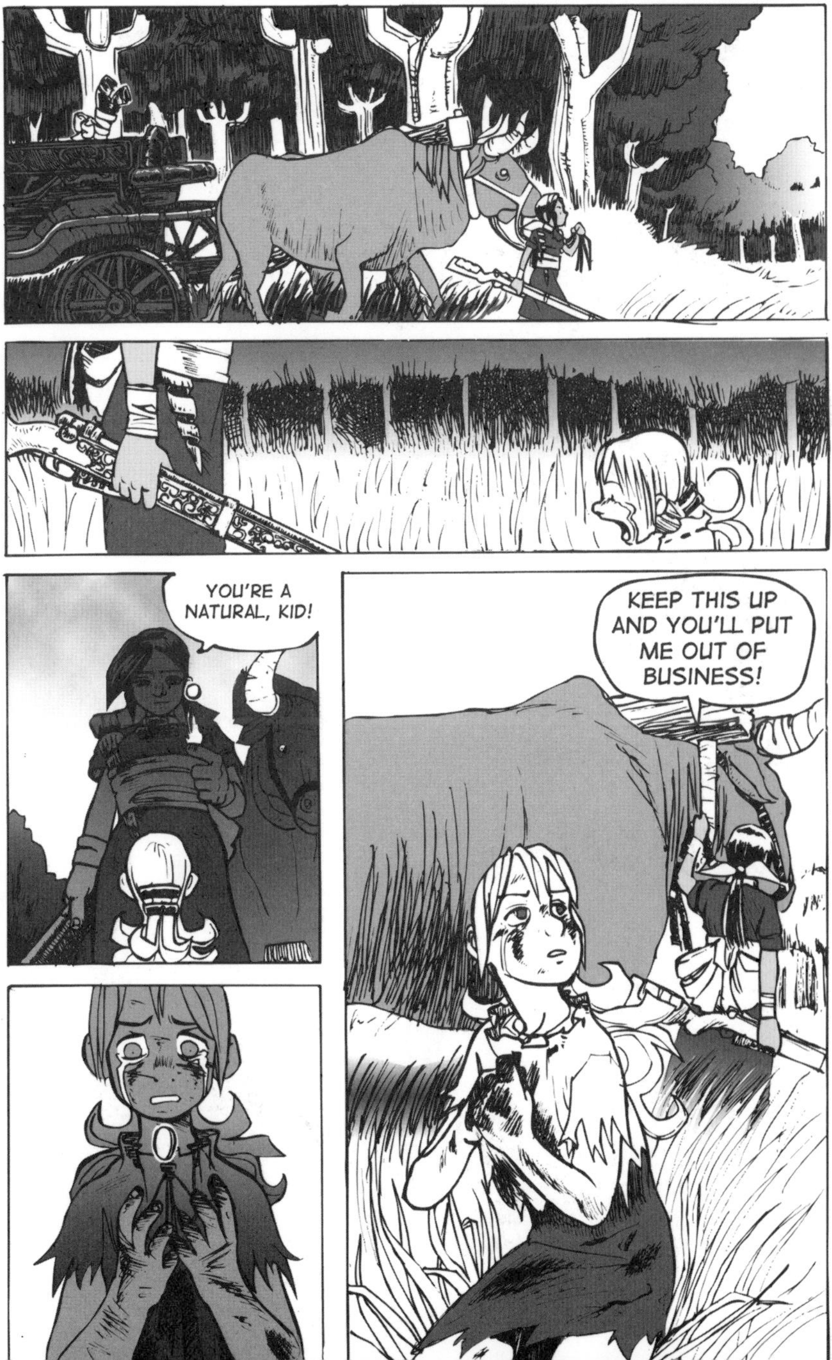
YOU'RE A NATURAL, KID!
KEEP THIS UP AND YOU'LL PUT ME OUT OF BUSINESS!

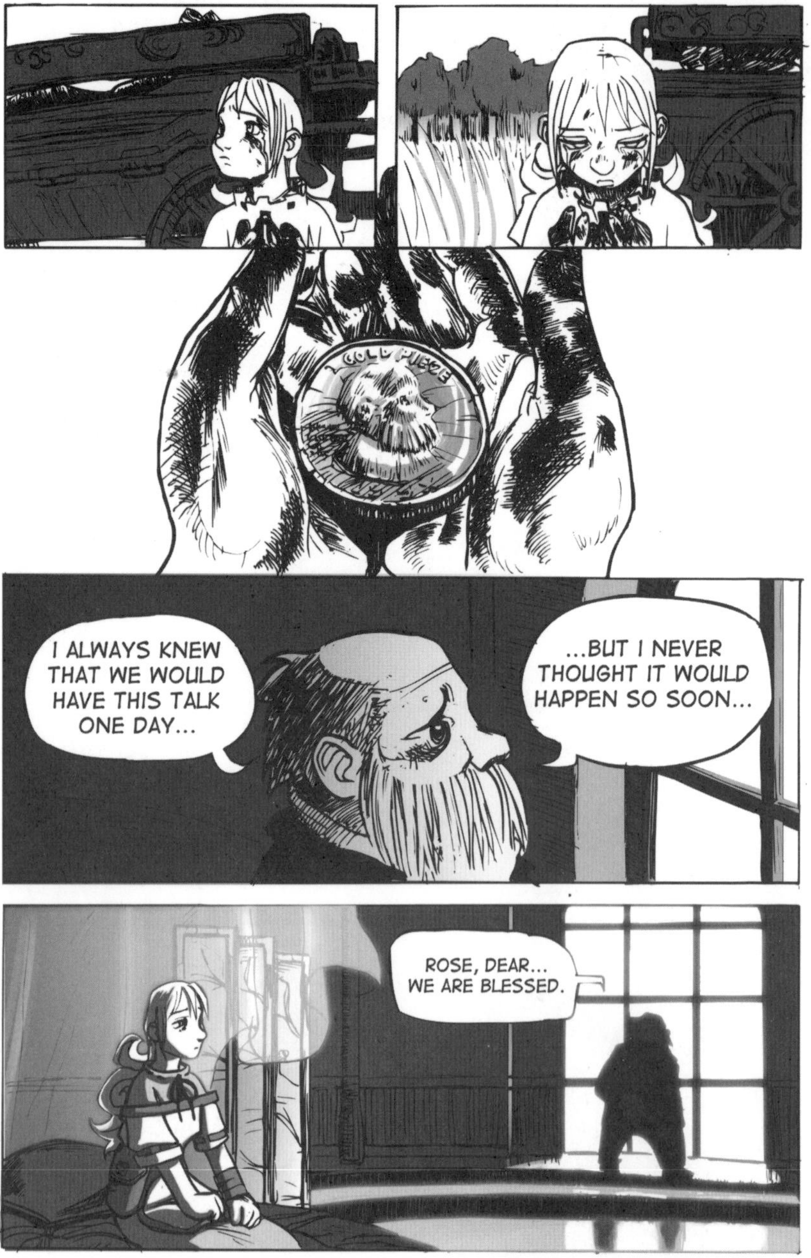
GOLD PIECE
I ALWAYS KNEW THAT WE WOULD HAVE THIS TALK ONE DAY...
...BUT I NEVER THOUGHT IT WOULD HAPPEN SO SOON...
ROSE, DEAR... WE ARE BLESSED.

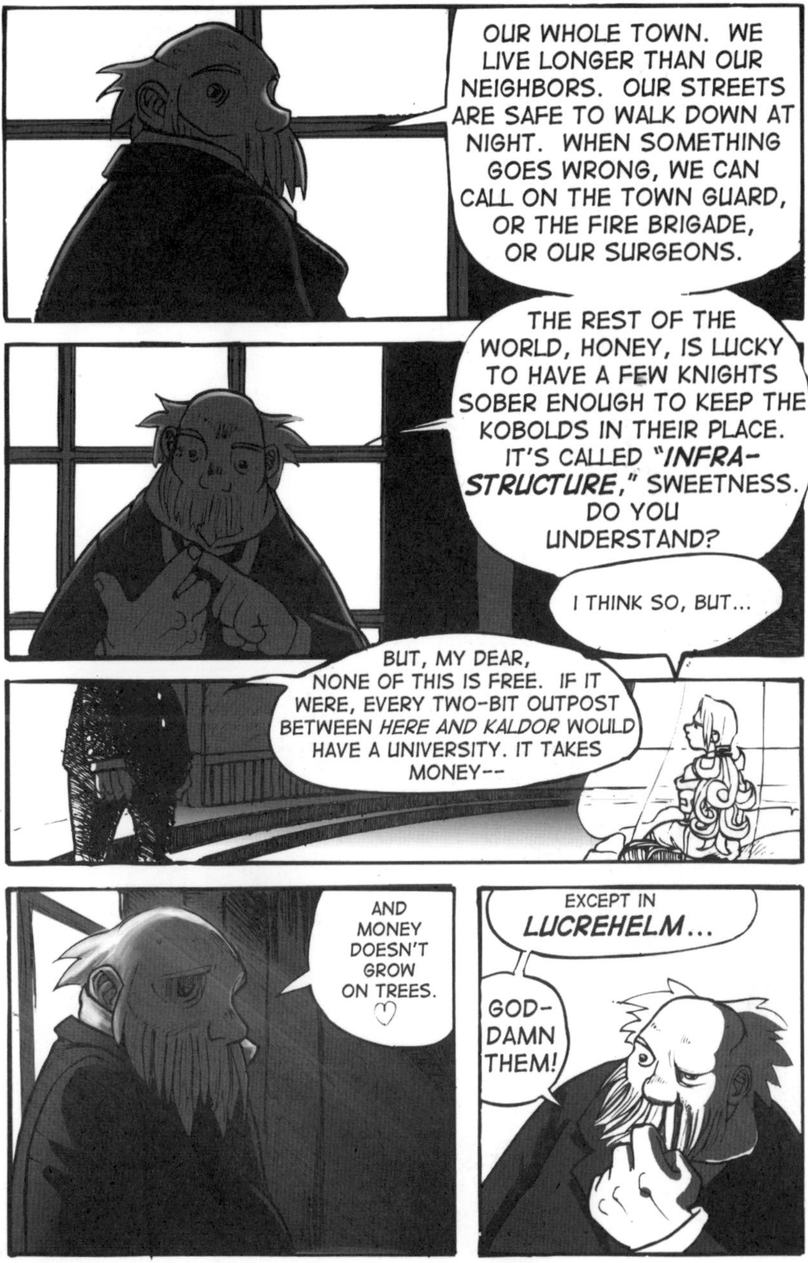
OUR WHOLE TOWN. WE LIVE LONGER THAN OUR NEIGHBORS. OUR STREETS ARE SAFE TO WALK DOWN AT NIGHT. WHEN SOMETHING GOES WRONG, WE CAN CALL ON THE TOWN GUARD, OR THE FIRE BRIGADE, OR OUR SURGEONS.
THE REST OF THE WORLD, HONEY, IS LUCKY TO HAVE A FEW KNIGHTS SOBER ENOUGH TO KEEP THE KOBOLDS IN THEIR PLACE. IT'S CALLED "INFRA-STRUCTURE," SWEETNESS. DO YOU UNDERSTAND?
I THINK SO, BUT...
BUT, MY DEAR, NONE OF THIS IS FREE. IF IT WERE, EVERY TWO-BIT OUTPOST BETWEEN HERE AND KALDOR WOULD HAVE A UNIVERSITY. IT TAKES MONEY--
AND MONEY DOESN'T GROW ON TREES. ♡
EXCEPT IN LUCREHELM...
GOD-DAMN THEM!

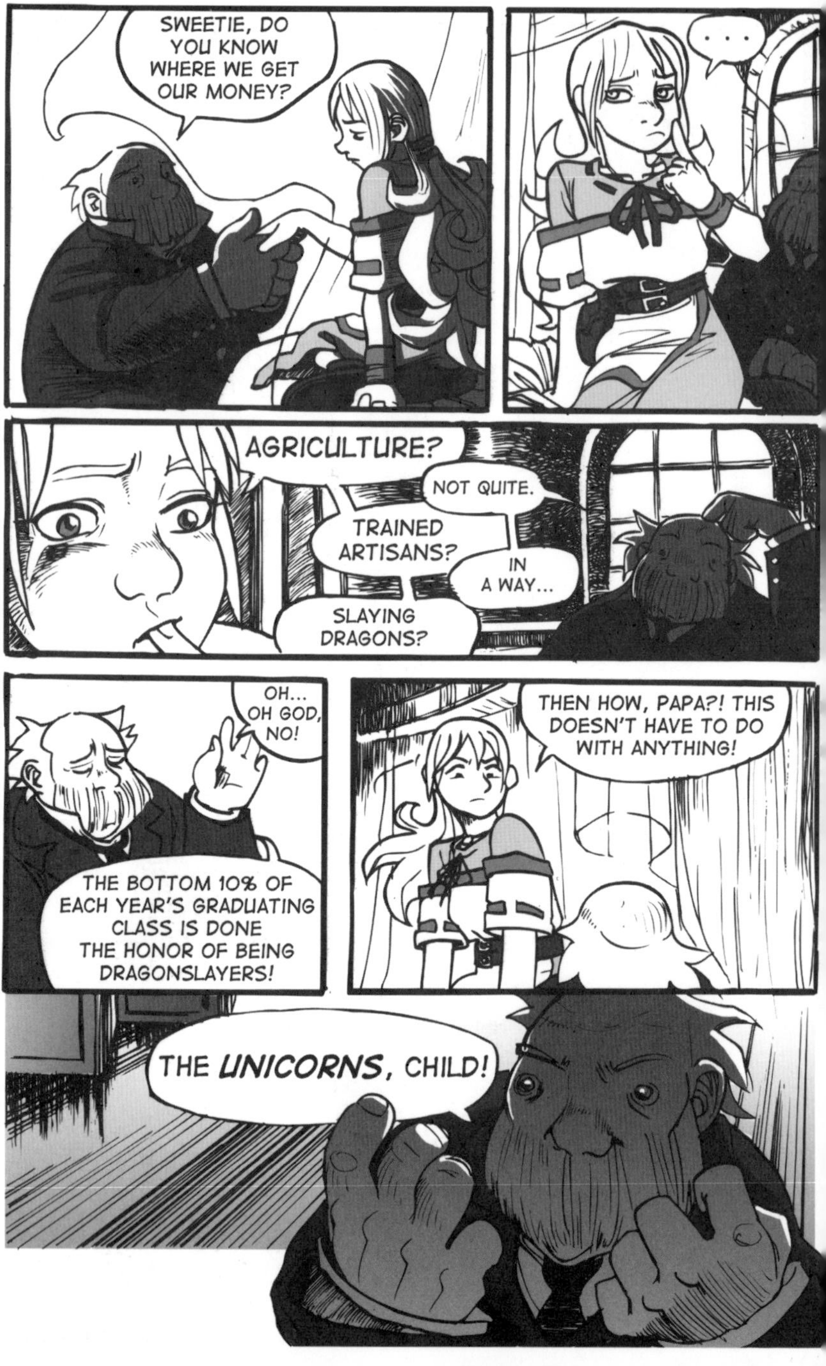
SWEETIE, DO YOU KNOW WHERE WE GET OUR MONEY?
. . .
AGRICULTURE?
NOT QUITE.
TRAINED ARTISANS?
IN A WAY...
SLAYING DRAGONS?
OH... OH GOD, NO!
THE BOTTOM 10% OF EACH YEAR'S GRADUATING CLASS IS DONE THE HONOR OF BEING DRAGONSLAYERS!
THEN HOW, PAPA?! THIS DOESN'T HAVE TO DO WITH ANYTHING!
THE *UNICORNS*, CHILD!

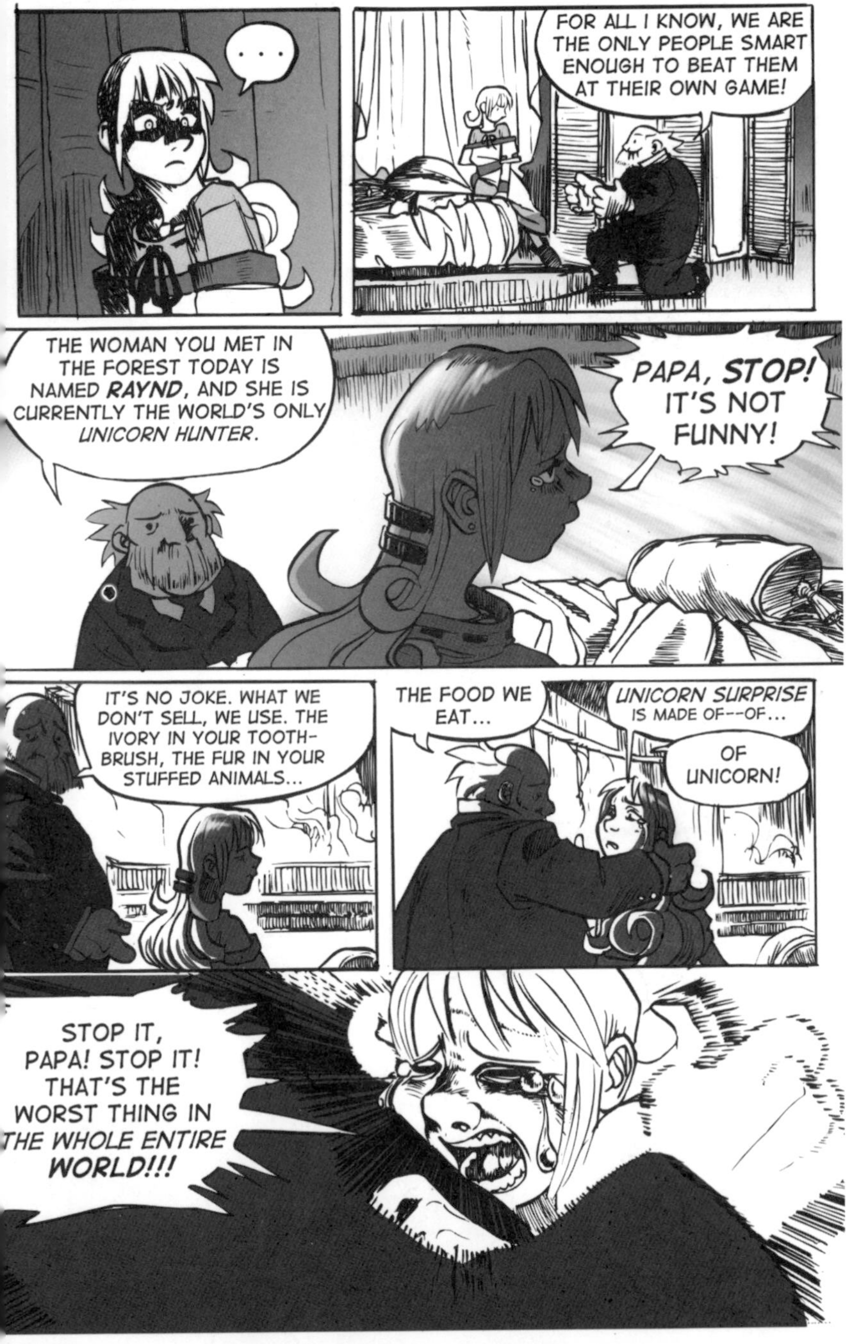

. . .
FOR ALL I KNOW, WE ARE THE ONLY PEOPLE SMART ENOUGH TO BEAT THEM AT THEIR OWN GAME!
THE WOMAN YOU MET IN THE FOREST TODAY IS NAMED RAYND, AND SHE IS CURRENTLY THE WORLD'S ONLY UNICORN HUNTER.
PAPA, STOP! IT'S NOT FUNNY!
IT'S NO JOKE. WHAT WE DON'T SELL, WE USE. THE IVORY IN YOUR TOOTH-BRUSH, THE FUR IN YOUR STUFFED ANIMALS...
THE FOOD WE EAT...
UNICORN SURPRISE IS MADE OF--OF...
OF UNICORN!
STOP IT, PAPA! STOP IT! THAT'S THE WORST THING IN THE WHOLE ENTIRE WORLD!!!

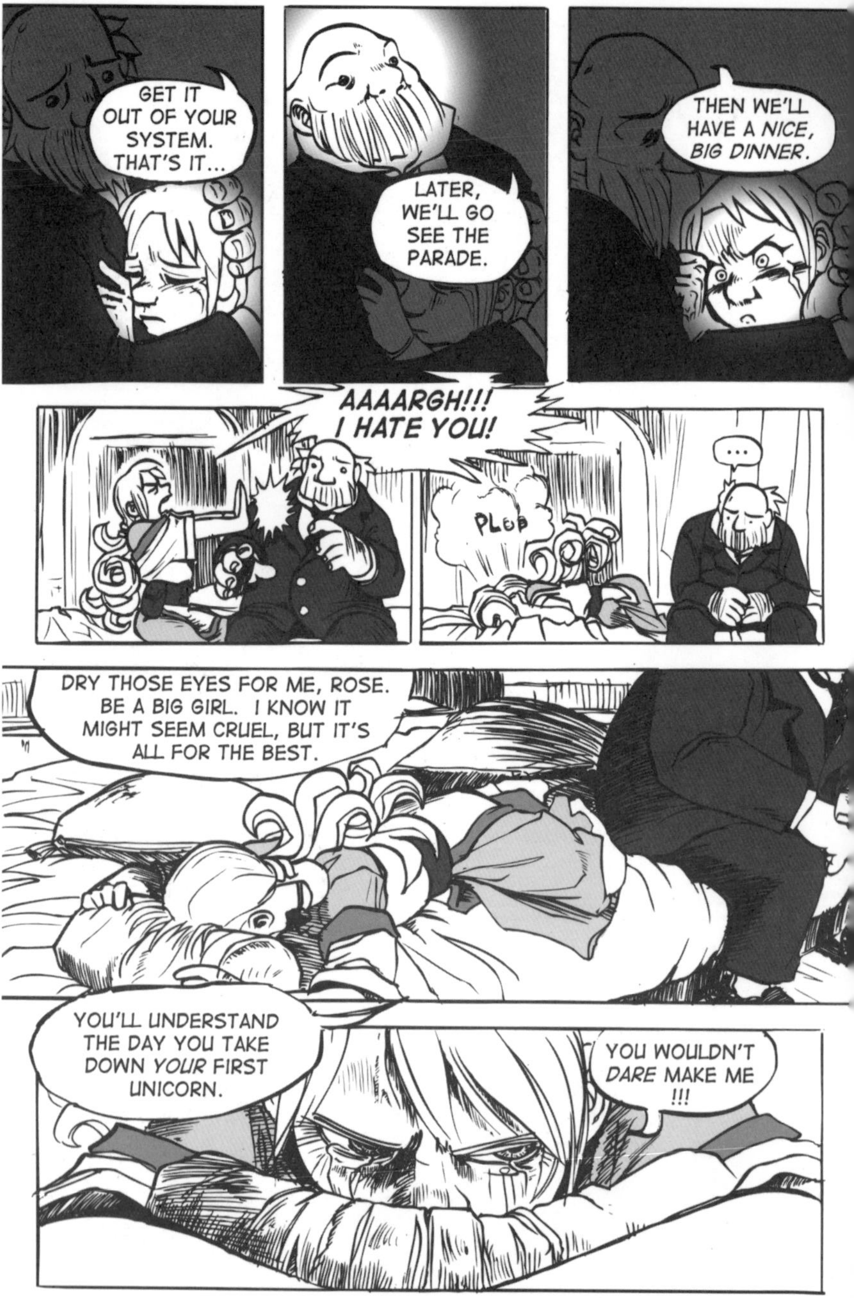
GET IT OUT OF YOUR SYSTEM. THAT'S IT...
LATER, WE'LL GO SEE THE PARADE.
THEN WE'LL HAVE A *NICE, BIG DINNER*.
AAAARGH!!! I HATE YOU!
PLOP
...
DRY THOSE EYES FOR ME, ROSE. BE A BIG GIRL. I KNOW IT MIGHT SEEM CRUEL, BUT IT'S ALL FOR THE BEST.
YOU'LL UNDERSTAND THE DAY YOU TAKE DOWN *YOUR* FIRST UNICORN.
YOU WOULDN'T *DARE* MAKE ME !!!

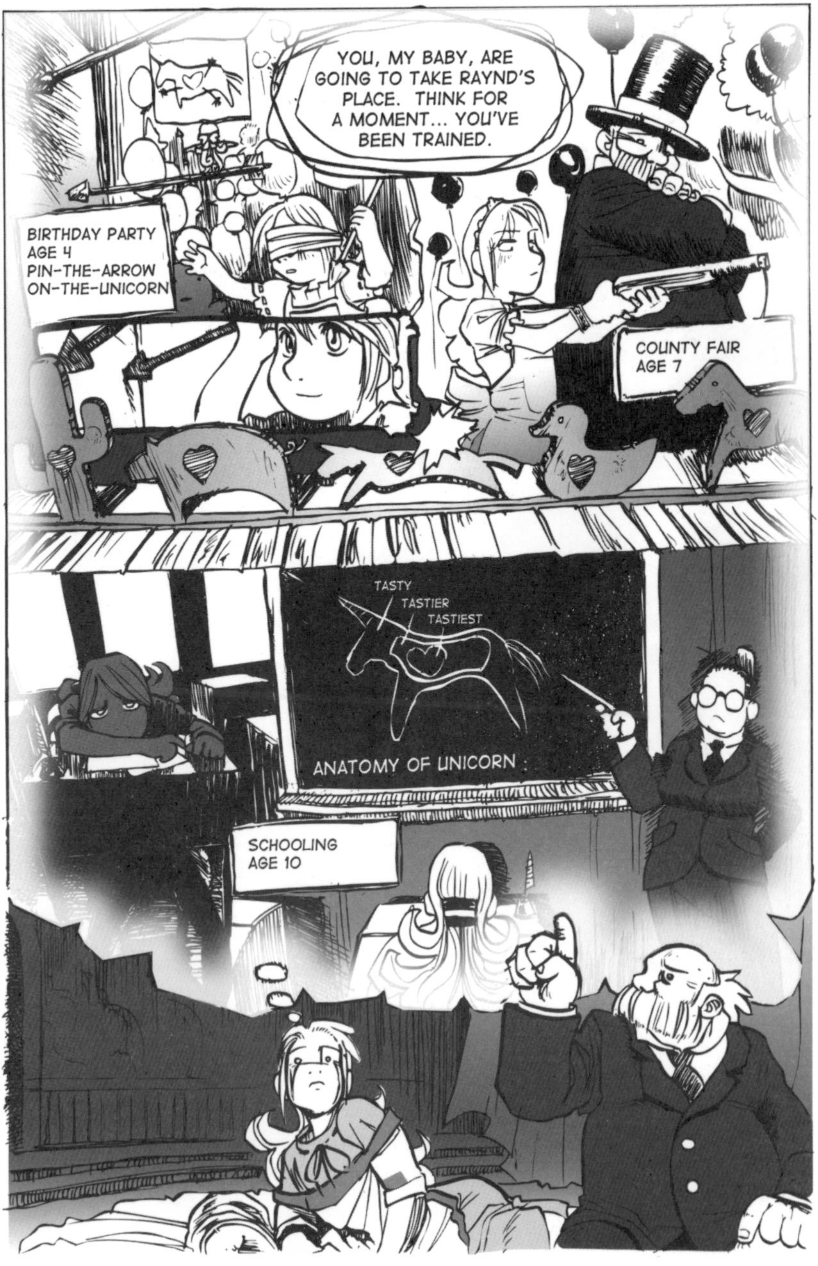
YOU, MY BABY, ARE GOING TO TAKE RAYND'S PLACE. THINK FOR A MOMENT... YOU'VE BEEN TRAINED.
BIRTHDAY PARTY
AGE 4
PIN-THE-ARROW
ON-THE-UNICORN
COUNTY FAIR
AGE 7
TASTY
TASTIER
TASTIEST
ANATOMY OF UNICORN
SCHOOLING
AGE 10

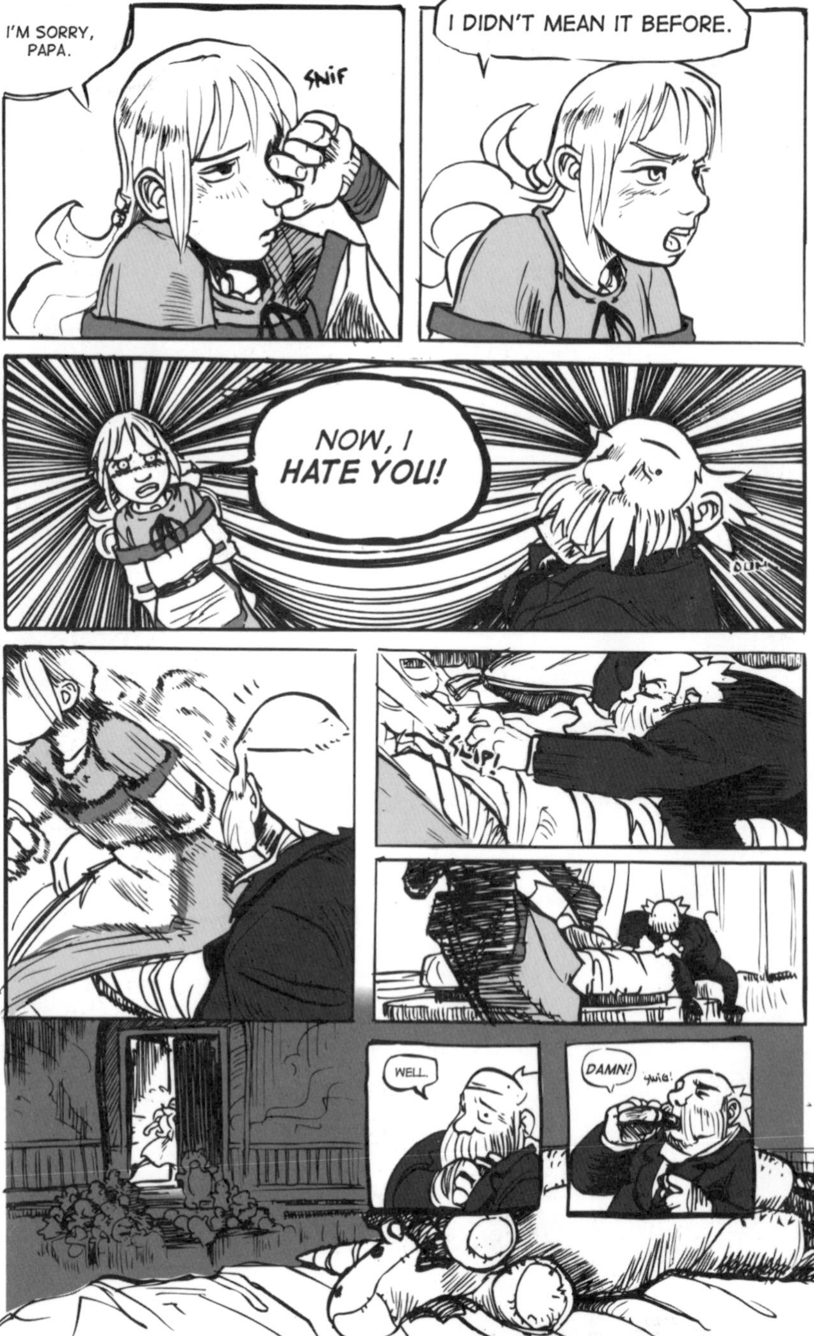
I'M SORRY, PAPA.
SNIF
I DIDN'T MEAN IT BEFORE.
NOW, I HATE YOU!
SLIP!
WELL.
DAMN!
SWIG!

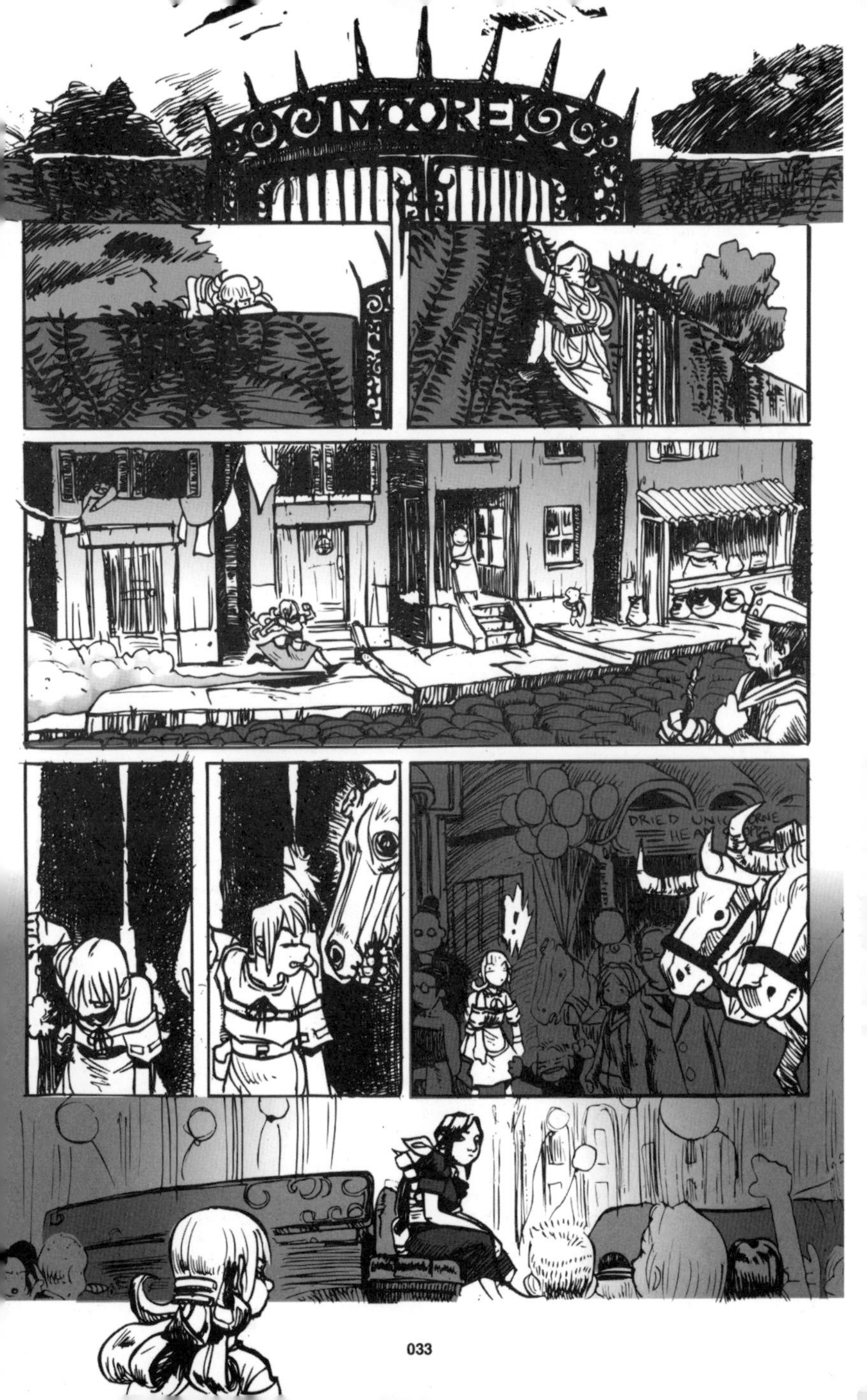
MOORE
DRIED UNI ORNE
HEA
!

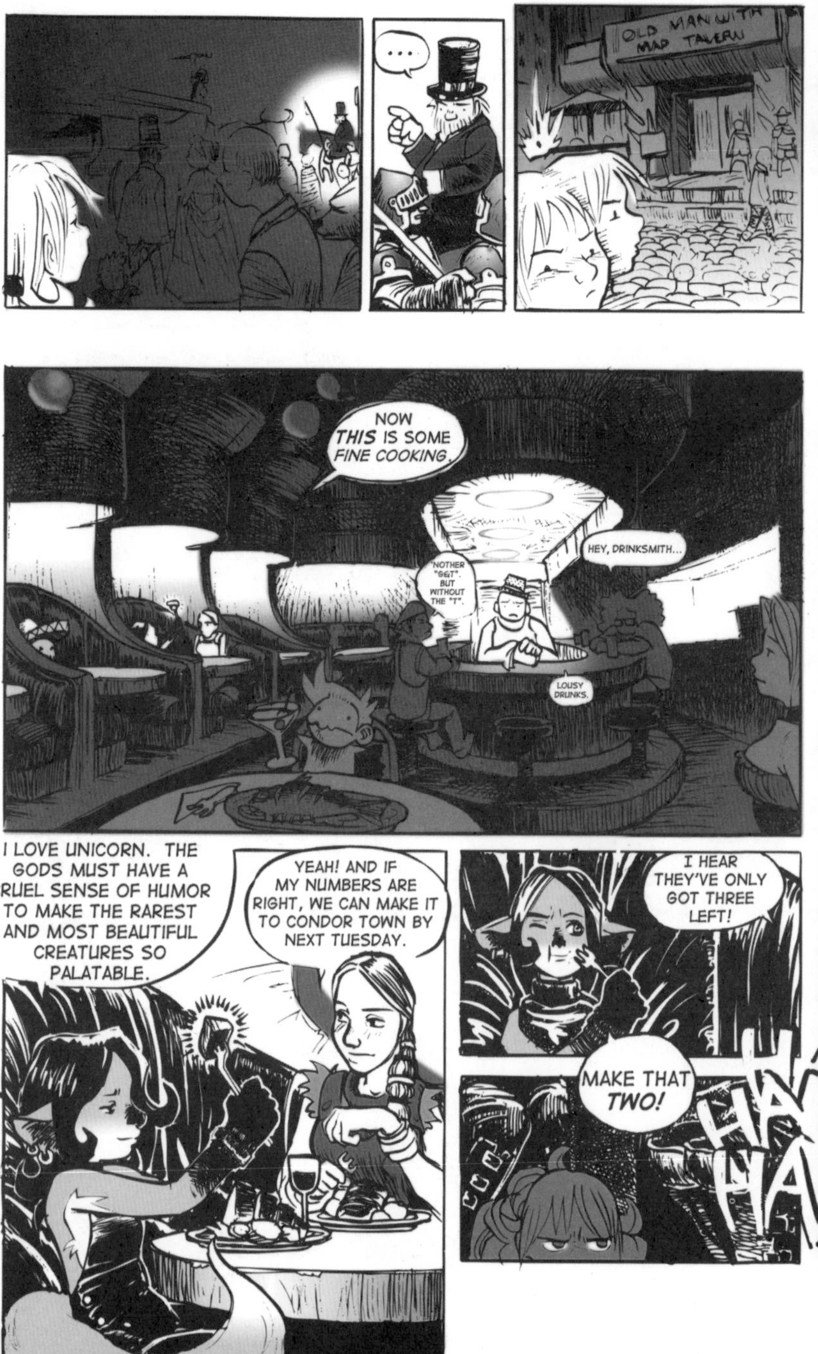
...
OLD MAN WITH MAP TAVERN
NOW THIS IS SOME FINE COOKING.
'NOTHER "G&T". BUT WITHOUT THE "T".
HEY, DRINKSMITH...
LOUSY DRUNKS.
I LOVE UNICORN. THE GODS MUST HAVE A CRUEL SENSE OF HUMOR TO MAKE THE RAREST AND MOST BEAUTIFUL CREATURES SO PALATABLE.
YEAH! AND IF MY NUMBERS ARE RIGHT, WE CAN MAKE IT TO CONDOR TOWN BY NEXT TUESDAY.
I HEAR THEY'VE ONLY GOT THREE LEFT!
MAKE THAT TWO!

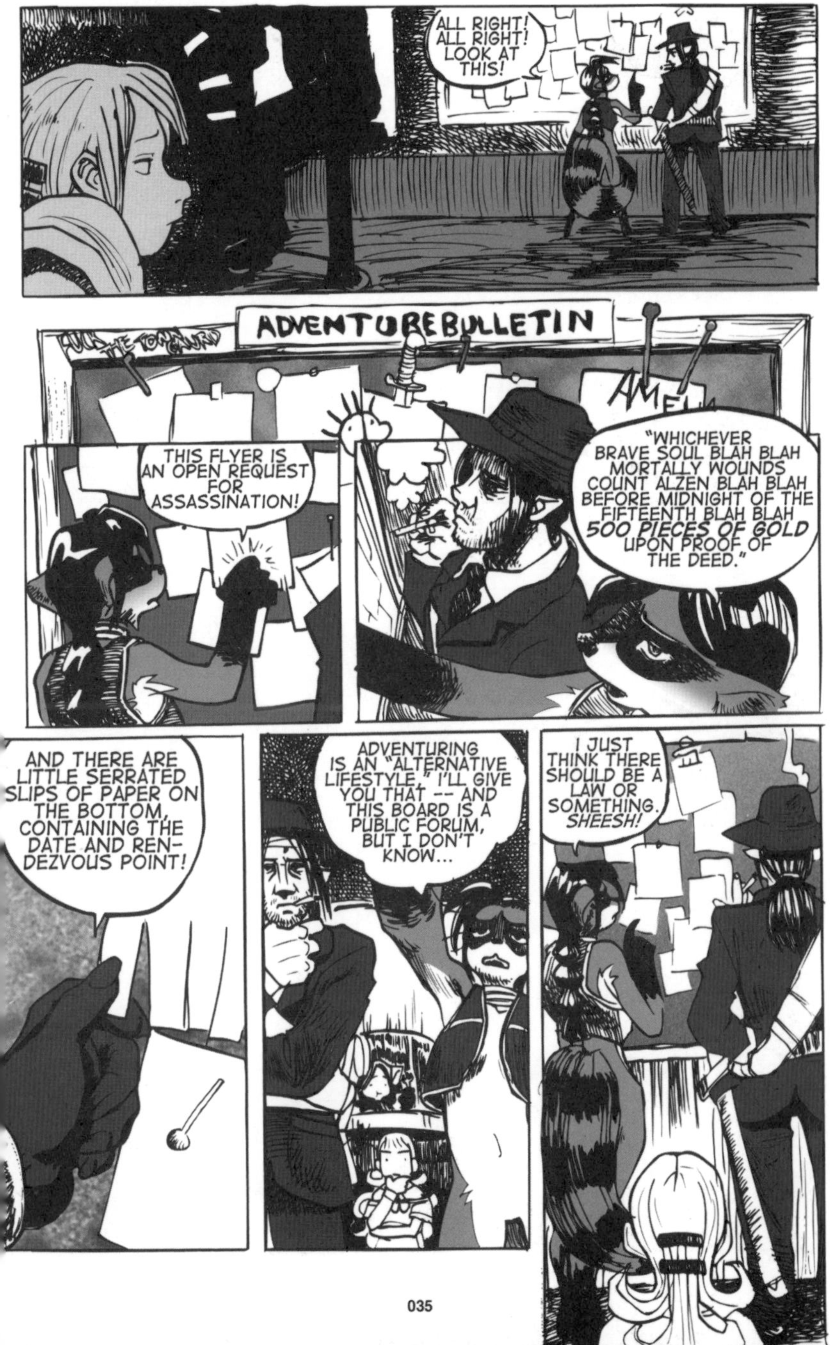
ALL RIGHT! ALL RIGHT! LOOK AT THIS!
ADVENTURE BULLETIN
THIS FLYER IS AN OPEN REQUEST FOR ASSASSINATION!
"WHICHEVER BRAVE SOUL BLAH BLAH MORTALLY WOUNDS COUNT ALZEN BLAH BLAH BEFORE MIDNIGHT OF THE FIFTEENTH BLAH BLAH *500 PIECES OF GOLD* UPON PROOF OF THE DEED."
AND THERE ARE LITTLE SERRATED SLIPS OF PAPER ON THE BOTTOM, CONTAINING THE DATE AND REN-DEZVOUS POINT!
ADVENTURING IS AN "ALTERNATIVE LIFESTYLE," I'LL GIVE YOU THAT -- AND THIS BOARD IS A PUBLIC FORUM, BUT I DON'T KNOW...
I JUST THINK THERE SHOULD BE A LAW OR SOMETHING. *SHEESH!*

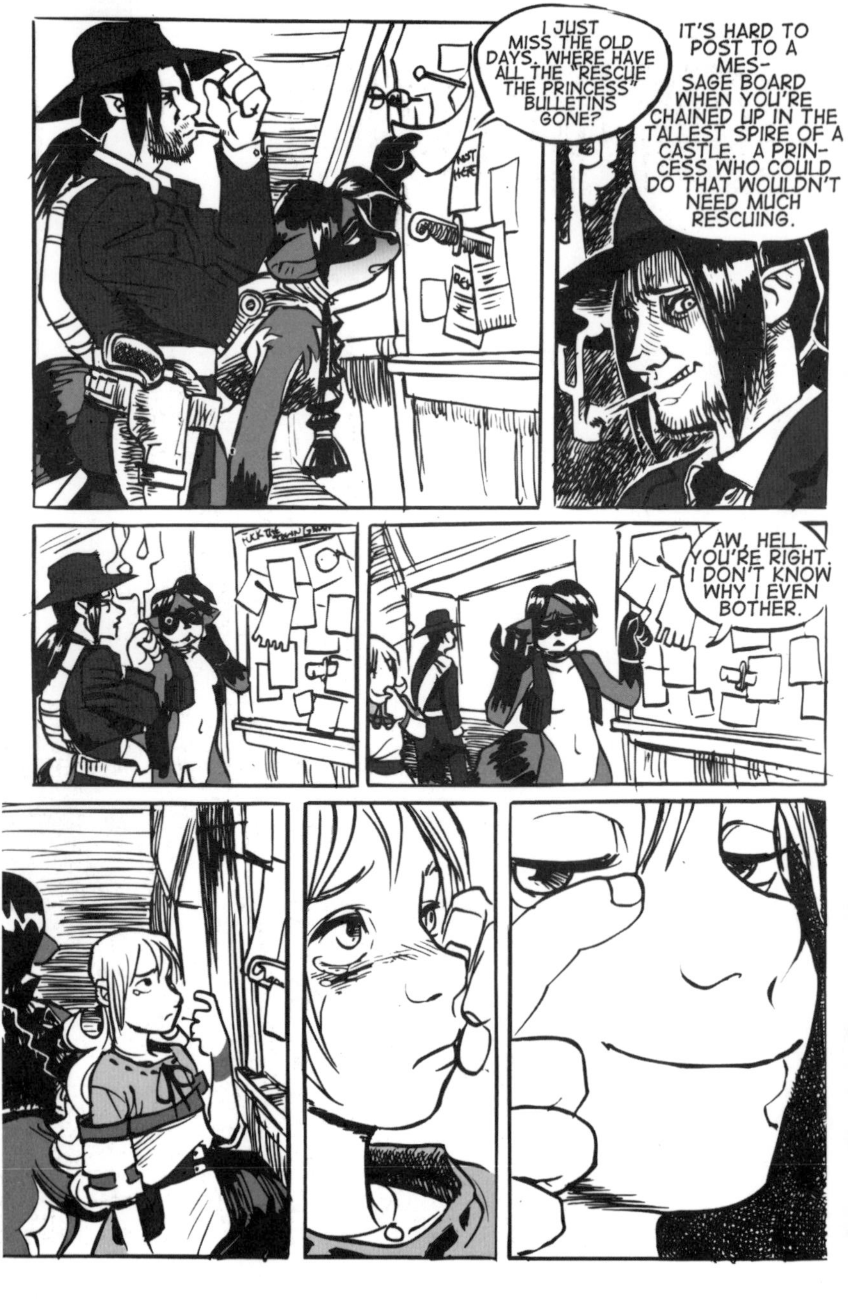
I JUST MISS THE OLD DAYS. WHERE HAVE ALL THE "RESCUE THE PRINCESS" BULLETINS GONE?
IT'S HARD TO POST TO A MES-SAGE BOARD WHEN YOU'RE CHAINED UP IN THE TALLEST SPIRE OF A CASTLE. A PRIN-CESS WHO COULD DO THAT WOULDN'T NEED MUCH RESCUING.
AW, HELL. YOU'RE RIGHT. I DON'T KNOW WHY I EVEN BOTHER.

LEGENDS FROM DARKWOOD

THE UNICORN HUNTERS : ISSUE TWO

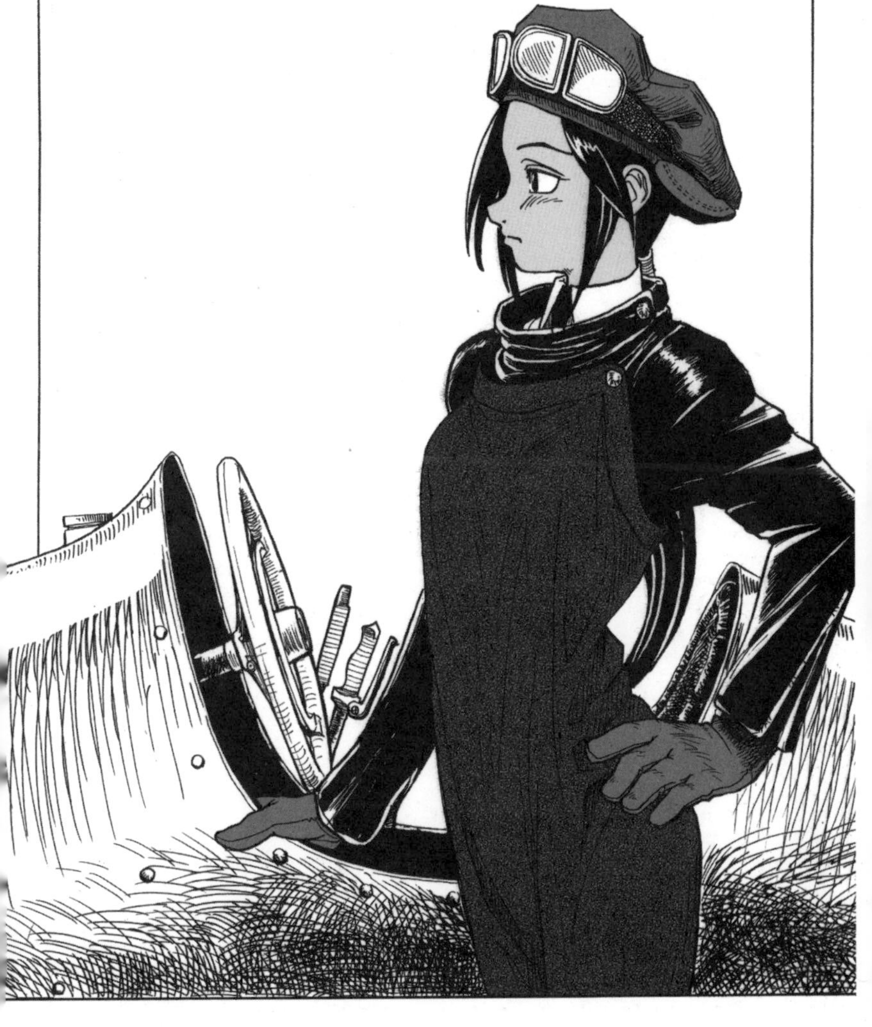

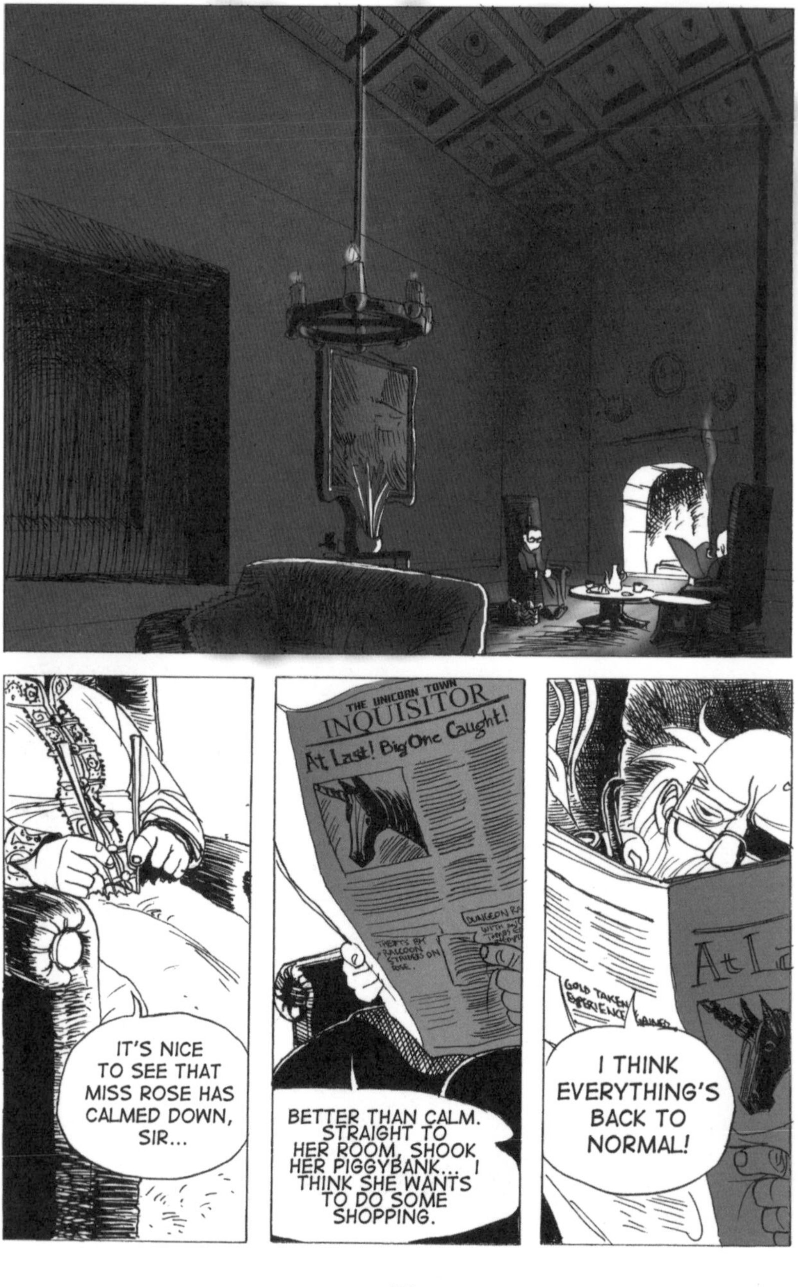
THE UNICORN TOWN
INQUISITOR
At Last! Big One Caught!
IT'S NICE TO SEE THAT MISS ROSE HAS CALMED DOWN, SIR...
BETTER THAN CALM. STRAIGHT TO HER ROOM, SHOOK HER PIGGYBANK... I THINK SHE WANTS TO DO SOME SHOPPING.
I THINK EVERYTHING'S BACK TO NORMAL!

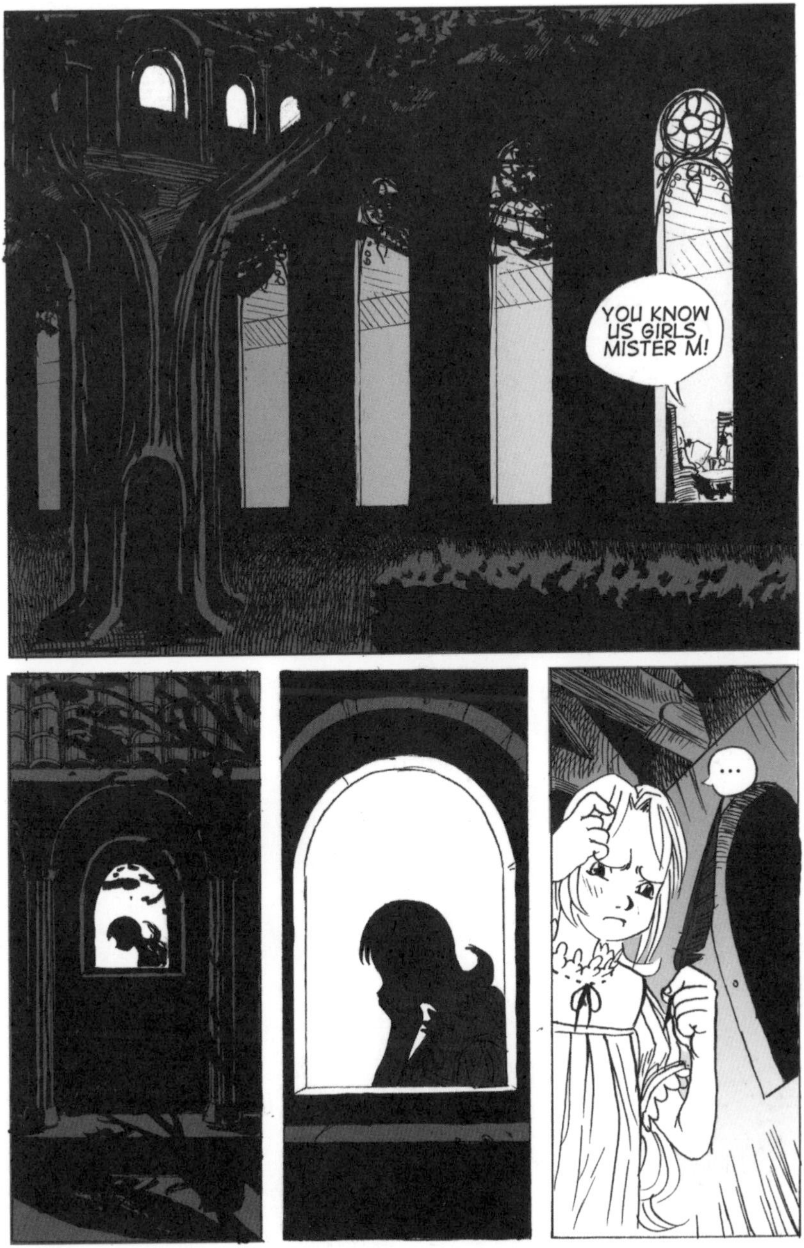
YOU KNOW US GIRLS, MISTER M!
...

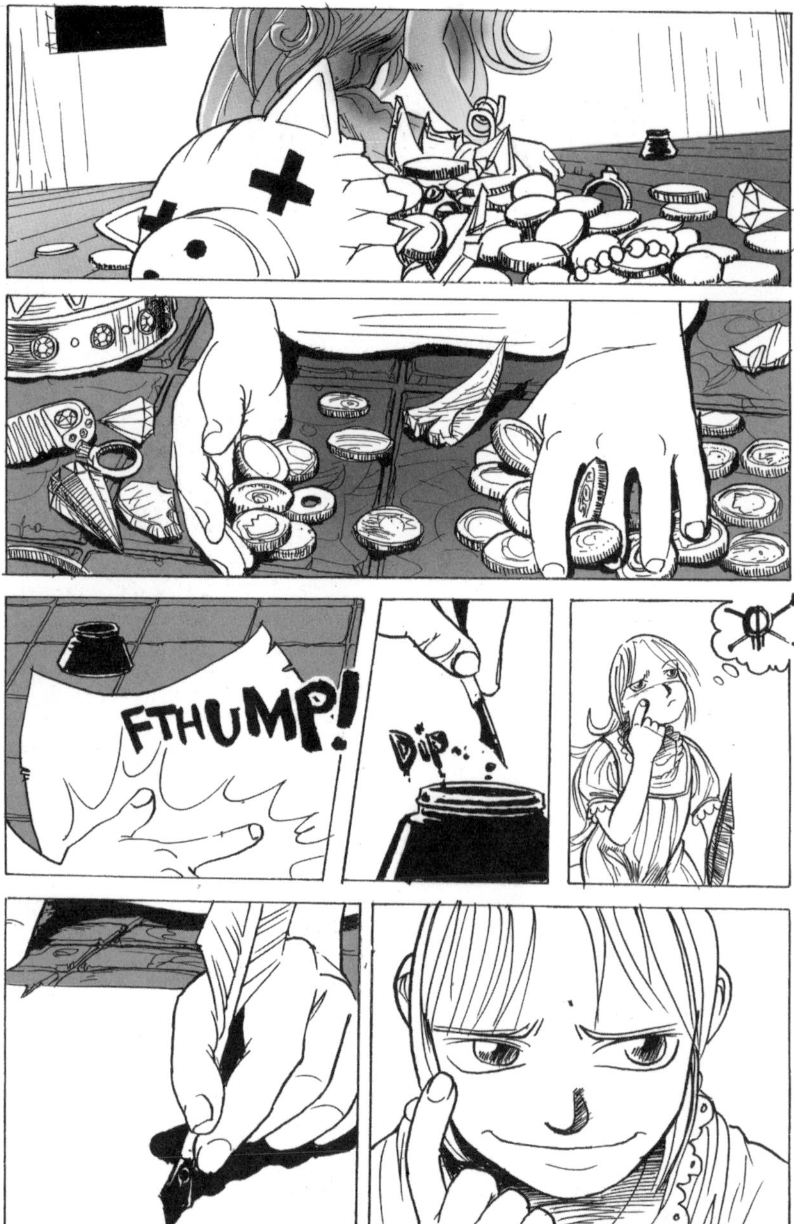
FTHUMP!
DIP...

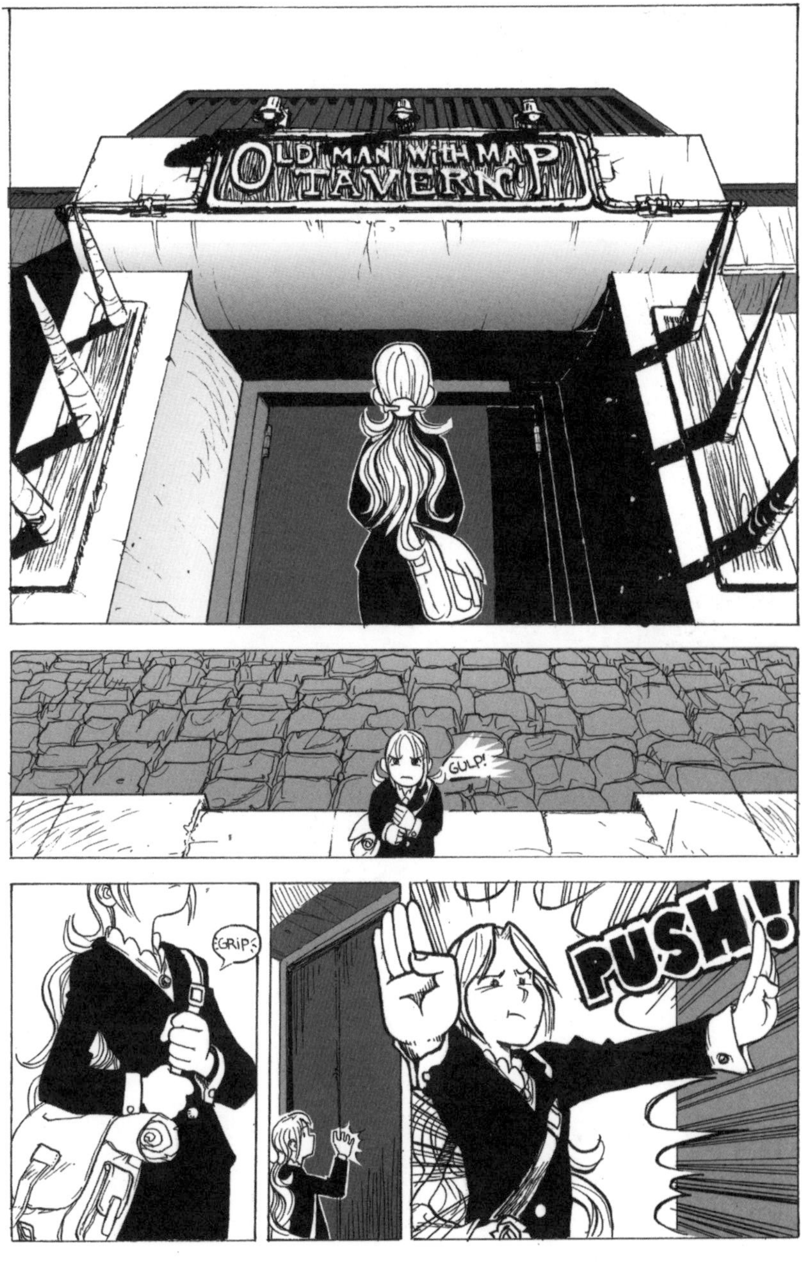
OLD MAN WITH MAP TAVERN
GULP!
GRIP
PUSH!

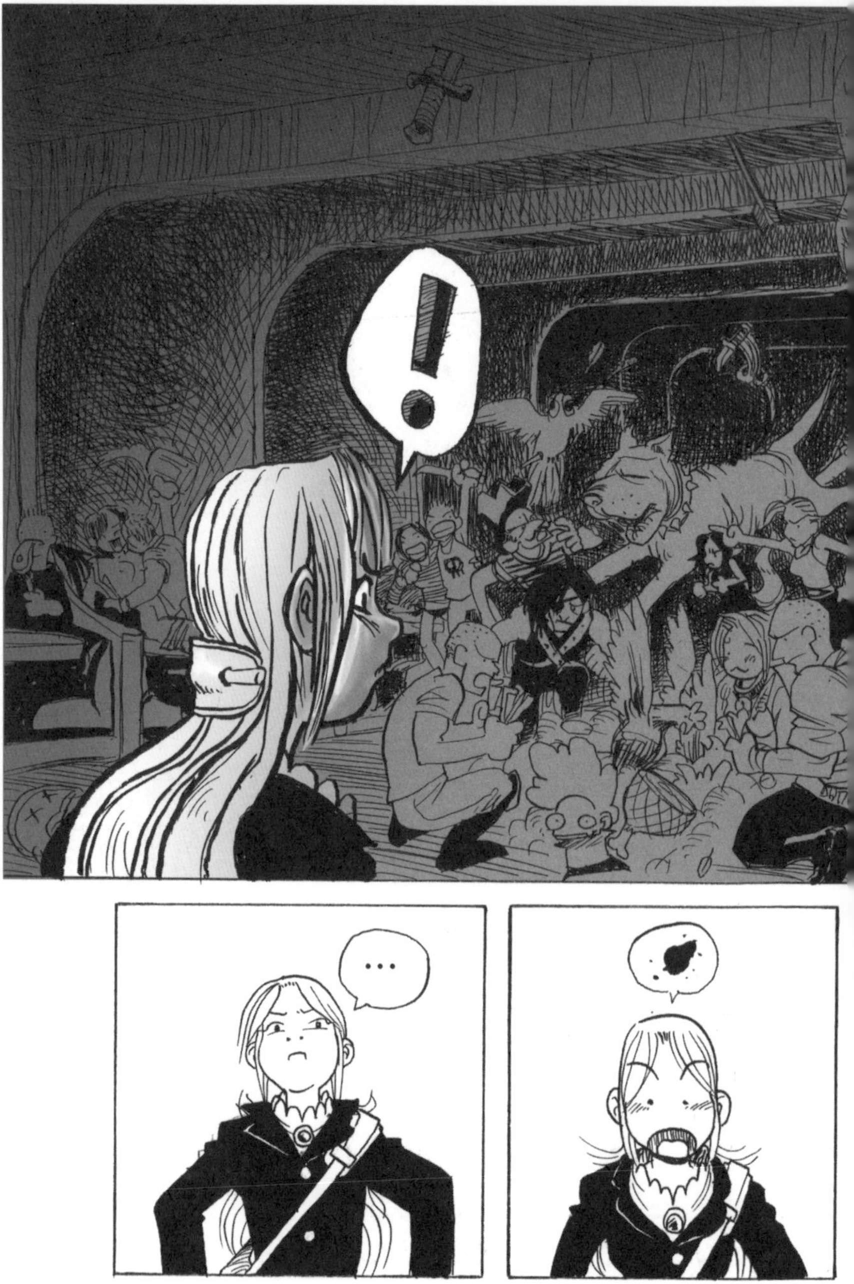
!
...

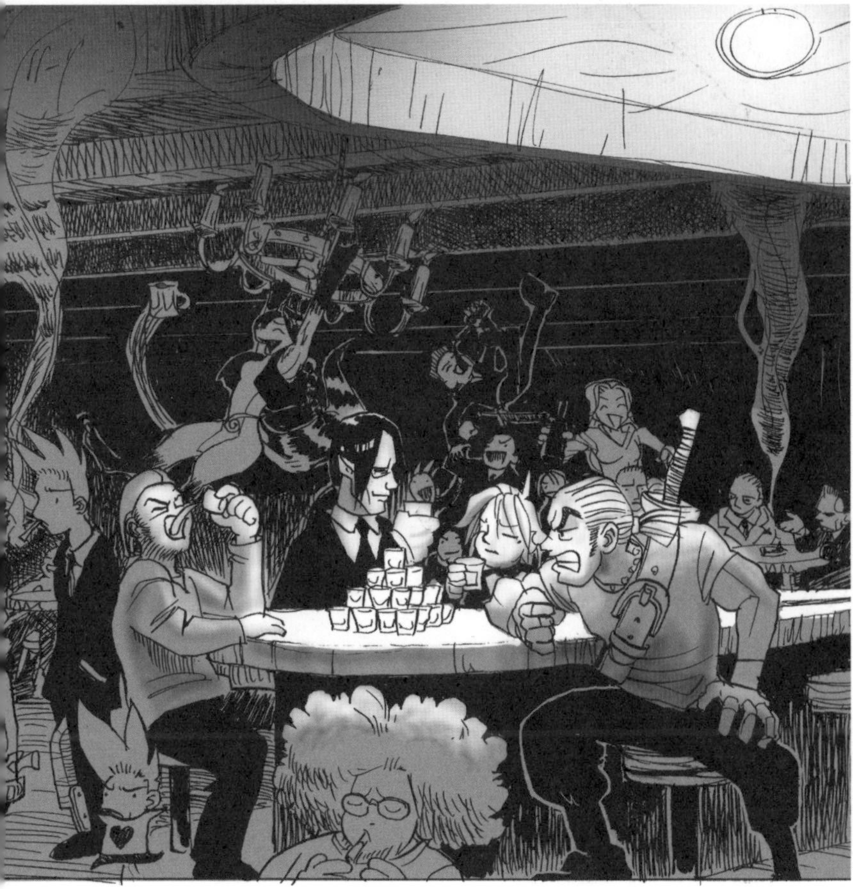

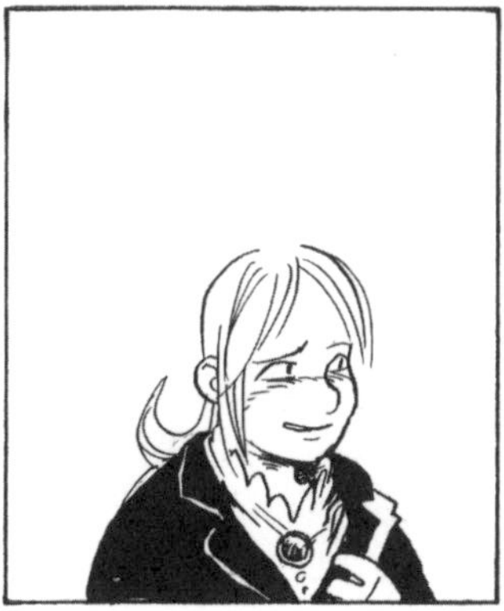

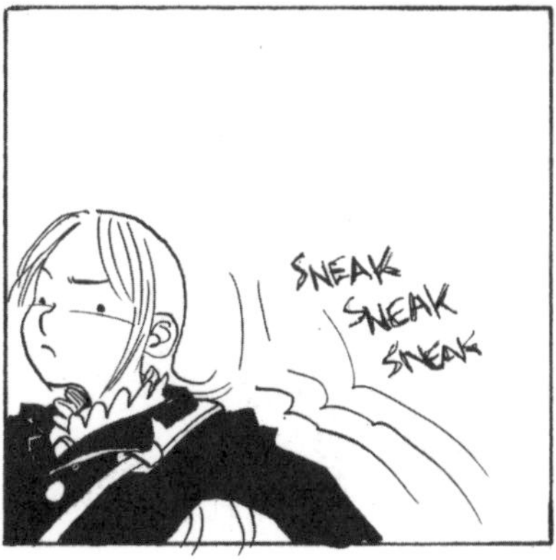
SNEAK
SNEAK
SNEAK

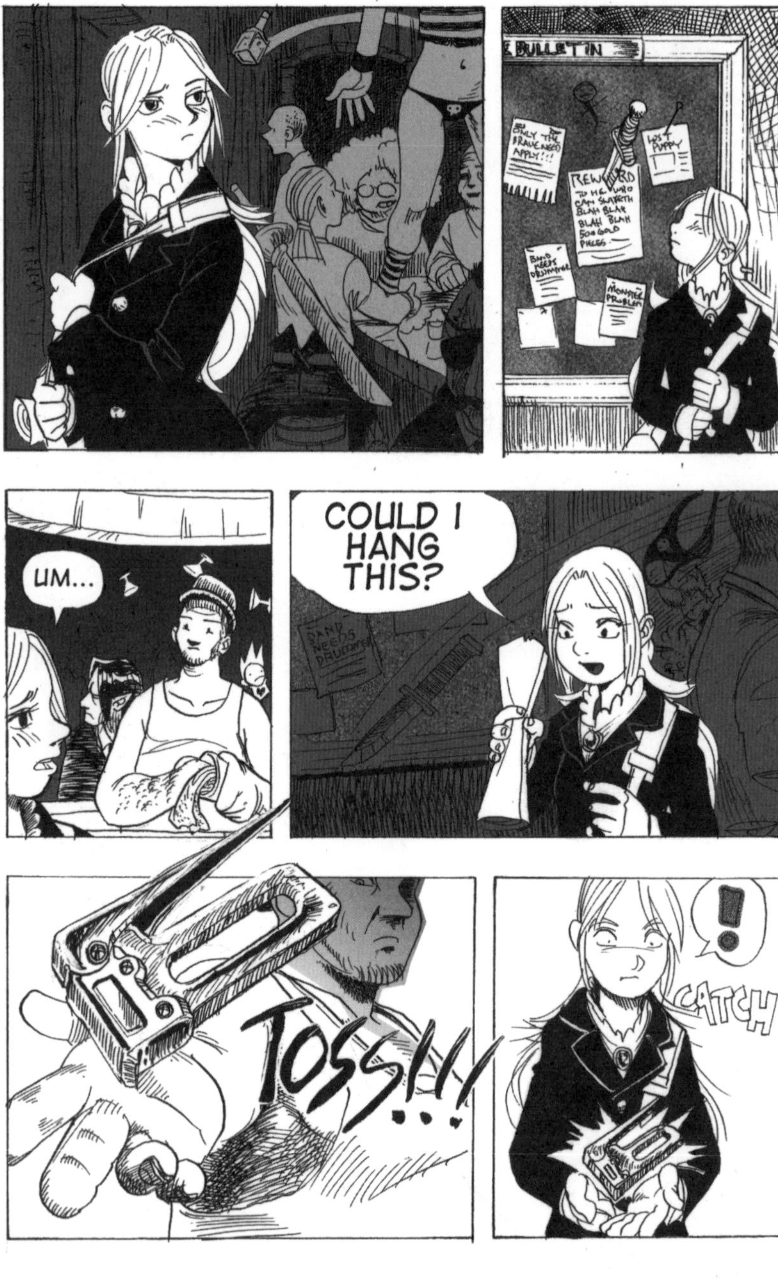
BULLETIN
ONLY THE BRAVE NEED APPLY!!!
REWARD TO HE WHO CAN SLAYETH BLAH BLAH BLAH BLAH 500 GOLD PIECES
LOST PUPPY
BAND NEEDS DRUMMER
MONSTER PROBLEM
UM...
COULD I HANG THIS?
BAND NEEDS DRUMMER
TOSS!!!
!
CATCH

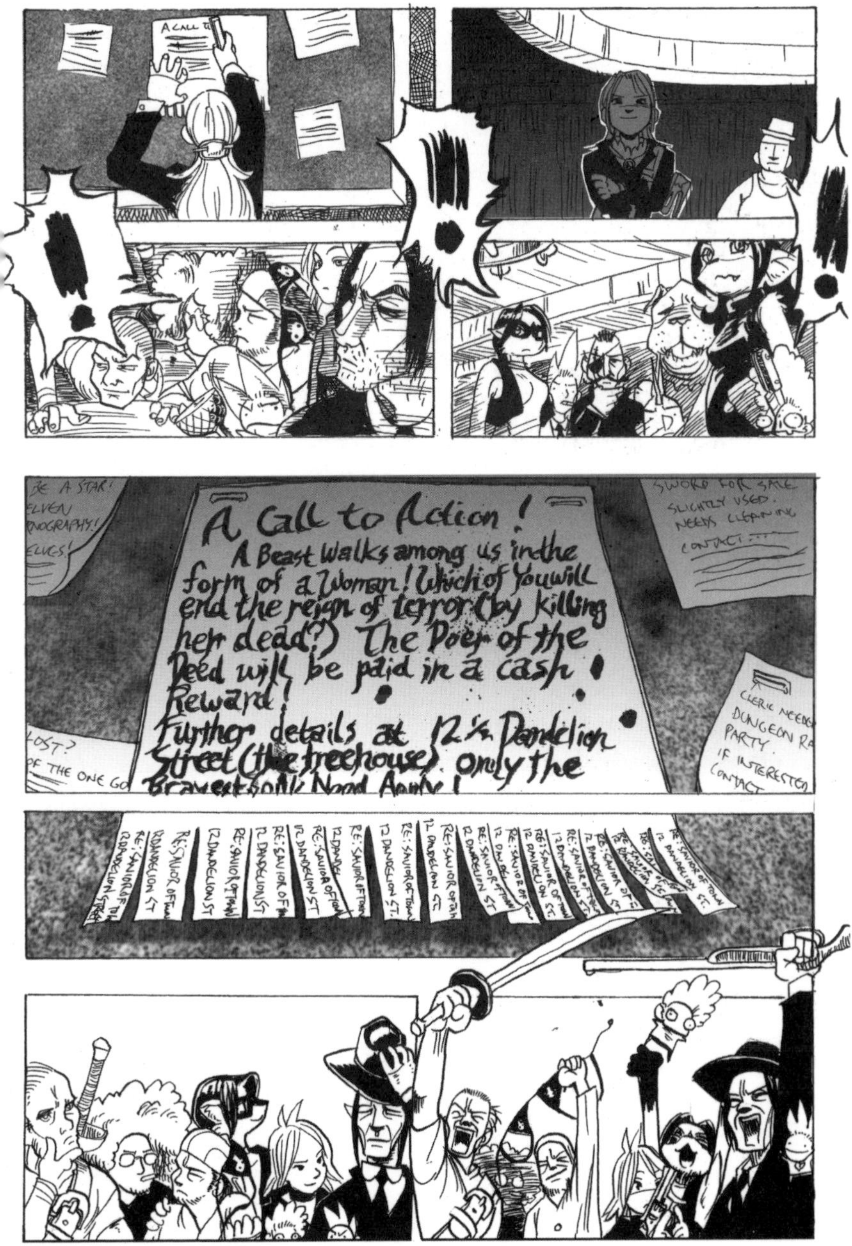
A CALL T
A Call to Action!
A Beast Walks among us in the form of a Woman! Which of You will end the reign of terror (by killing her dead?) The Doer of the Deed will be paid in a cash Reward!
Further details at 12½ Dandelion Street (the treehouse) only the Bravest Folk Need Apply!
BE A STAR!
SWORD FOR SALE
SLIGHTLY USED.
NEEDS CLEANING
CONTACT....
DUNGEON
PARTY.
IF INTERESTED
CONTACT
LOST?
OF THE ONE
RE: SAVIOR OF TOWN
12 DANDELION ST.

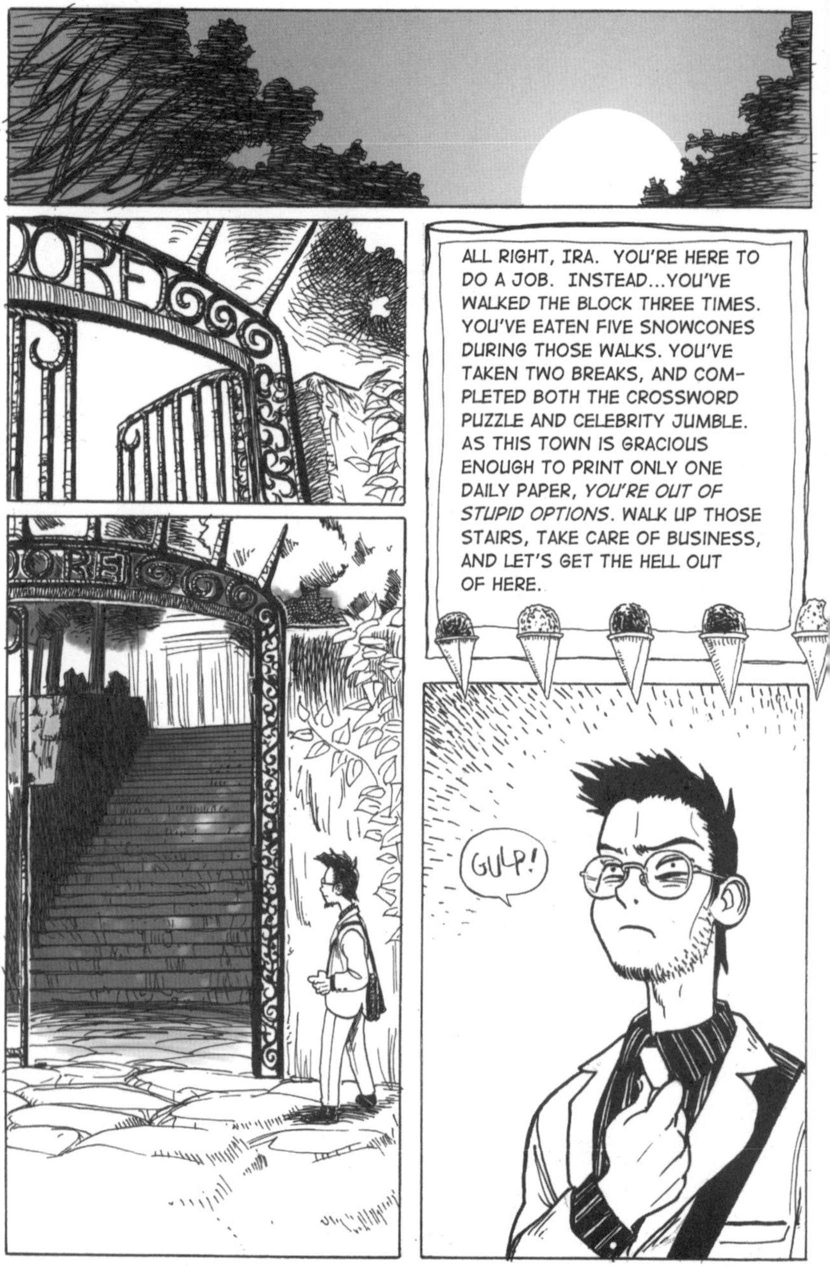
ALL RIGHT, IRA. YOU'RE HERE TO DO A JOB. INSTEAD...YOU'VE WALKED THE BLOCK THREE TIMES. YOU'VE EATEN FIVE SNOWCONES DURING THOSE WALKS. YOU'VE TAKEN TWO BREAKS, AND COMPLETED BOTH THE CROSSWORD PUZZLE AND CELEBRITY JUMBLE. AS THIS TOWN IS GRACIOUS ENOUGH TO PRINT ONLY ONE DAILY PAPER, *YOU'RE OUT OF STUPID OPTIONS*. WALK UP THOSE STAIRS, TAKE CARE OF BUSINESS, AND LET'S GET THE HELL OUT OF HERE.
GULP!

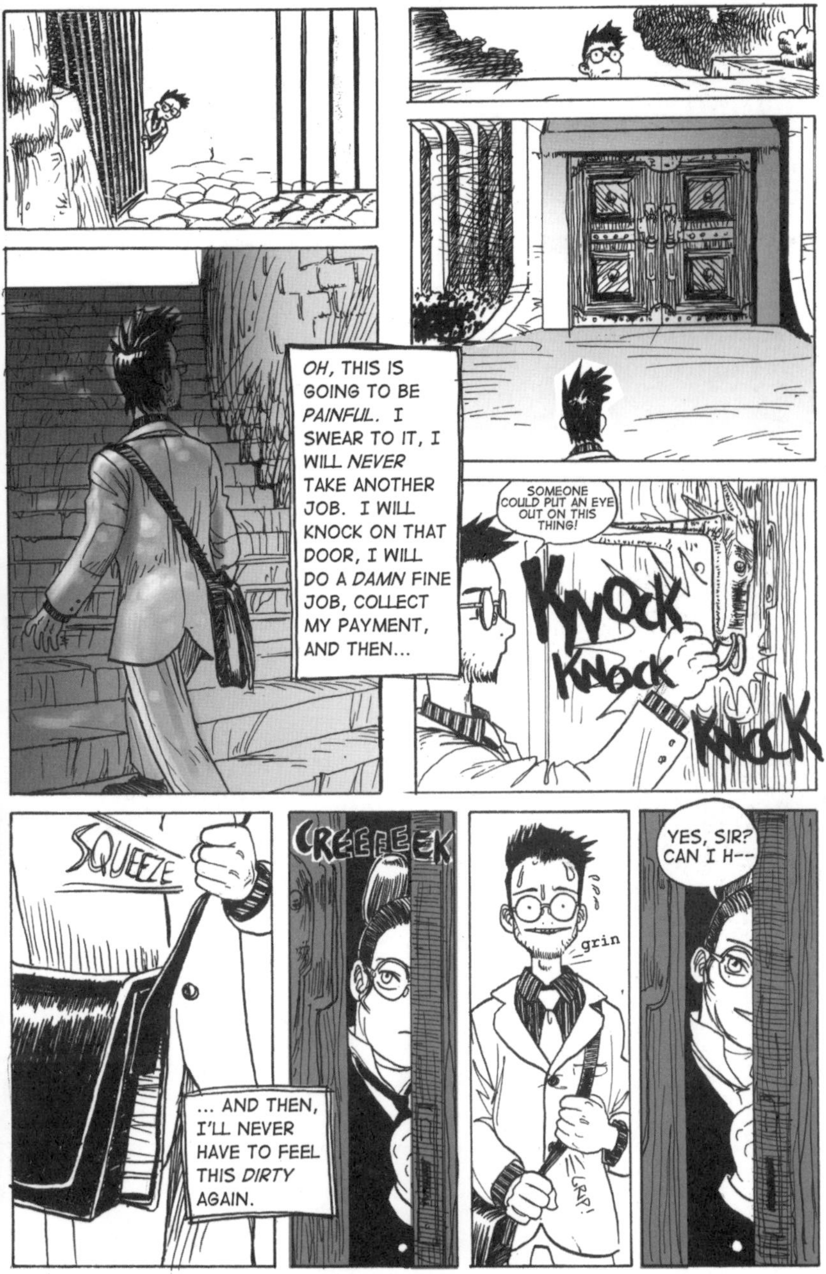
OH, THIS IS GOING TO BE PAINFUL. I SWEAR TO IT, I WILL NEVER TAKE ANOTHER JOB. I WILL KNOCK ON THAT DOOR, I WILL DO A DAMN FINE JOB, COLLECT MY PAYMENT, AND THEN...
SOMEONE COULD PUT AN EYE OUT ON THIS THING!
KNOCK
KNOCK
KNOCK
SQUEEZE
... AND THEN, I'LL NEVER HAVE TO FEEL THIS DIRTY AGAIN.
CREEEEEK
grin
GRIP!
YES, SIR? CAN I H--

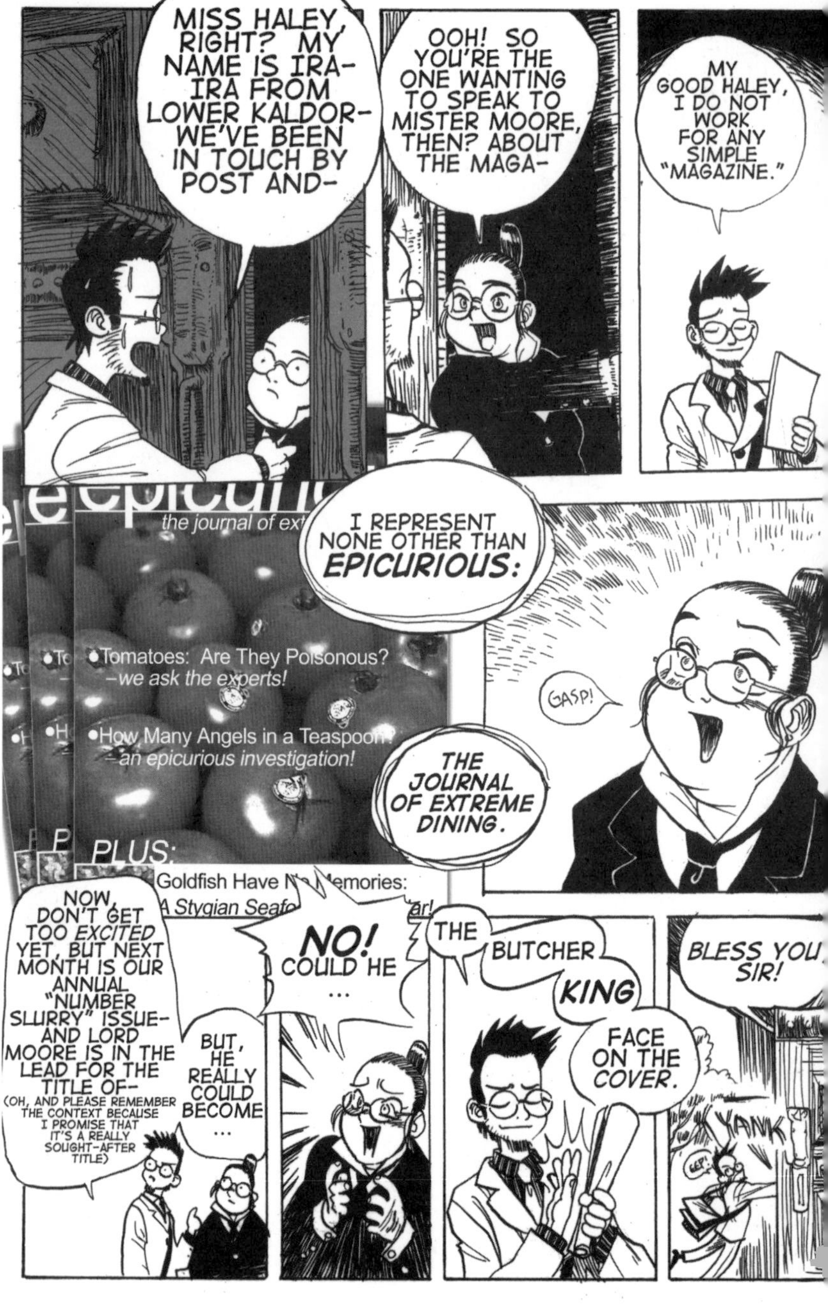
MISS HALEY, RIGHT? MY NAME IS IRA-IRA FROM LOWER KALDOR- WE'VE BEEN IN TOUCH BY POST AND-
OOH! SO YOU'RE THE ONE WANTING TO SPEAK TO MISTER MOORE, THEN? ABOUT THE MAGA-
MY GOOD HALEY, I DO NOT WORK FOR ANY SIMPLE "MAGAZINE."
I REPRESENT NONE OTHER THAN EPICURIOUS:
epicurious
the journal of ext
•Tomatoes: Are They Poisonous? –we ask the experts!
•How Many Angels in a Teaspoon? –an epicurious investigation!
PLUS:
GASP!
THE JOURNAL OF EXTREME DINING.
NOW, DON'T GET TOO EXCITED YET, BUT NEXT MONTH IS OUR ANNUAL "NUMBER SLURRY" ISSUE- AND LORD MOORE IS IN THE LEAD FOR THE TITLE OF-
(OH, AND PLEASE REMEMBER THE CONTEXT BECAUSE I PROMISE THAT IT'S A REALLY SOUGHT-AFTER TITLE)
BUT, HE REALLY COULD BECOME ...
NO! COULD HE ...
THE
BUTCHER
KING
FACE ON THE COVER.
BLESS YOU, SIR!
YANK

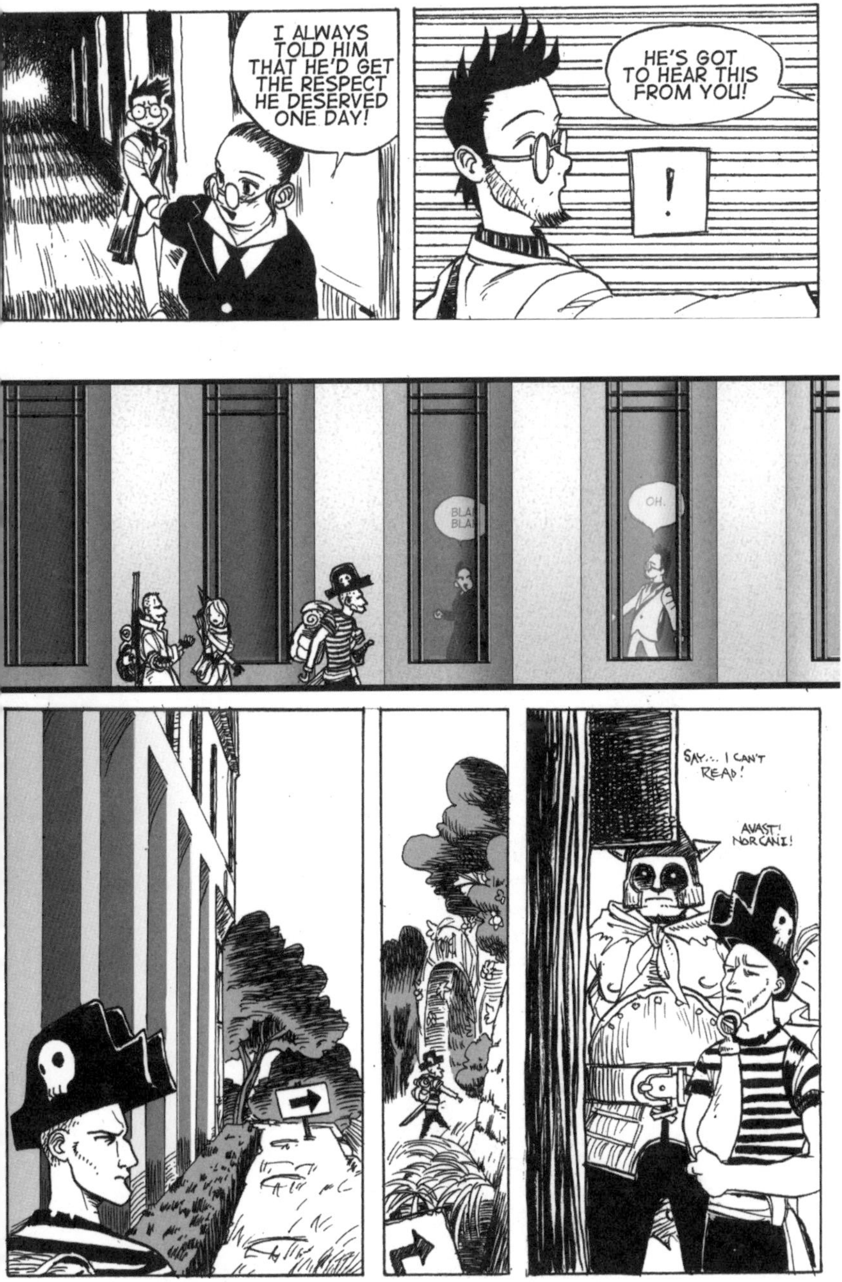
I ALWAYS TOLD HIM THAT HE'D GET THE RESPECT HE DESERVED ONE DAY!
HE'S GOT TO HEAR THIS FROM YOU!
!
BLA BLA
OH.
SAY.... I CAN'T READ!
AVAST! NORCANI!

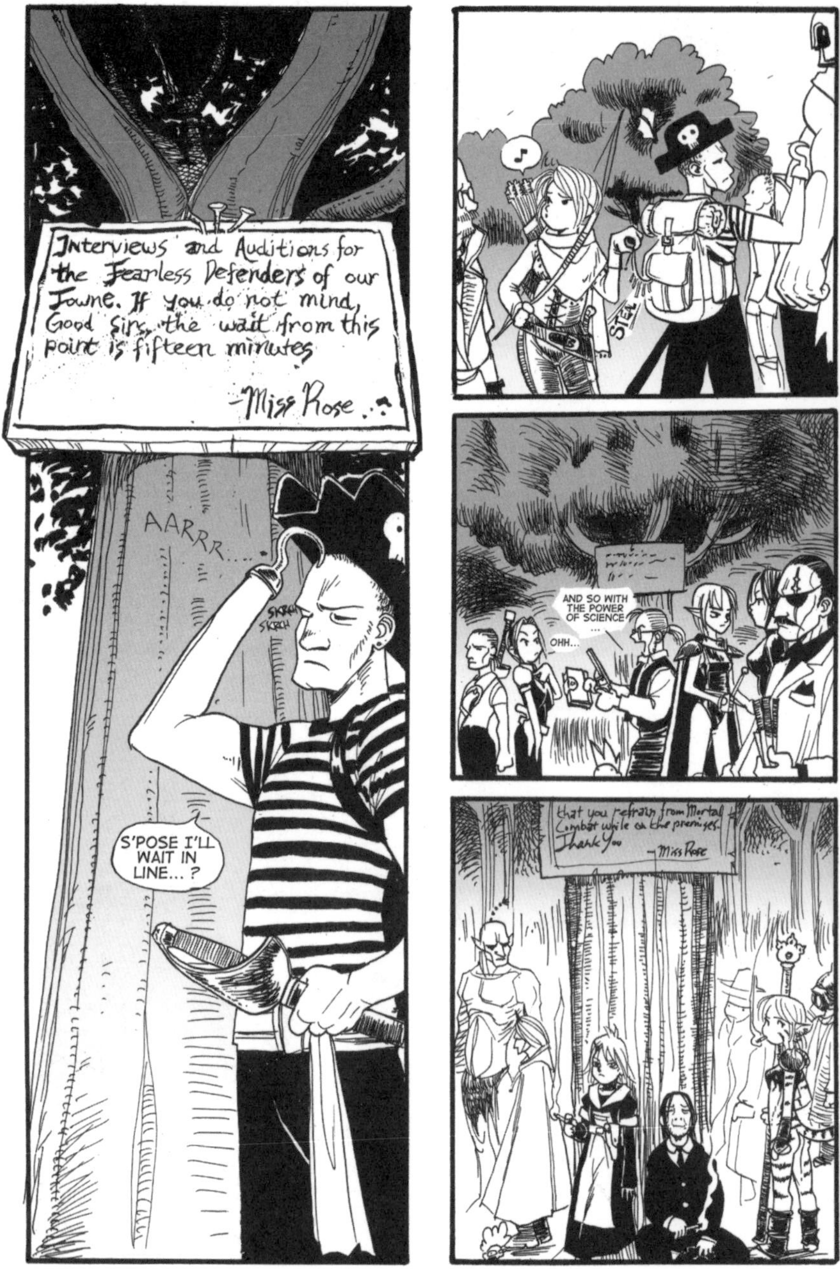
Interviews and Auditions for the Fearless Defenders of our Towne. If you do not mind, Good Sirs, the wait from this point is fifteen minutes
-Miss Rose
AARRR....
SKRCH
SKRCH
S'POSE I'LL WAIT IN LINE... ?
STEAL
AND SO WITH THE POWER OF SCIENCE ...
OHH...
that you refrain from Mortal Combat while on the premises. Thank You
-Miss Rose

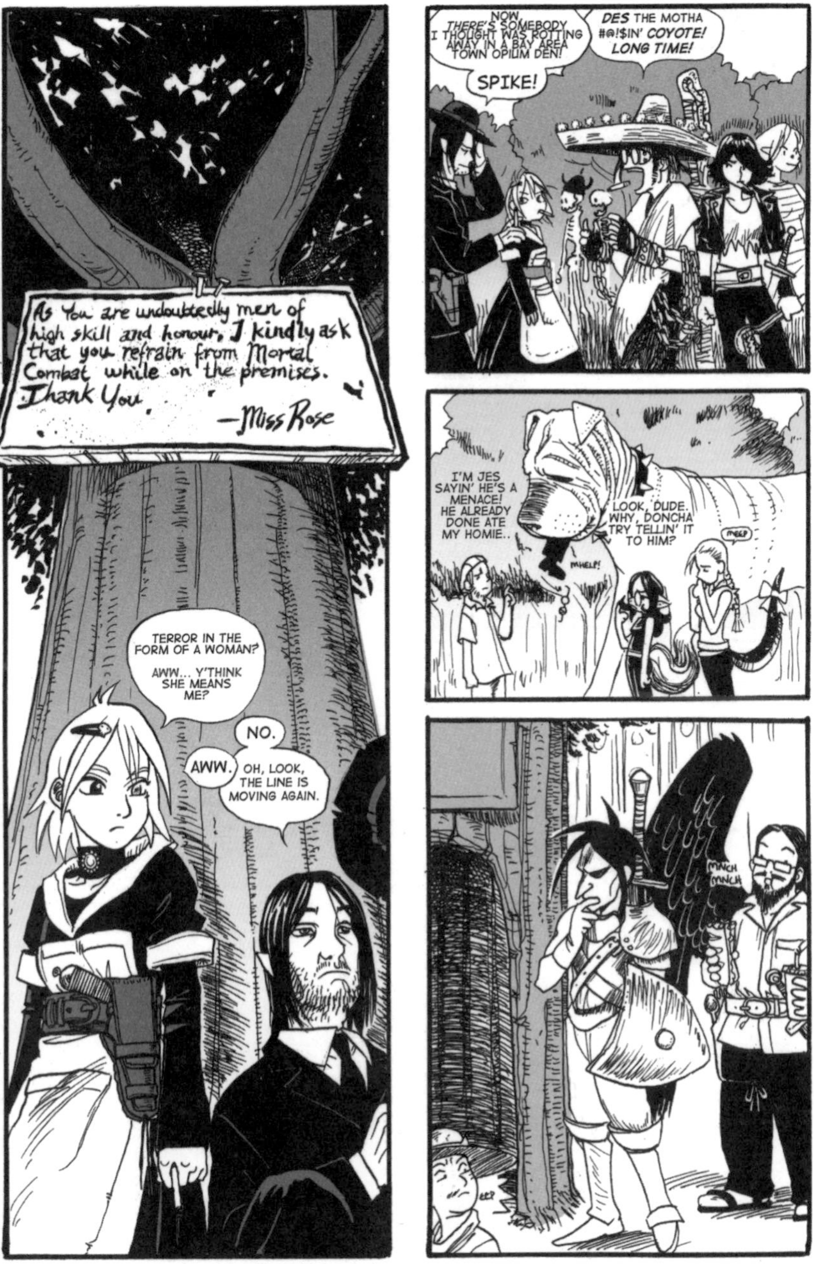

As You are undoubtedly men of high skill and honour, I kindly ask that you refrain from Mortal Combat while on the premises. Thank You. —Miss Rose
TERROR IN THE FORM OF A WOMAN? AWW... Y'THINK SHE MEANS ME?
NO.
AWW.
OH, LOOK, THE LINE IS MOVING AGAIN.
NOW, THERE'S SOMEBODY I THOUGHT WAS ROTTING AWAY IN A BAY AREA TOWN OPIUM DEN!
SPIKE!
DES THE MOTHA #@!$IN' COYOTE! LONG TIME!
I'M JES SAYIN' HE'S A MENACE! HE ALREADY DONE ATE MY HOMIE..
MHELP!
LOOK, DUDE. WHY, DONCHA TRY TELLIN' IT TO HIM?
MEEP
MNCH MNCH
EEP

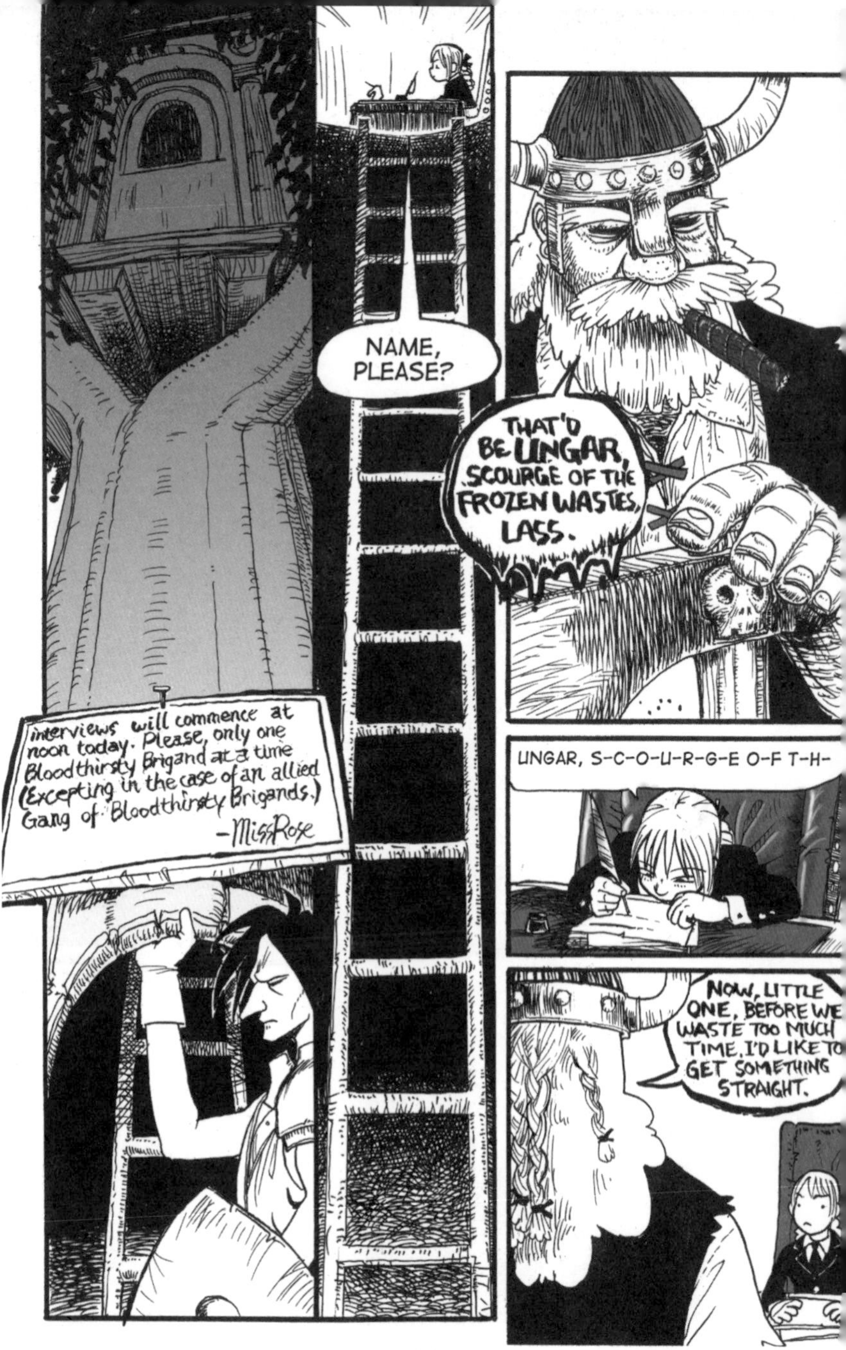

interviews will commence at noon today. Please, only one Bloodthirsty Brigand at a time (Excepting in the case of an allied Gang of Bloodthirsty Brigands.)
-MissRose
NAME, PLEASE?
THAT'D BE UNGAR, SCOURGE OF THE FROZEN WASTES, LASS.
UNGAR, S-C-O-U-R-G-E O-F T-H-
NOW, LITTLE ONE, BEFORE WE WASTE TOO MUCH TIME, I'D LIKE TO GET SOMETHING STRAIGHT.

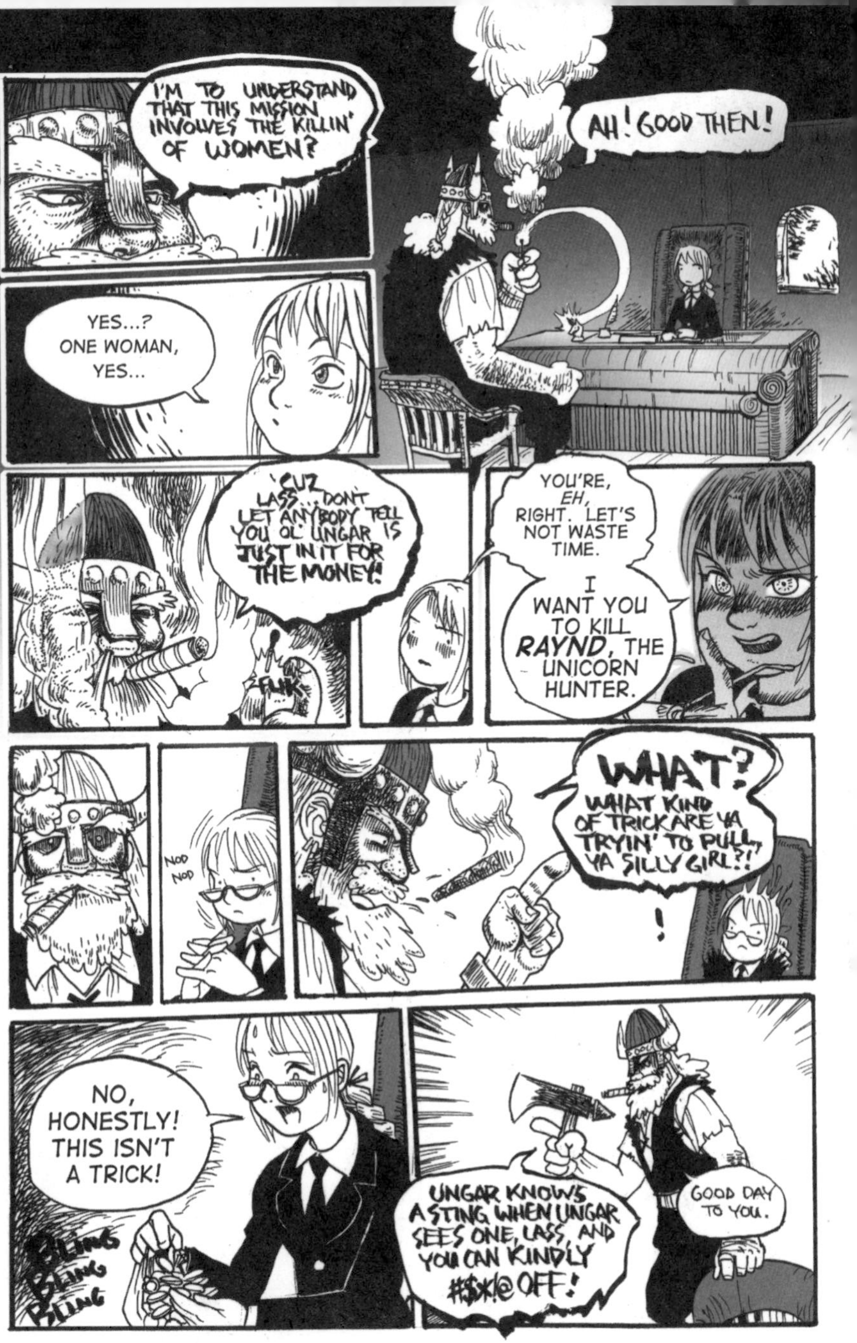
I'M TO UNDERSTAND THAT THIS MISSION INVOLVES THE KILLIN' OF WOMEN?
AH! GOOD THEN!
YES...? ONE WOMAN, YES...
'CUZ LASS... DON'T LET ANYBODY TELL YOU OL' UNGAR IS JUST IN IT FOR THE MONEY!
FLIK
YOU'RE, EH, RIGHT. LET'S NOT WASTE TIME.
I WANT YOU TO KILL RAYND, THE UNICORN HUNTER.
NOD NOD
WHAT? WHAT KIND OF TRICK ARE YA TRYIN' TO PULL, YA SILLY GIRL?!
!
NO, HONESTLY! THIS ISN'T A TRICK!
BLING BLING BLING
UNGAR KNOWS A STING WHEN UNGAR SEES ONE, LASS, AND YOU CAN KINDLY #$*!@ OFF!
GOOD DAY TO YOU.

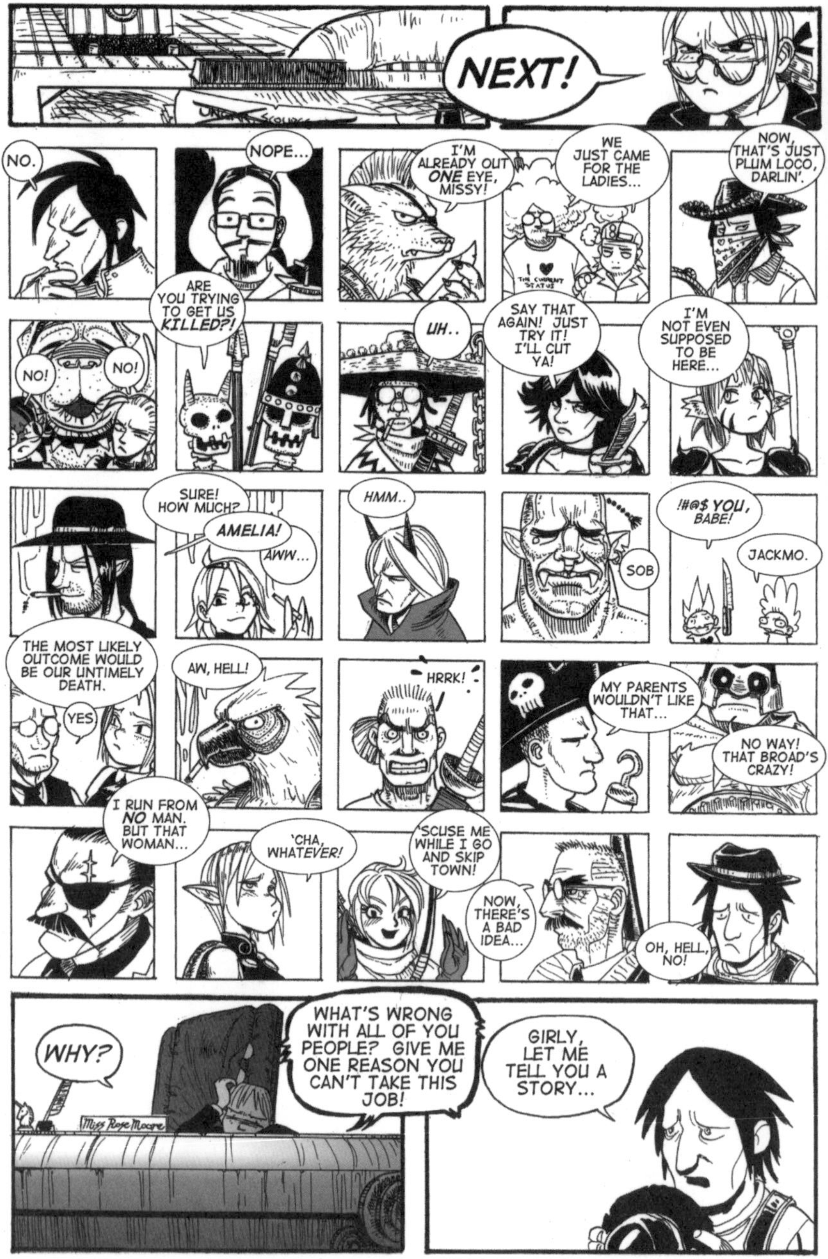
NEXT!
NO.
NOPE...
I'M ALREADY OUT ONE EYE, MISSY!
WE JUST CAME FOR THE LADIES...
NOW, THAT'S JUST PLUM LOCO, DARLIN'.
NO!
NO!
ARE YOU TRYING TO GET US KILLED?!
UH..
SAY THAT AGAIN! JUST TRY IT! I'LL CUT YA!
I'M NOT EVEN SUPPOSED TO BE HERE...
SURE! HOW MUCH?
AMELIA!
AWW...
HMM..
SOB
!#@$ YOU, BABE!
JACKMO.
THE MOST LIKELY OUTCOME WOULD BE OUR UNTIMELY DEATH.
YES.
AW, HELL!
HRRK!
MY PARENTS WOULDN'T LIKE THAT...
NO WAY! THAT BROAD'S CRAZY!
I RUN FROM NO MAN. BUT THAT WOMAN...
'CHA, WHATEVER!
'SCUSE ME WHILE I GO AND SKIP TOWN!
NOW, THERE'S A BAD IDEA...
OH, HELL, NO!
WHY?
Miss Rose Moore
WHAT'S WRONG WITH ALL OF YOU PEOPLE? GIVE ME ONE REASON YOU CAN'T TAKE THIS JOB!
GIRLY, LET ME TELL YOU A STORY...

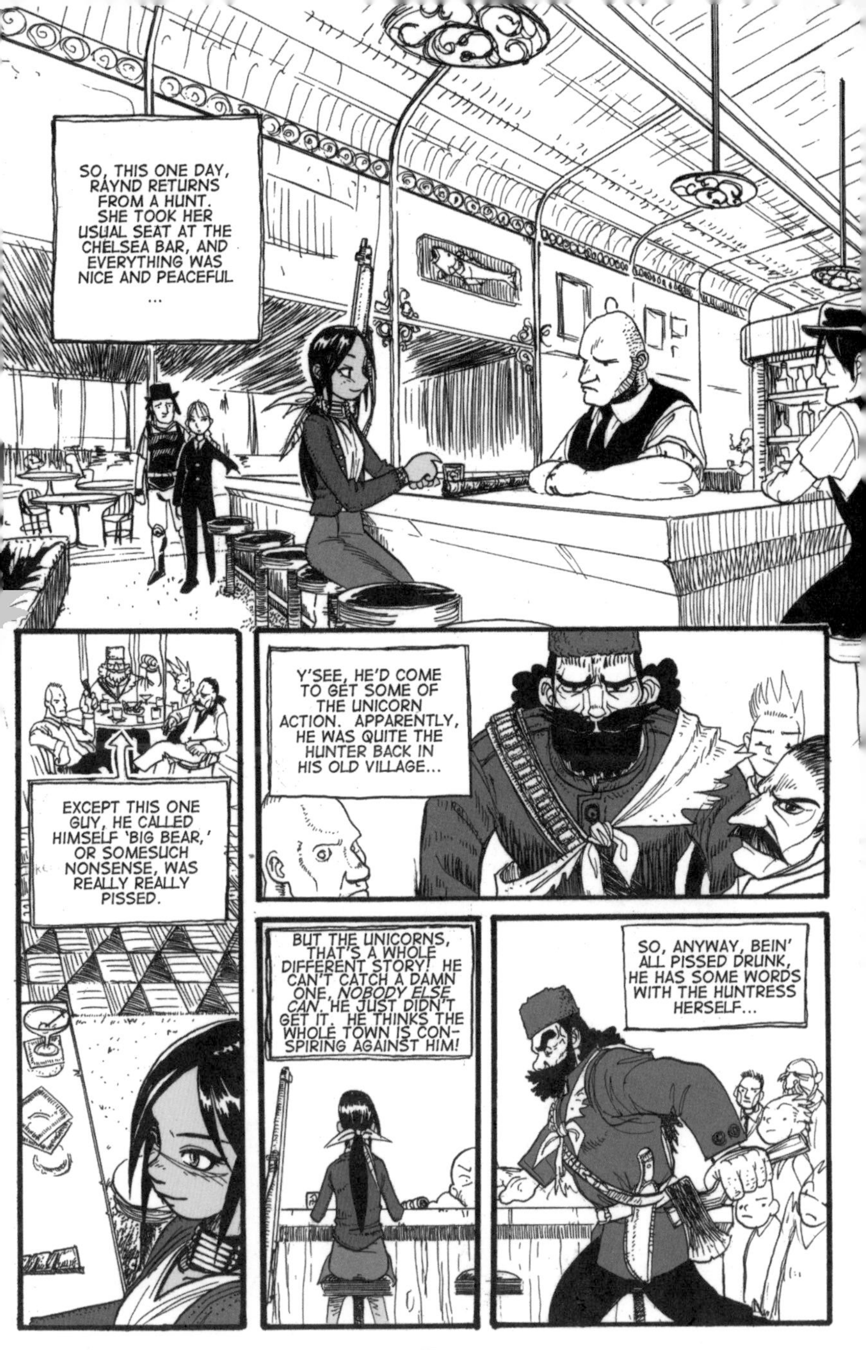
SO, THIS ONE DAY, RAYND RETURNS FROM A HUNT. SHE TOOK HER USUAL SEAT AT THE CHELSEA BAR, AND EVERYTHING WAS NICE AND PEACEFUL ...
EXCEPT THIS ONE GUY, HE CALLED HIMSELF 'BIG BEAR,' OR SOMESUCH NONSENSE, WAS REALLY REALLY PISSED.
Y'SEE, HE'D COME TO GET SOME OF THE UNICORN ACTION. APPARENTLY, HE WAS QUITE THE HUNTER BACK IN HIS OLD VILLAGE...
BUT THE UNICORNS, THAT'S A WHOLE DIFFERENT STORY! HE CAN'T CATCH A DAMN ONE, *NOBODY ELSE CAN*. HE JUST DIDN'T GET IT. HE THINKS THE WHOLE TOWN IS CONSPIRING AGAINST HIM!
SO, ANYWAY, BEIN' ALL PISSED DRUNK, HE HAS SOME WORDS WITH THE HUNTRESS HERSELF...

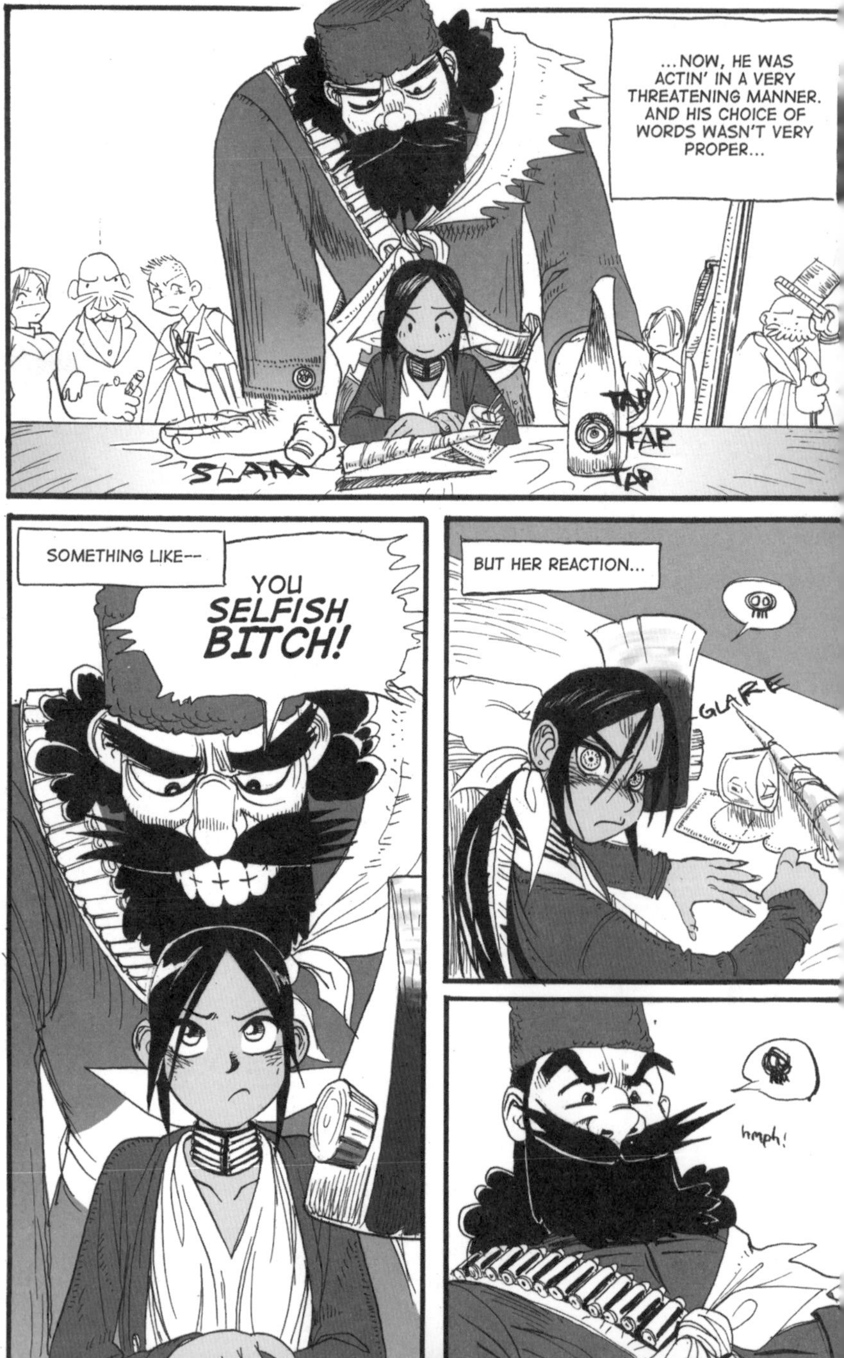
...NOW, HE WAS ACTIN' IN A VERY THREATENING MANNER. AND HIS CHOICE OF WORDS WASN'T VERY PROPER...
SLAM
TAP
TAP
TAP
SOMETHING LIKE--
YOU SELFISH BITCH!
BUT HER REACTION...
GLARE
hmph!

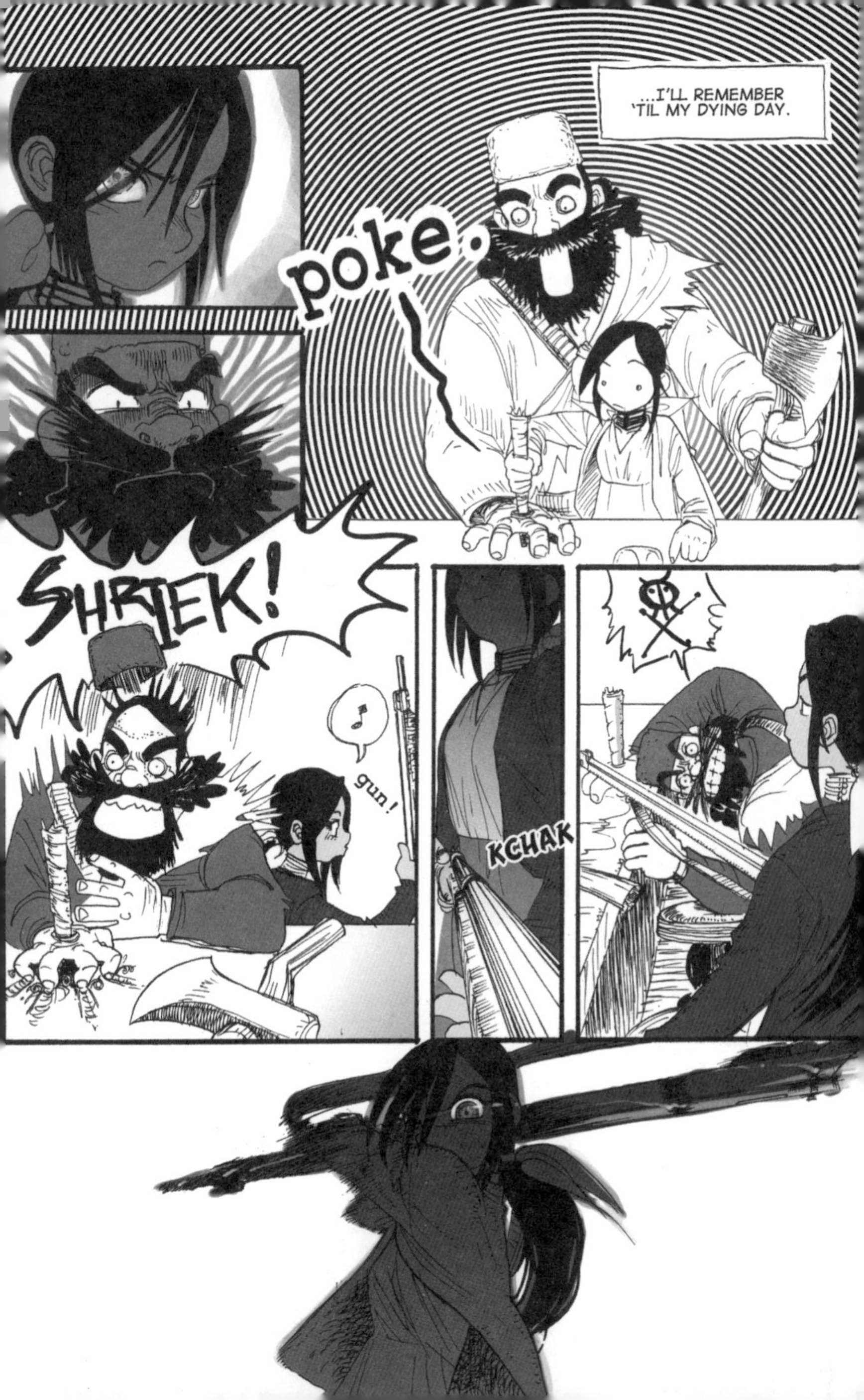
...I'LL REMEMBER 'TIL MY DYING DAY.
poke.
SHRIEK!
gun!
KCHAK

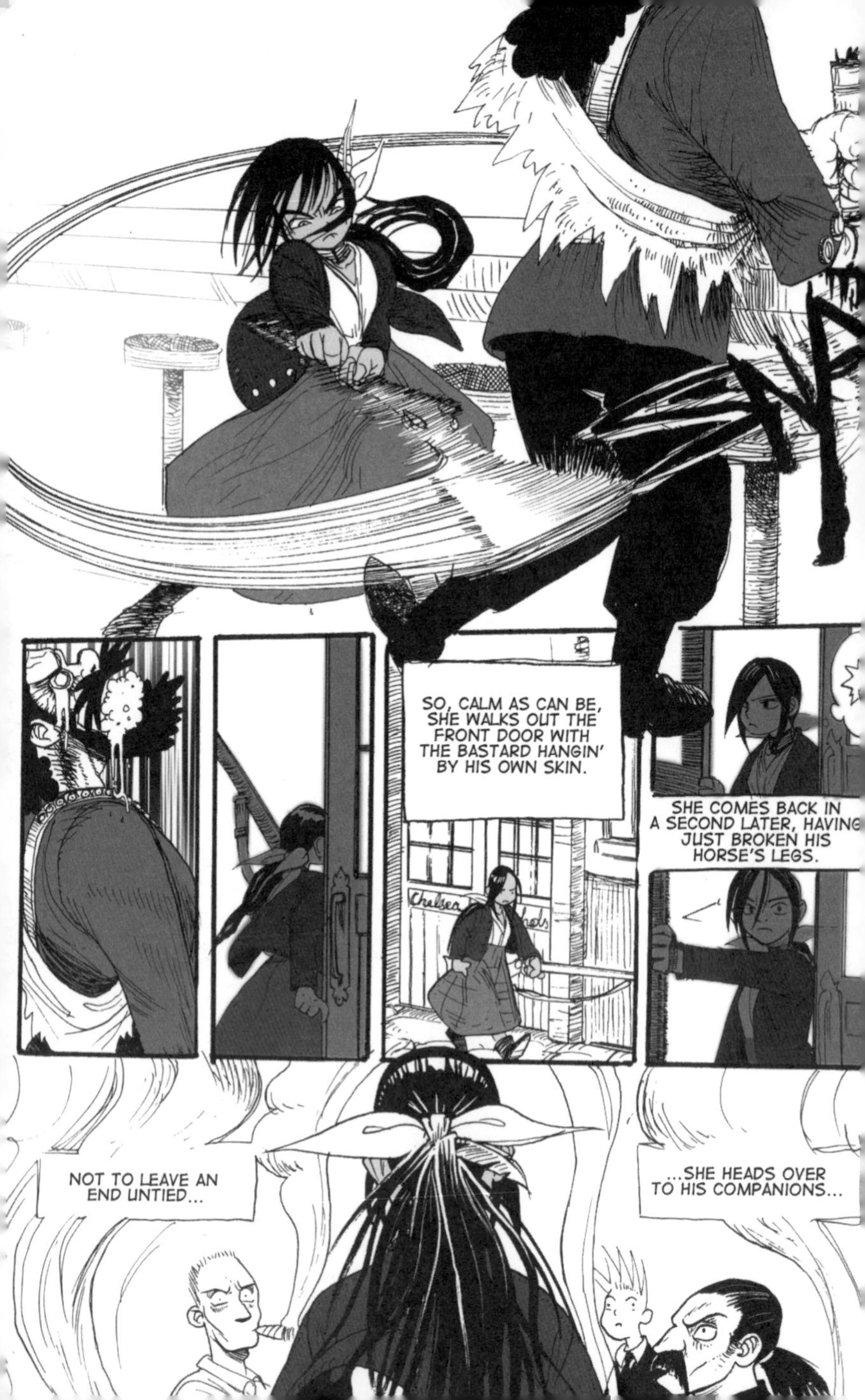
SO, CALM AS CAN BE, SHE WALKS OUT THE FRONT DOOR WITH THE BASTARD HANGIN' BY HIS OWN SKIN.
SHE COMES BACK IN A SECOND LATER, HAVING JUST BROKEN HIS HORSE'S LEGS.
NOT TO LEAVE AN END UNTIED...
...SHE HEADS OVER TO HIS COMPANIONS...

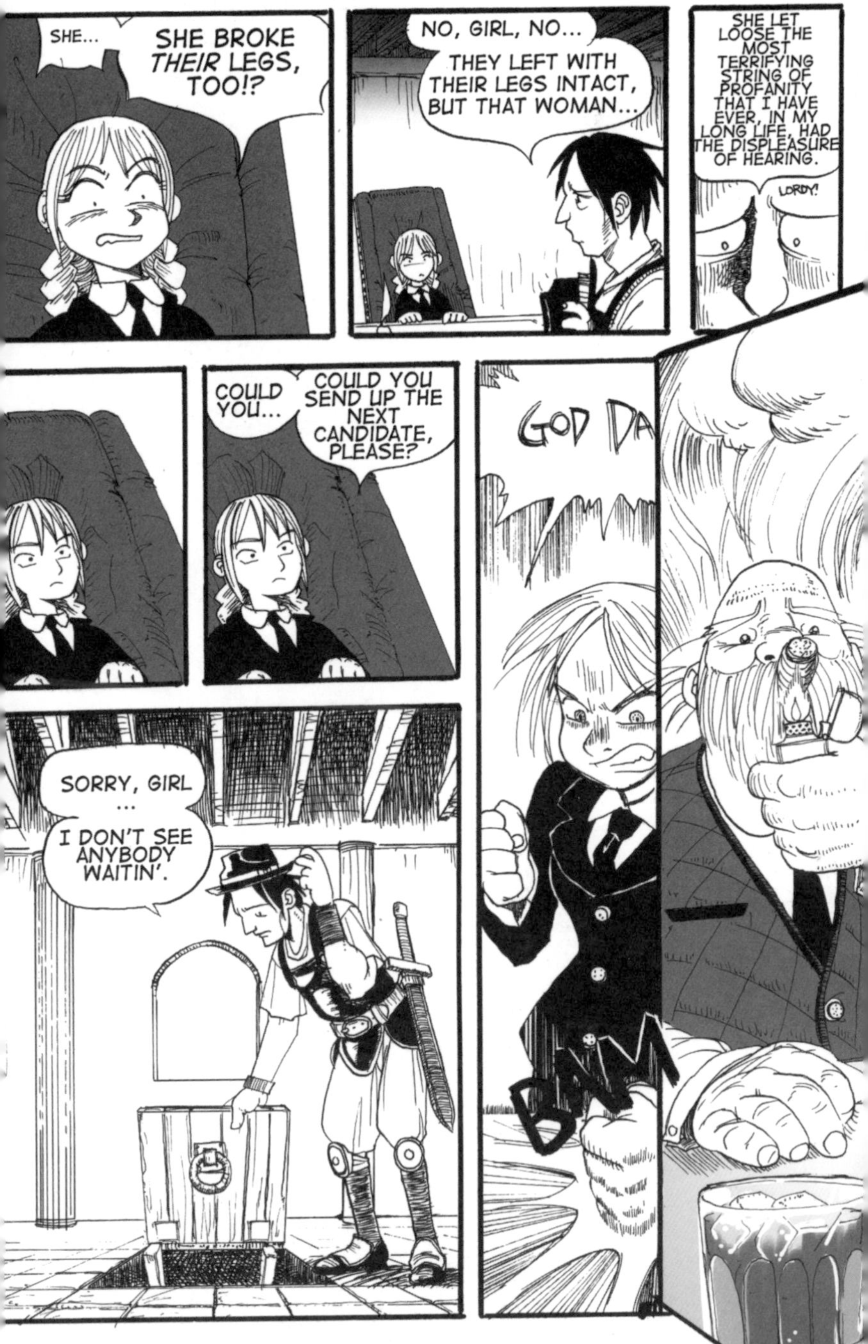
SHE...
SHE BROKE THEIR LEGS, TOO!?
NO, GIRL, NO...
THEY LEFT WITH THEIR LEGS INTACT, BUT THAT WOMAN...
SHE LET LOOSE THE MOST TERRIFYING STRING OF PROFANITY THAT I HAVE EVER, IN MY LONG LIFE, HAD THE DISPLEASURE OF HEARING.
LORDY!
COULD YOU...
COULD YOU SEND UP THE NEXT CANDIDATE, PLEASE?
GOD DA
BAM
SORRY, GIRL ...
I DON'T SEE ANYBODY WAITIN'.

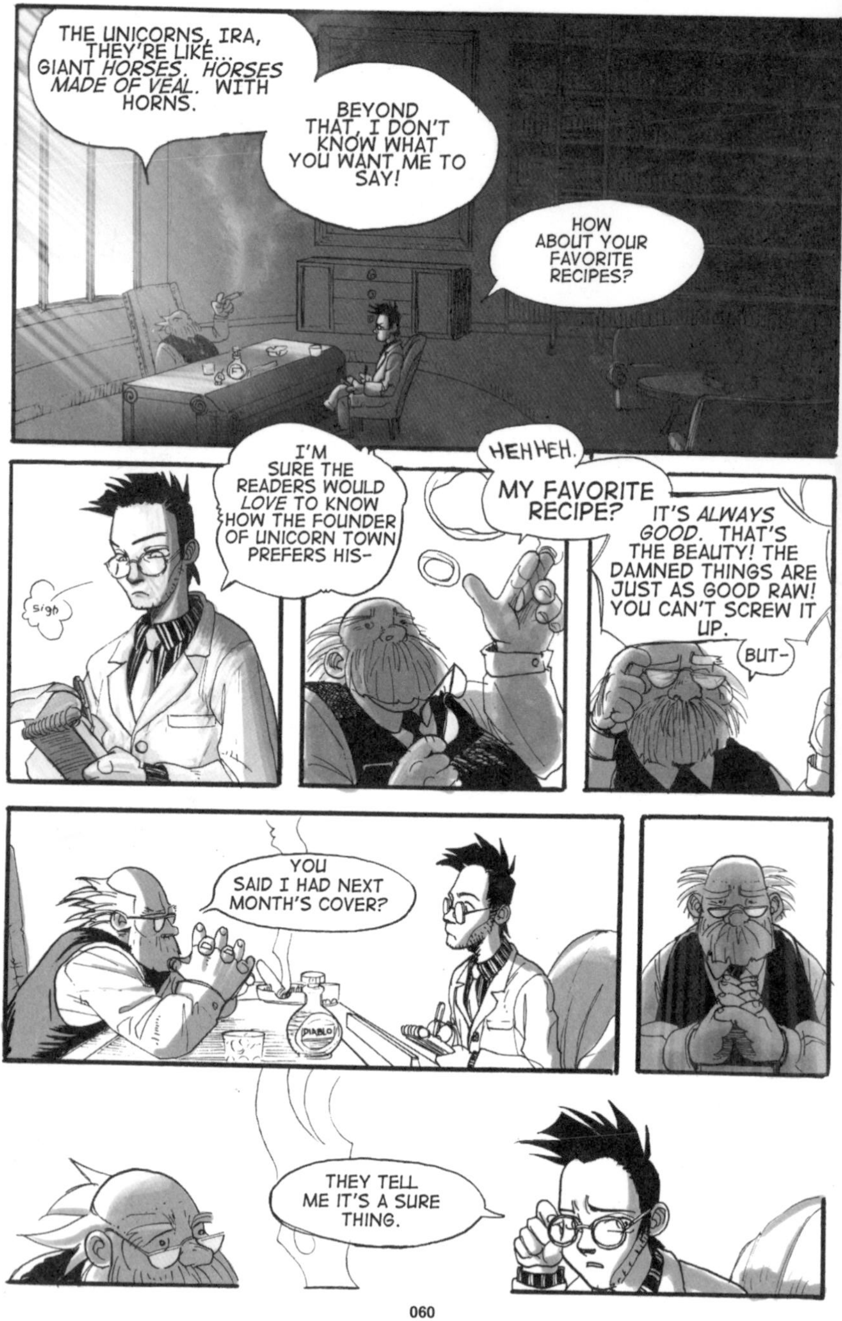
THE UNICORNS, IRA, THEY'RE LIKE... GIANT HORSES. HORSES MADE OF VEAL. WITH HORNS.
BEYOND THAT, I DON'T KNOW WHAT YOU WANT ME TO SAY!
HOW ABOUT YOUR FAVORITE RECIPES?
sigh
I'M SURE THE READERS WOULD LOVE TO KNOW HOW THE FOUNDER OF UNICORN TOWN PREFERS HIS-
HEHHEH.
MY FAVORITE RECIPE?
IT'S ALWAYS GOOD. THAT'S THE BEAUTY! THE DAMNED THINGS ARE JUST AS GOOD RAW! YOU CAN'T SCREW IT UP.
BUT-
YOU SAID I HAD NEXT MONTH'S COVER?
DIABLO
THEY TELL ME IT'S A SURE THING.

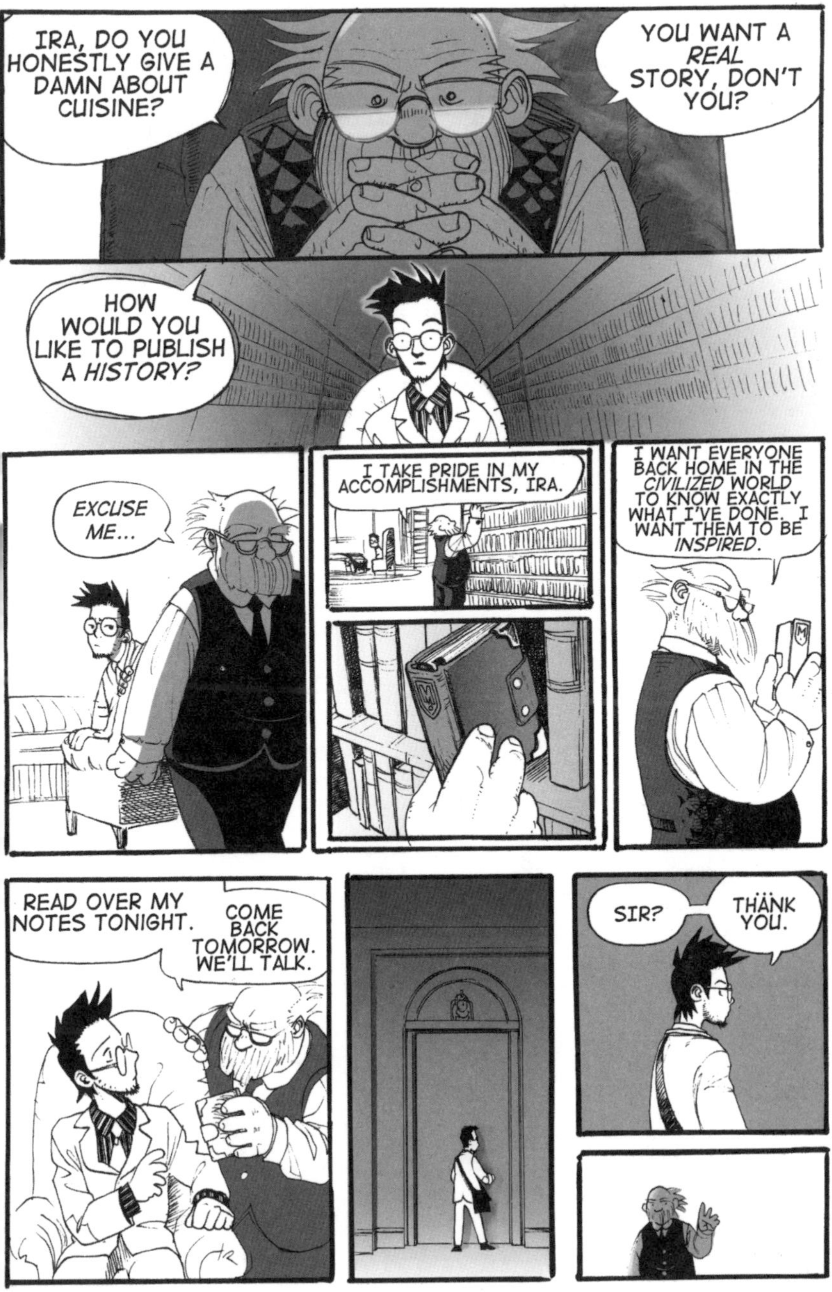
IRA, DO YOU HONESTLY GIVE A DAMN ABOUT CUISINE?
YOU WANT A *REAL* STORY, DON'T YOU?
HOW WOULD YOU LIKE TO PUBLISH A *HISTORY?*
EXCUSE ME...
I TAKE PRIDE IN MY ACCOMPLISHMENTS, IRA.
I WANT EVERYONE BACK HOME IN THE *CIVILIZED* WORLD TO KNOW EXACTLY WHAT I'VE DONE. I WANT THEM TO BE *INSPIRED*.
READ OVER MY NOTES TONIGHT.
COME BACK TOMORROW. WE'LL TALK.
SIR?
THÄNK YOU.

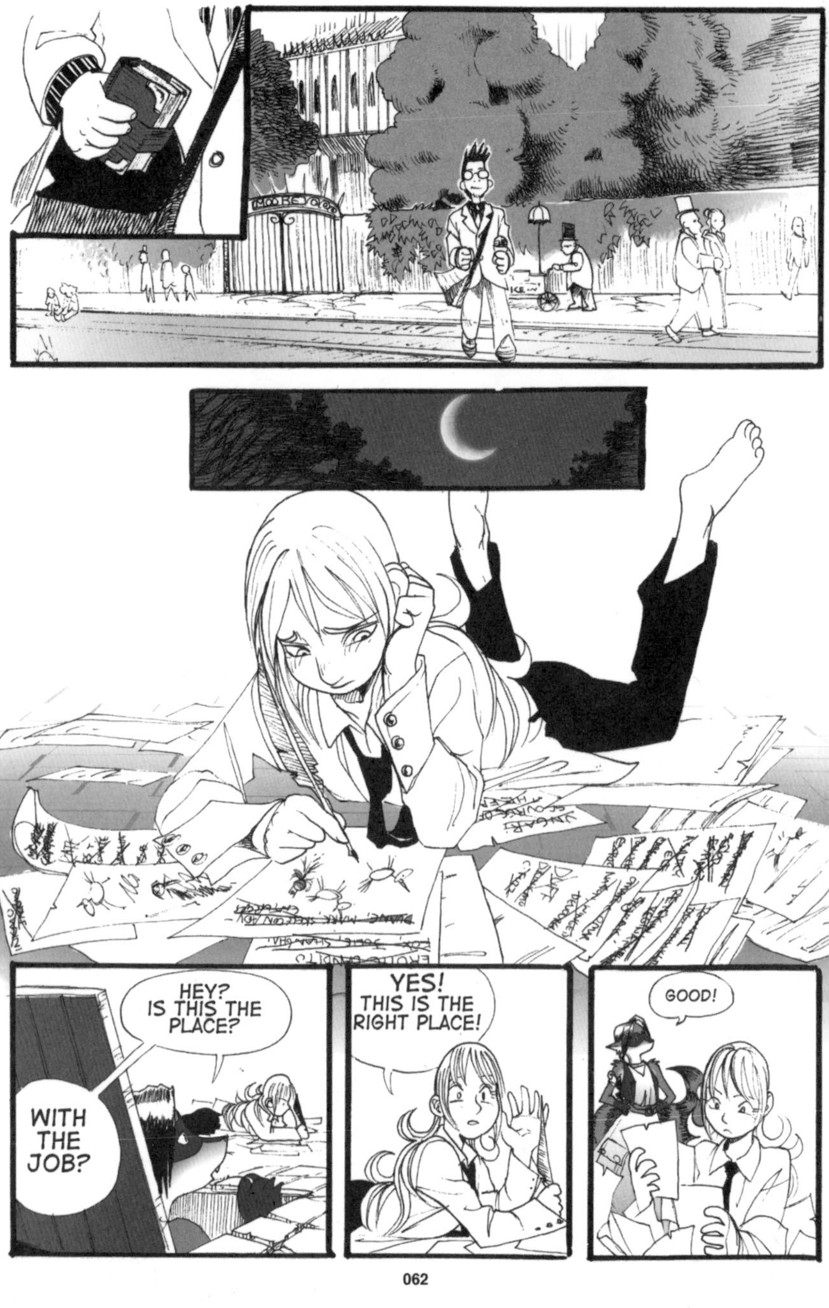
HEY? IS THIS THE PLACE?
WITH THE JOB?
YES! THIS IS THE RIGHT PLACE!
GOOD!

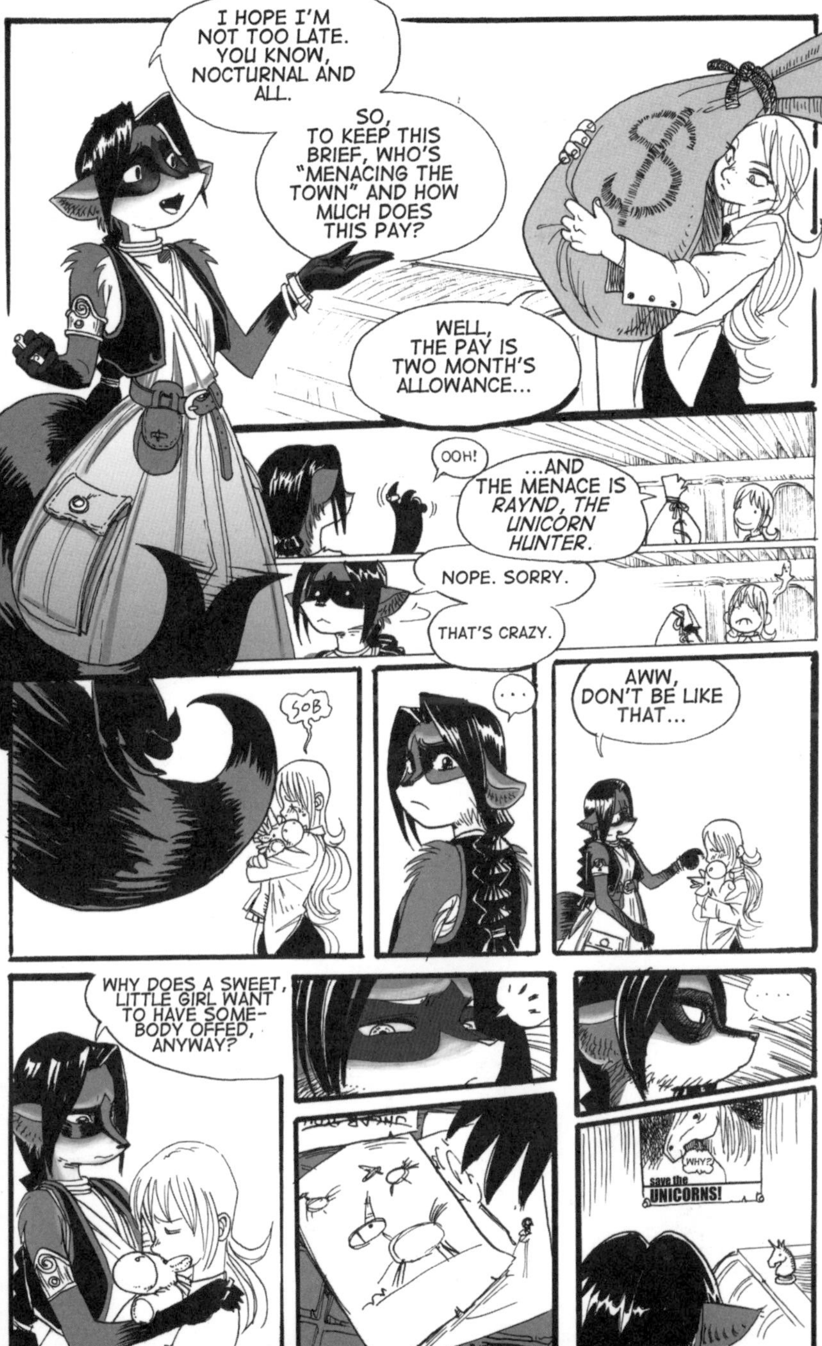
I HOPE I'M NOT TOO LATE. YOU KNOW, NOCTURNAL AND ALL.
SO, TO KEEP THIS BRIEF, WHO'S "MENACING THE TOWN" AND HOW MUCH DOES THIS PAY?
WELL, THE PAY IS TWO MONTH'S ALLOWANCE...
OOH!
...AND THE MENACE IS RAYND, THE UNICORN HUNTER.
NOPE. SORRY.
THAT'S CRAZY.
SOB
. . .
AWW, DON'T BE LIKE THAT...
WHY DOES A SWEET, LITTLE GIRL WANT TO HAVE SOME-BODY OFFED, ANYWAY?
WHY?
save the UNICORNS!

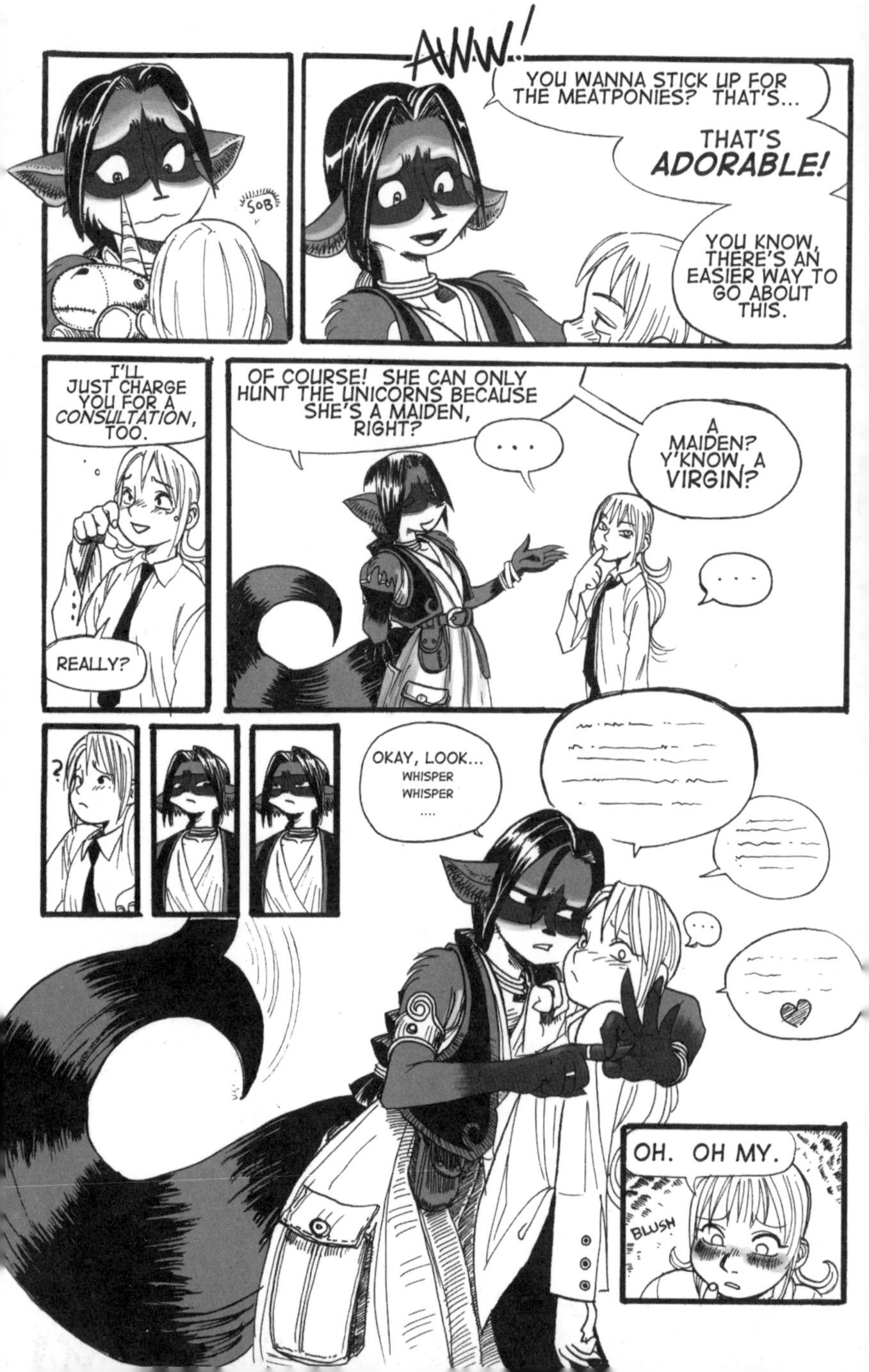
SOB
AWW!
YOU WANNA STICK UP FOR THE MEATPONIES? THAT'S...
THAT'S ADORABLE!
YOU KNOW, THERE'S AN EASIER WAY TO GO ABOUT THIS.
I'LL JUST CHARGE YOU FOR A CONSULTATION, TOO.
REALLY?
OF COURSE! SHE CAN ONLY HUNT THE UNICORNS BECAUSE SHE'S A MAIDEN, RIGHT?
. . .
A MAIDEN? Y'KNOW, A VIRGIN?
. . .
?
OKAY, LOOK... WHISPER WHISPER ....
...
OH. OH MY.
BLUSH

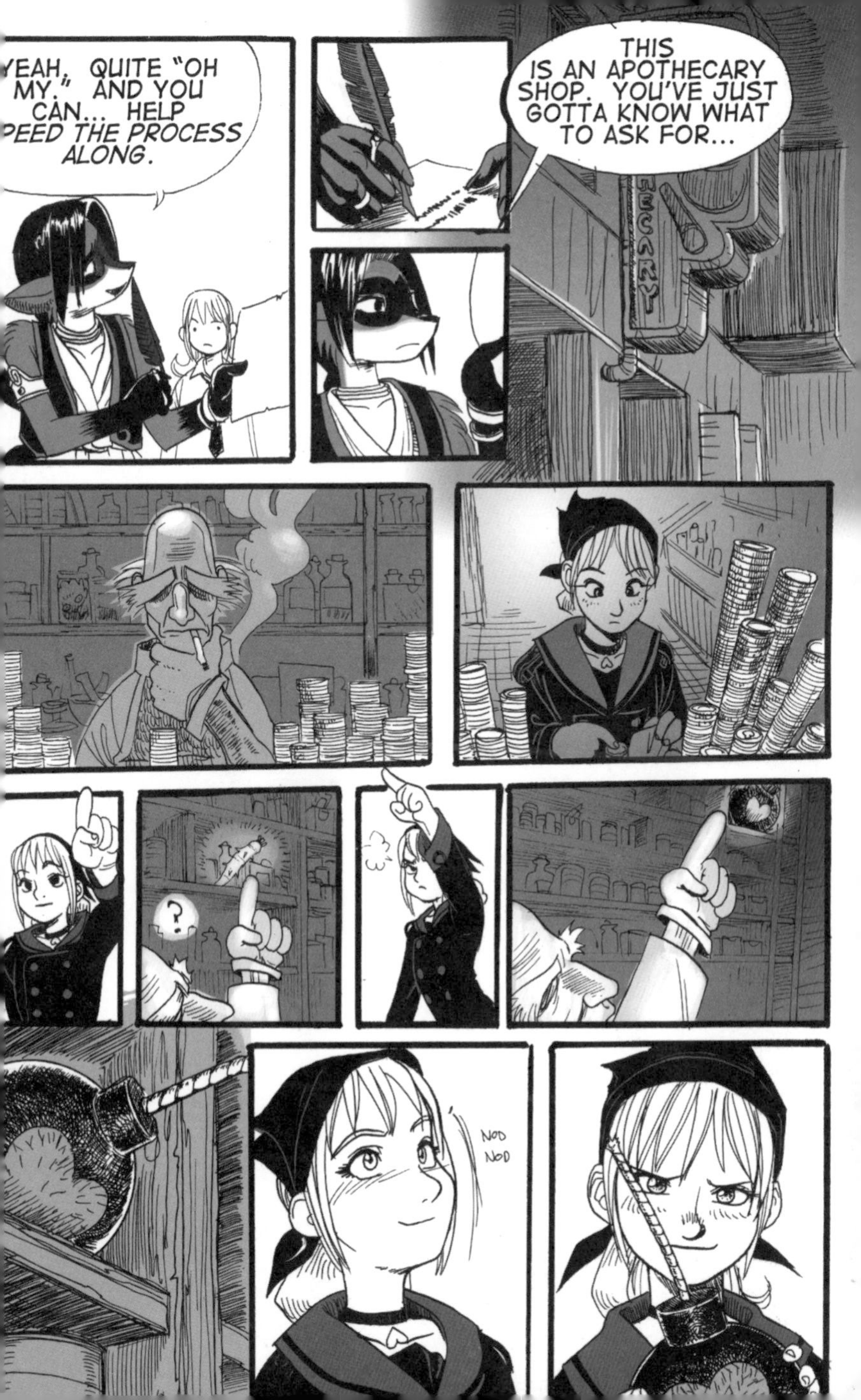
YEAH, QUITE "OH MY." AND YOU CAN... HELP PEED THE PROCESS ALONG.
THIS IS AN APOTHECARY SHOP. YOU'VE JUST GOTTA KNOW WHAT TO ASK FOR...
NOD NOD

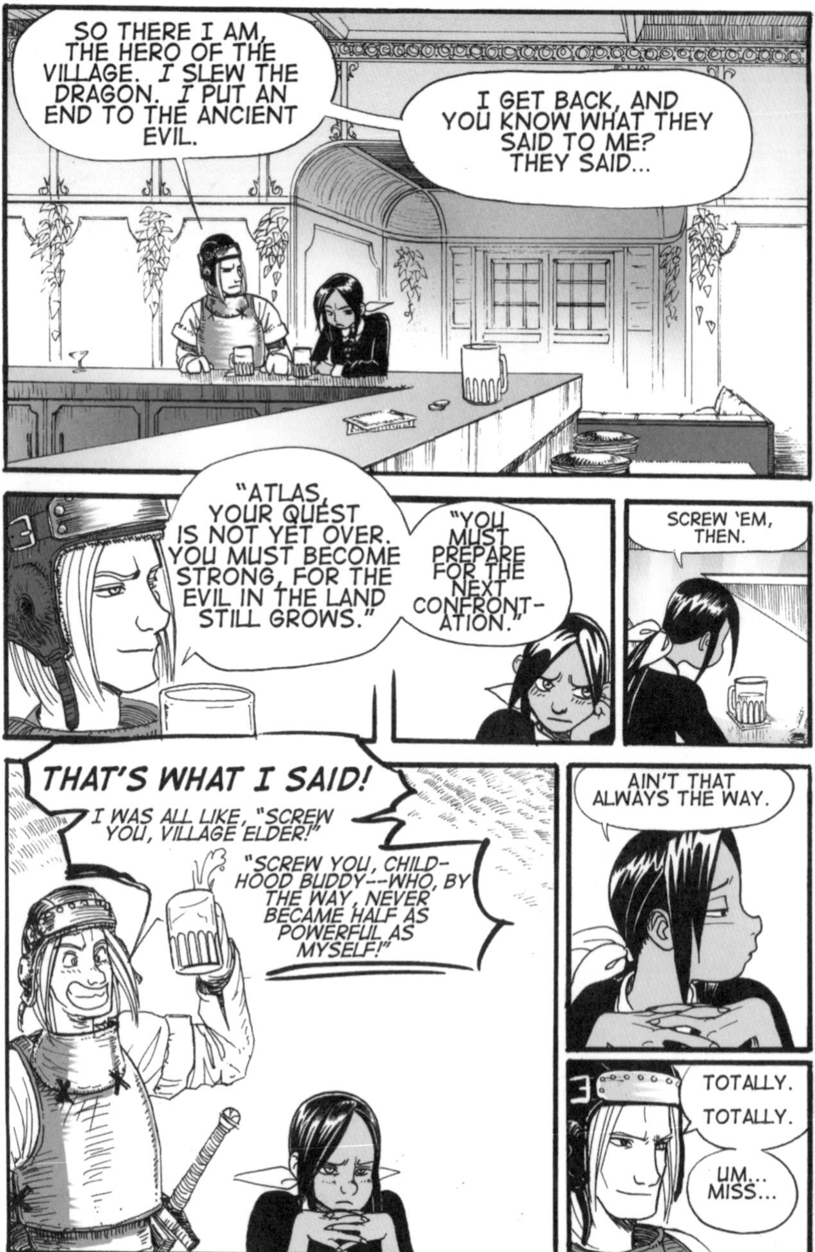
SO THERE I AM, THE HERO OF THE VILLAGE. *I* SLEW THE DRAGON. *I* PUT AN END TO THE ANCIENT EVIL.
I GET BACK, AND YOU KNOW WHAT THEY SAID TO ME? THEY SAID...
"ATLAS, YOUR QUEST IS NOT YET OVER. YOU MUST BECOME STRONG, FOR THE EVIL IN THE LAND STILL GROWS."
"YOU MUST PREPARE FOR THE NEXT CONFRONT-ATION."
SCREW 'EM, THEN.
THAT'S WHAT I SAID!
I WAS ALL LIKE, "SCREW YOU, VILLAGE ELDER!"
"SCREW YOU, CHILD-HOOD BUDDY--WHO, BY THE WAY, NEVER BECAME HALF AS POWERFUL AS MYSELF!"
AIN'T THAT ALWAYS THE WAY.
TOTALLY.
TOTALLY.
UM... MISS...

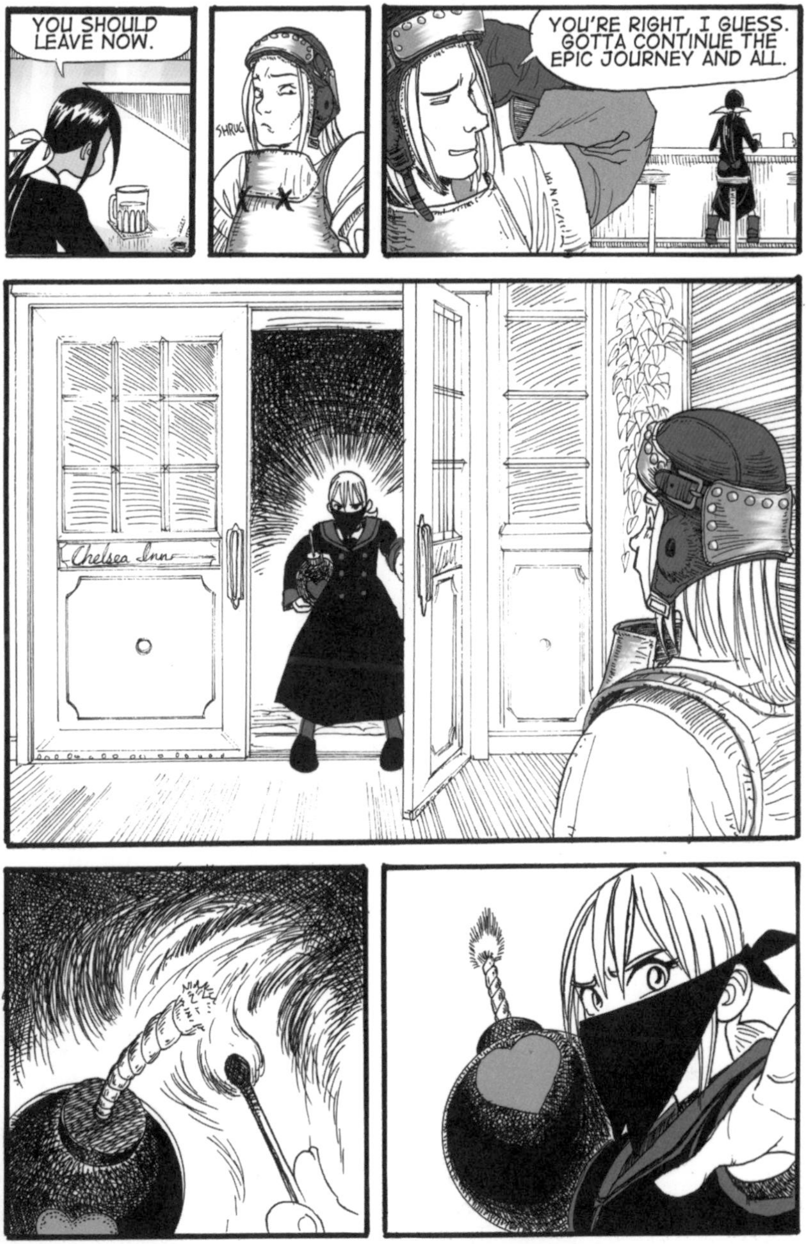
YOU SHOULD LEAVE NOW.
SHRUG
YOU'RE RIGHT, I GUESS. GOTTA CONTINUE THE EPIC JOURNEY AND ALL.
Chelsea Inn

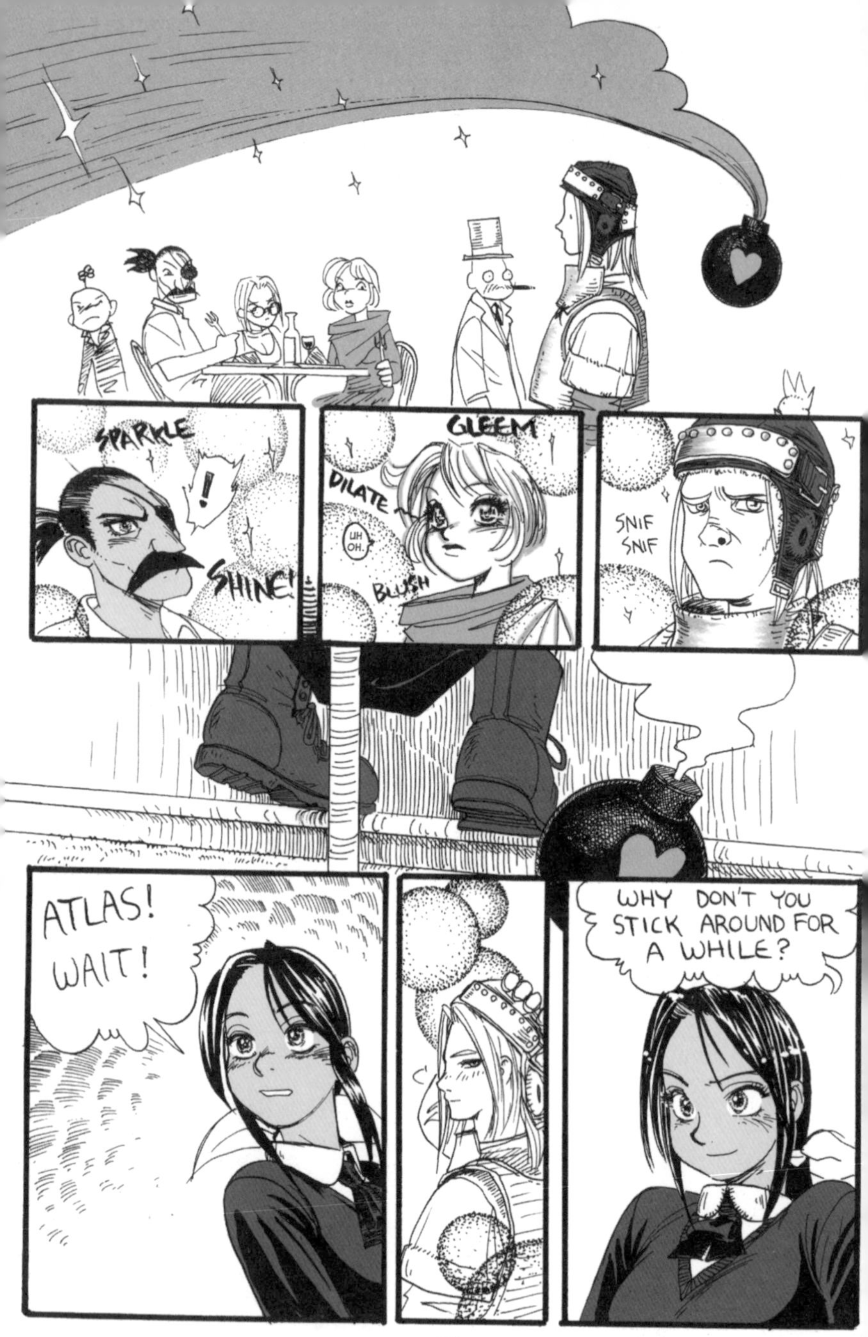
SPARKLE
!
SHINE!
GLEEM
DILATE
UH OH.
BLUSH
SNIF
SNIF
ATLAS! WAIT!
WHY DON'T YOU STICK AROUND FOR A WHILE?

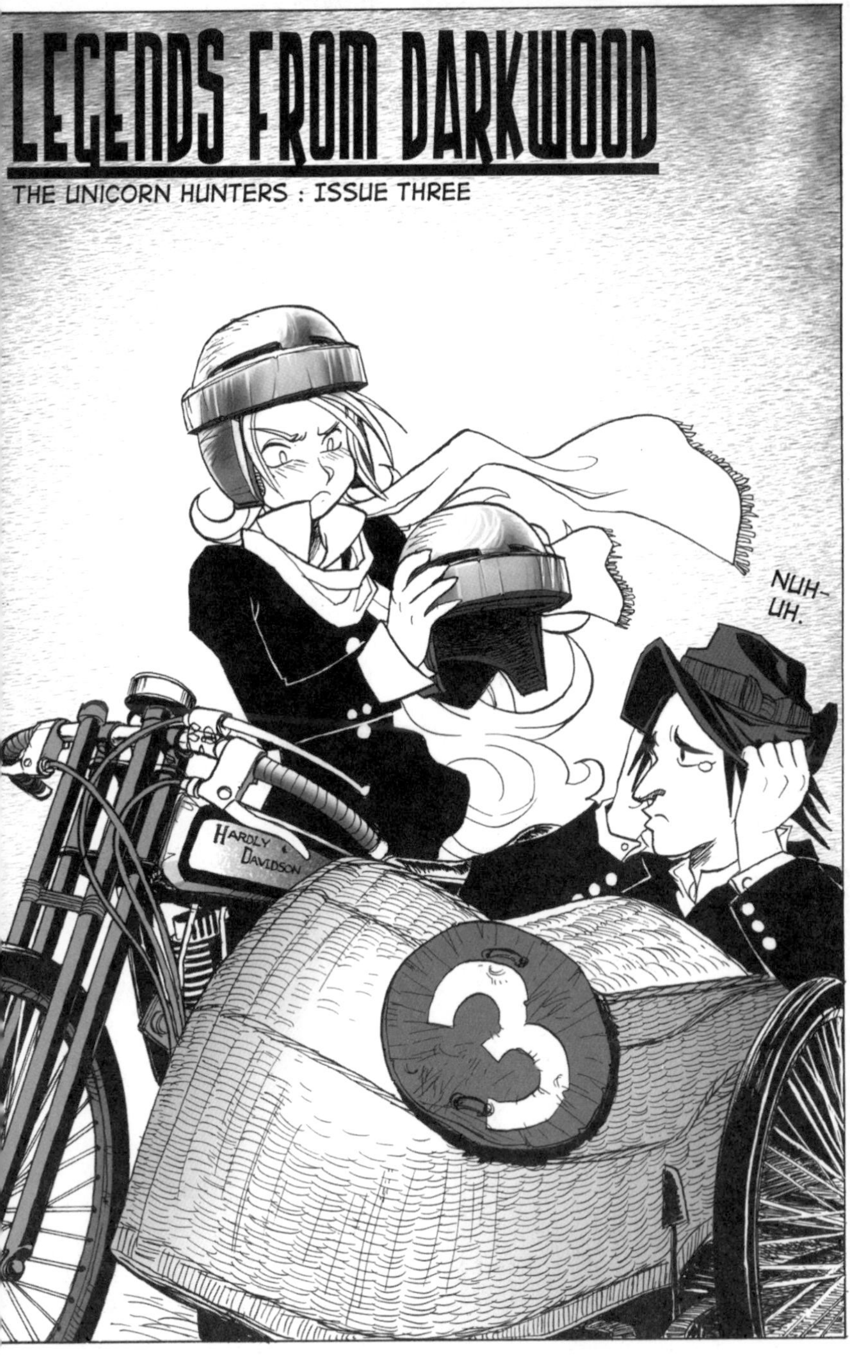
LEGENDS FROM DARKWOOD
THE UNICORN HUNTERS : ISSUE THREE
NUH-UH.
HARDLY DAVIDSON
3

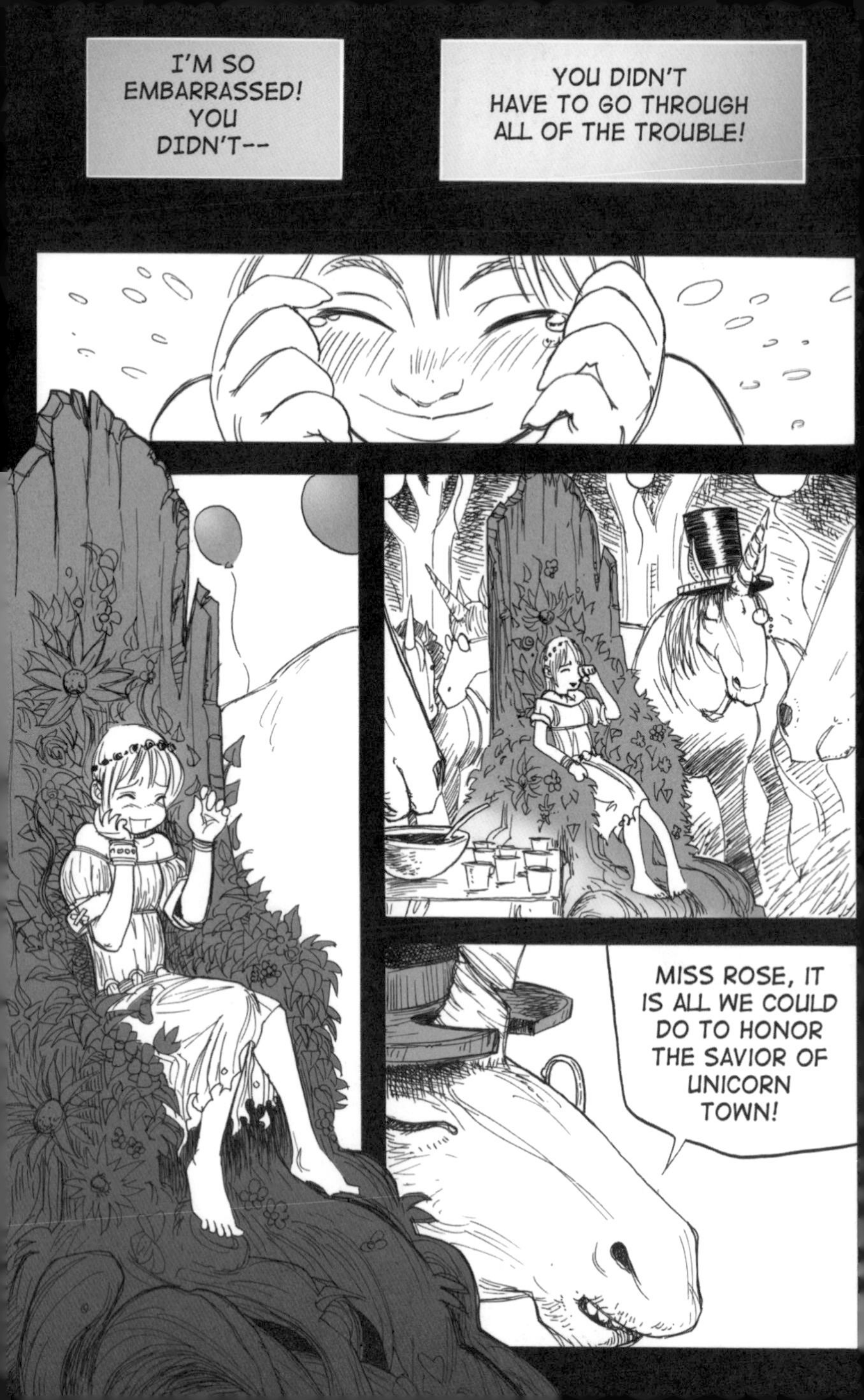
I'M SO EMBARRASSED! YOU DIDN'T--
YOU DIDN'T HAVE TO GO THROUGH ALL OF THE TROUBLE!
MISS ROSE, IT IS ALL WE COULD DO TO HONOR THE SAVIOR OF UNICORN TOWN!

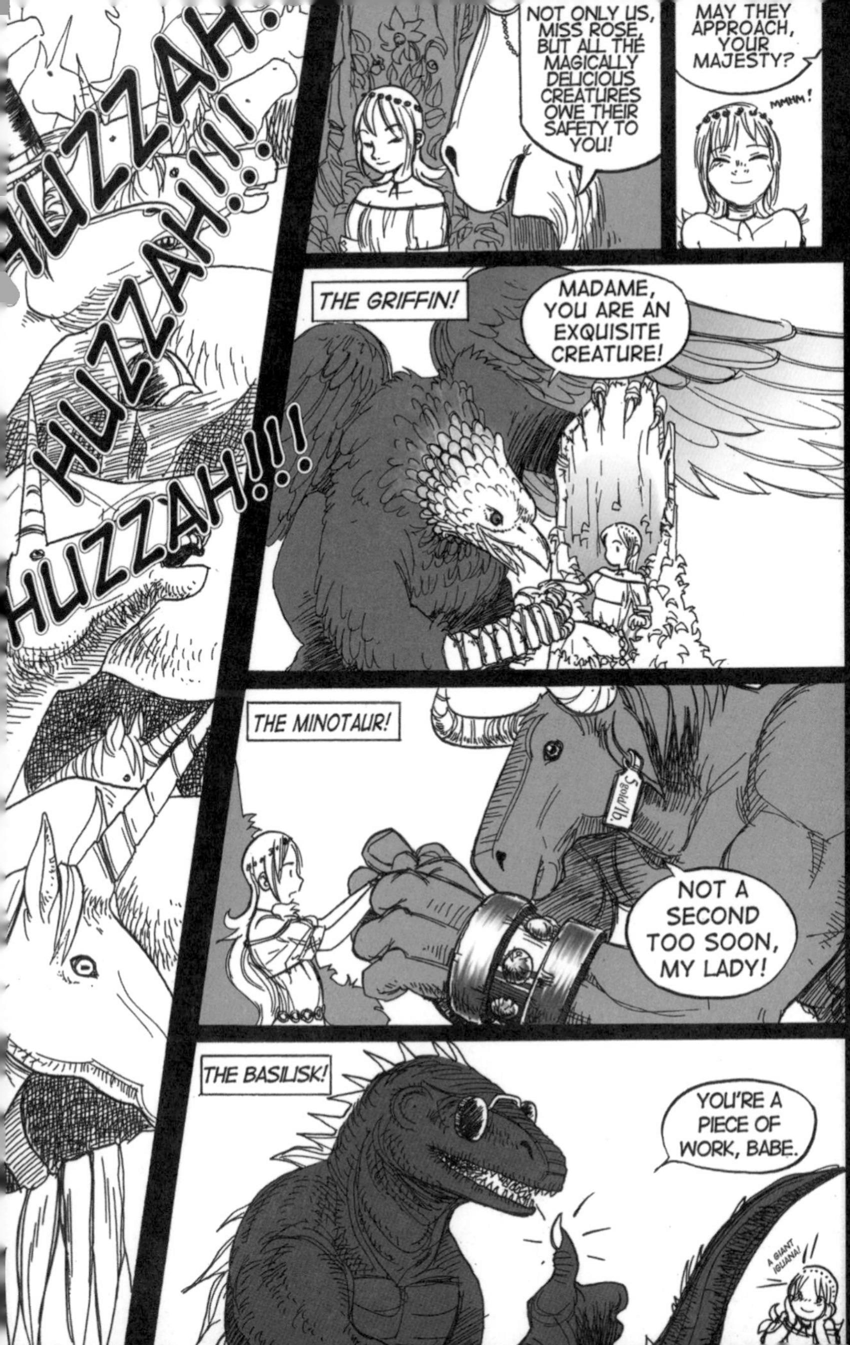
HUZZAH!!!
HUZZAH!!!
HUZZAH!!!
HUZZAH!!!
NOT ONLY US, MISS ROSE, BUT ALL THE MAGICALLY DELICIOUS CREATURES OWE THEIR SAFETY TO YOU!
MAY THEY APPROACH, YOUR MAJESTY?
MMHM!
THE GRIFFIN!
MADAME, YOU ARE AN EXQUISITE CREATURE!
THE MINOTAUR!
5 gold/lb.
NOT A SECOND TOO SOON, MY LADY!
THE BASILISK!
YOU'RE A PIECE OF WORK, BABE.
A GIANT IGUANA!

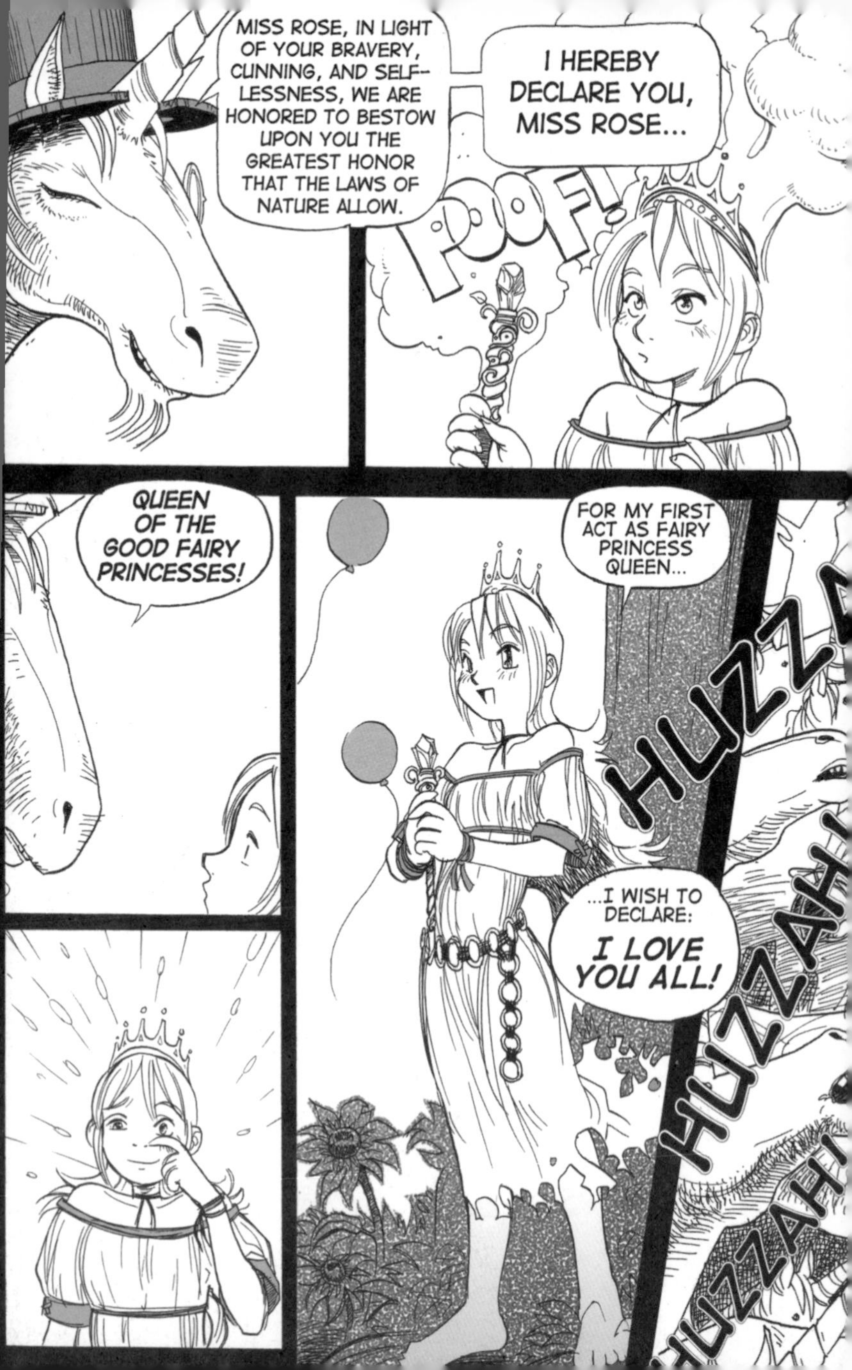
MISS ROSE, IN LIGHT OF YOUR BRAVERY, CUNNING, AND SELF-LESSNESS, WE ARE HONORED TO BESTOW UPON YOU THE GREATEST HONOR THAT THE LAWS OF NATURE ALLOW.
I HEREBY DECLARE YOU, MISS ROSE...
POOF!
QUEEN OF THE GOOD FAIRY PRINCESSES!
FOR MY FIRST ACT AS FAIRY PRINCESS QUEEN...
...I WISH TO DECLARE: I LOVE YOU ALL!
HUZZA
HUZZAH
HUZZAH
HUZZAH

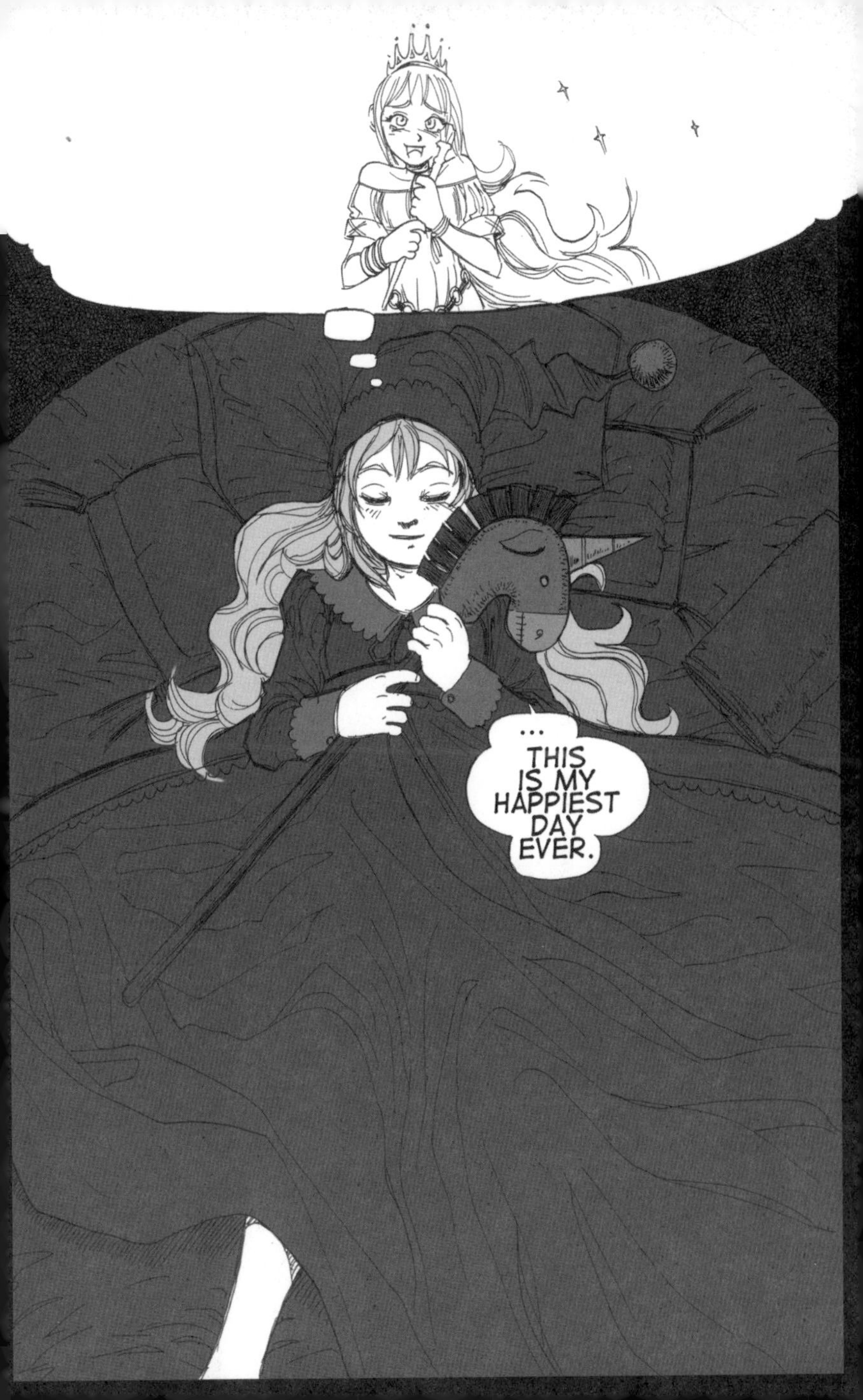
... THIS IS MY HAPPIEST DAY EVER.

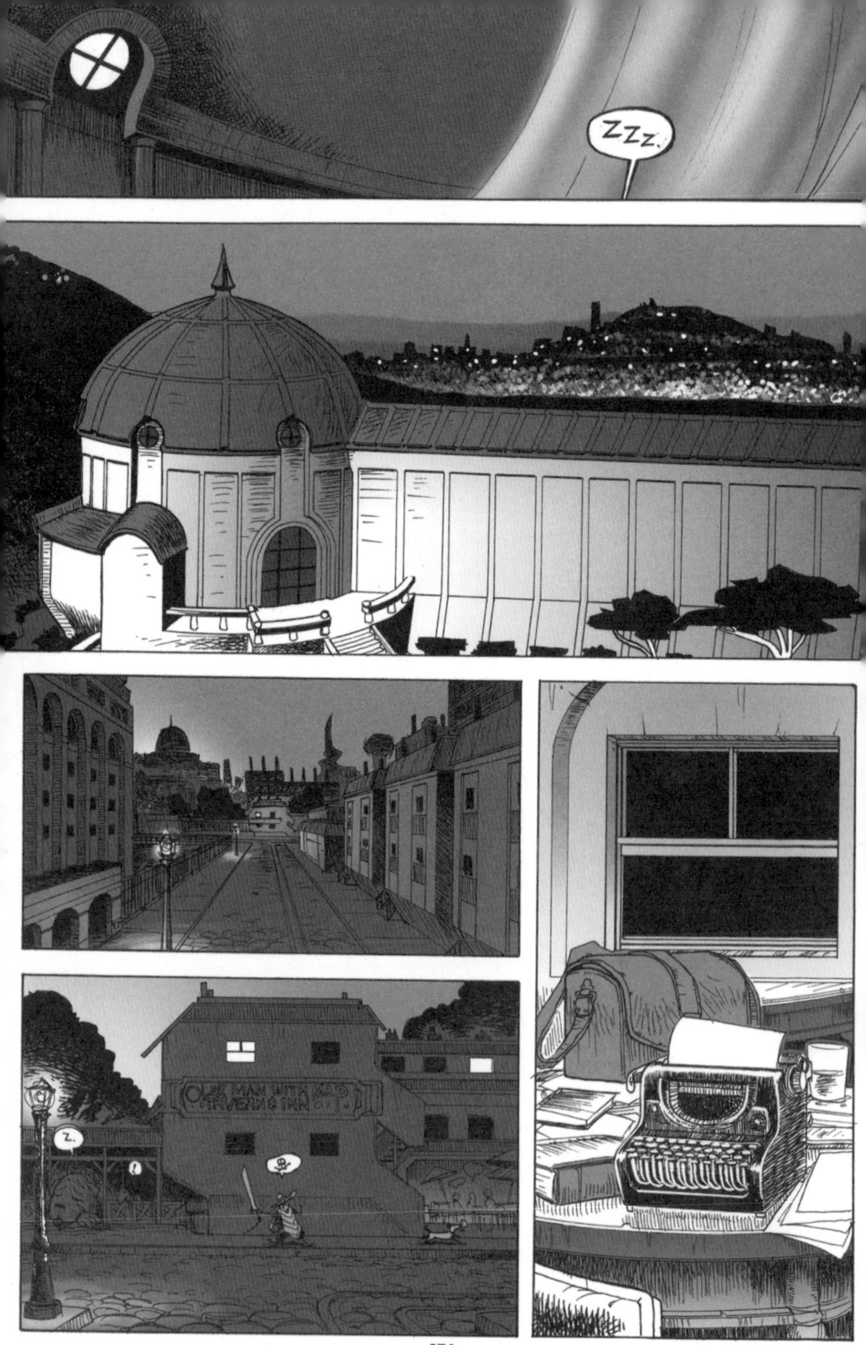
ZZZ.
OLE MAN WITH MAP
TAVERN & INN
Z.
!

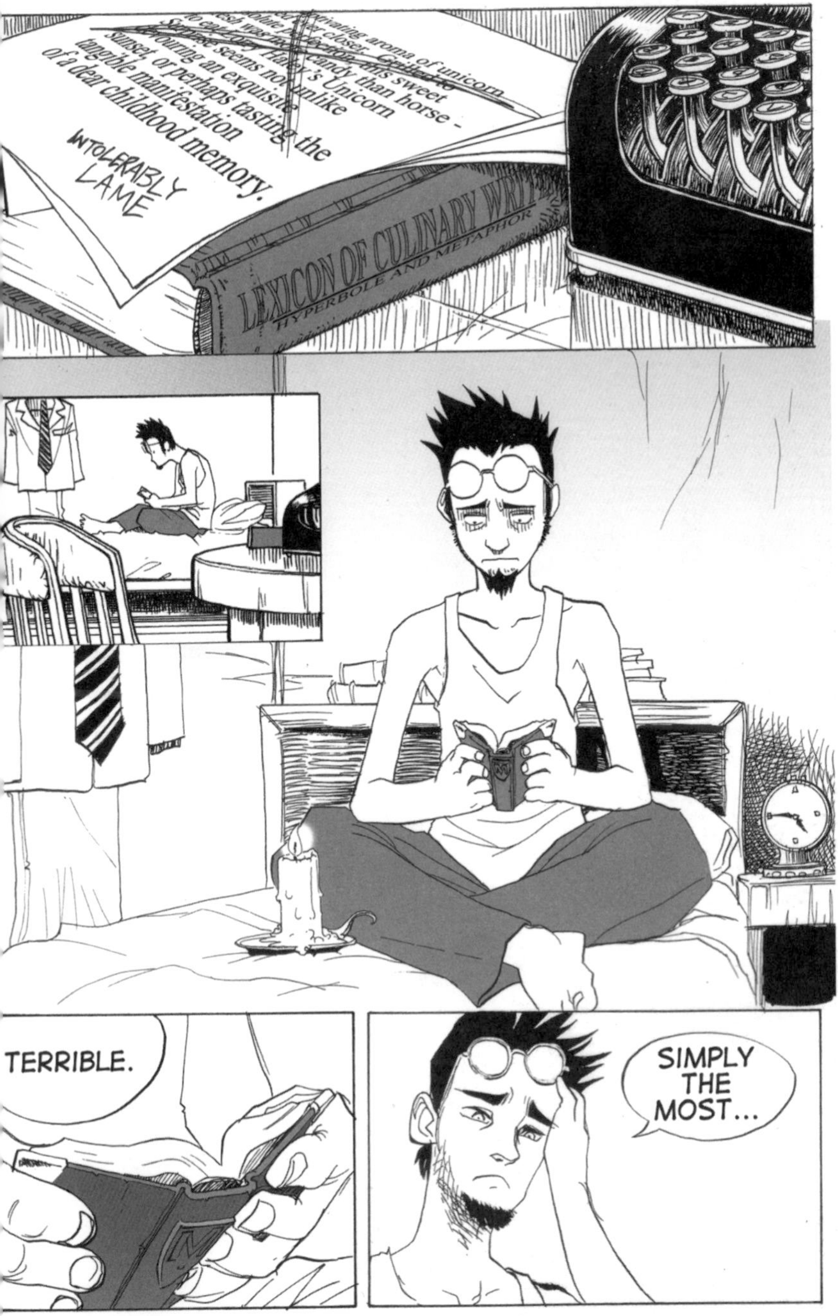

sunset, or perhaps tasting the
tangible manifestation
of a dear childhood memory.
INTOLERABLY LAME
LEXICON OF CULINARY WRIT
HYPERBOLE AND METAPHOR
TERRIBLE.
SIMPLY THE MOST...

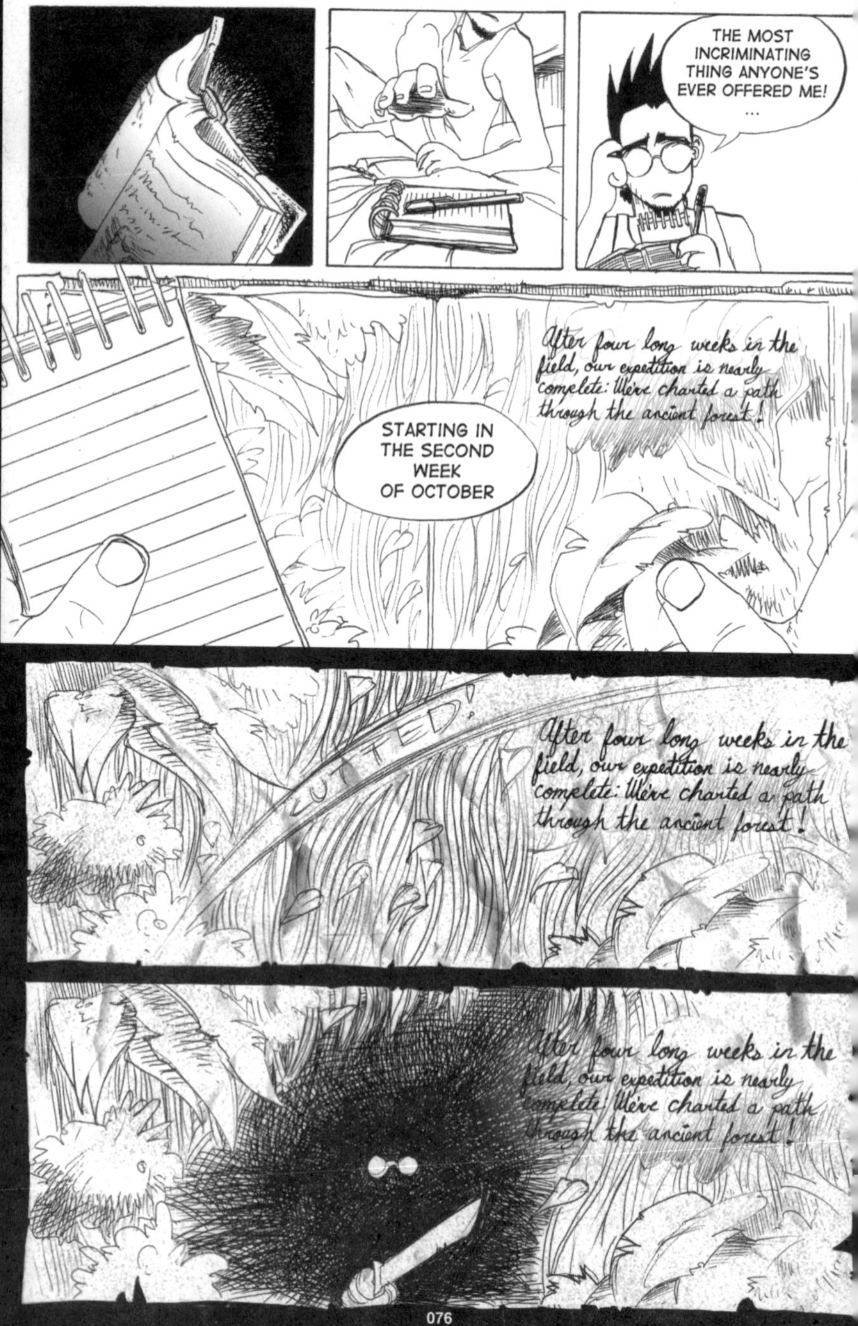
THE MOST INCRIMINATING THING ANYONE'S EVER OFFERED ME!
...
After four long weeks in the field, our expedition is nearly complete: We've charted a path through the ancient forest!
STARTING IN THE SECOND WEEK OF OCTOBER
After four long weeks in the field, our expedition is nearly complete: We've charted a path through the ancient forest!
After four long weeks in the field, our expedition is nearly complete: We've charted a path through the ancient forest!

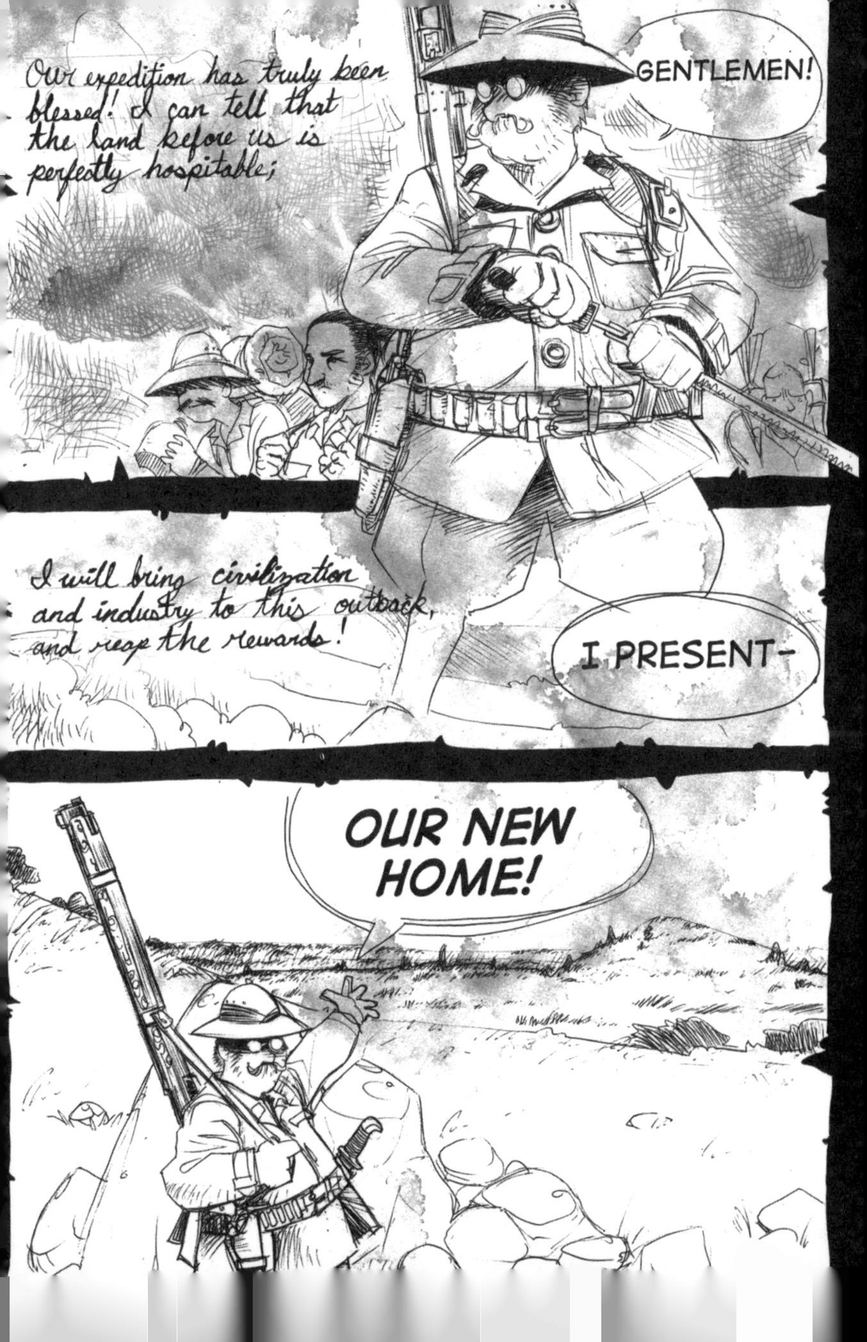
Our expedition has truly been blessed! I can tell that the land before us is perfectly hospitable;
GENTLEMEN!
I will bring civilization and industry to this outback, and reap the rewards!
I PRESENT-
OUR NEW HOME!

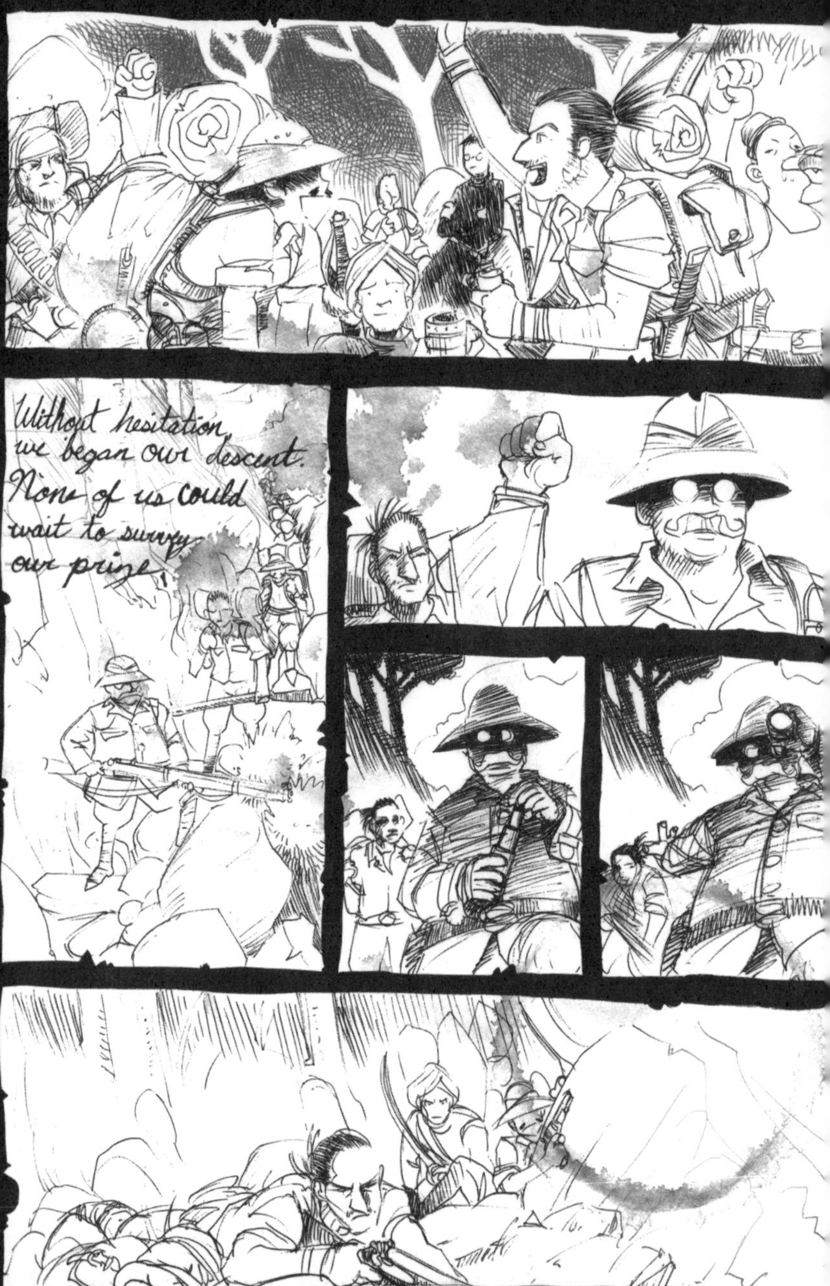
Without hesitation, we began our descent. None of us could wait to survey our prize.

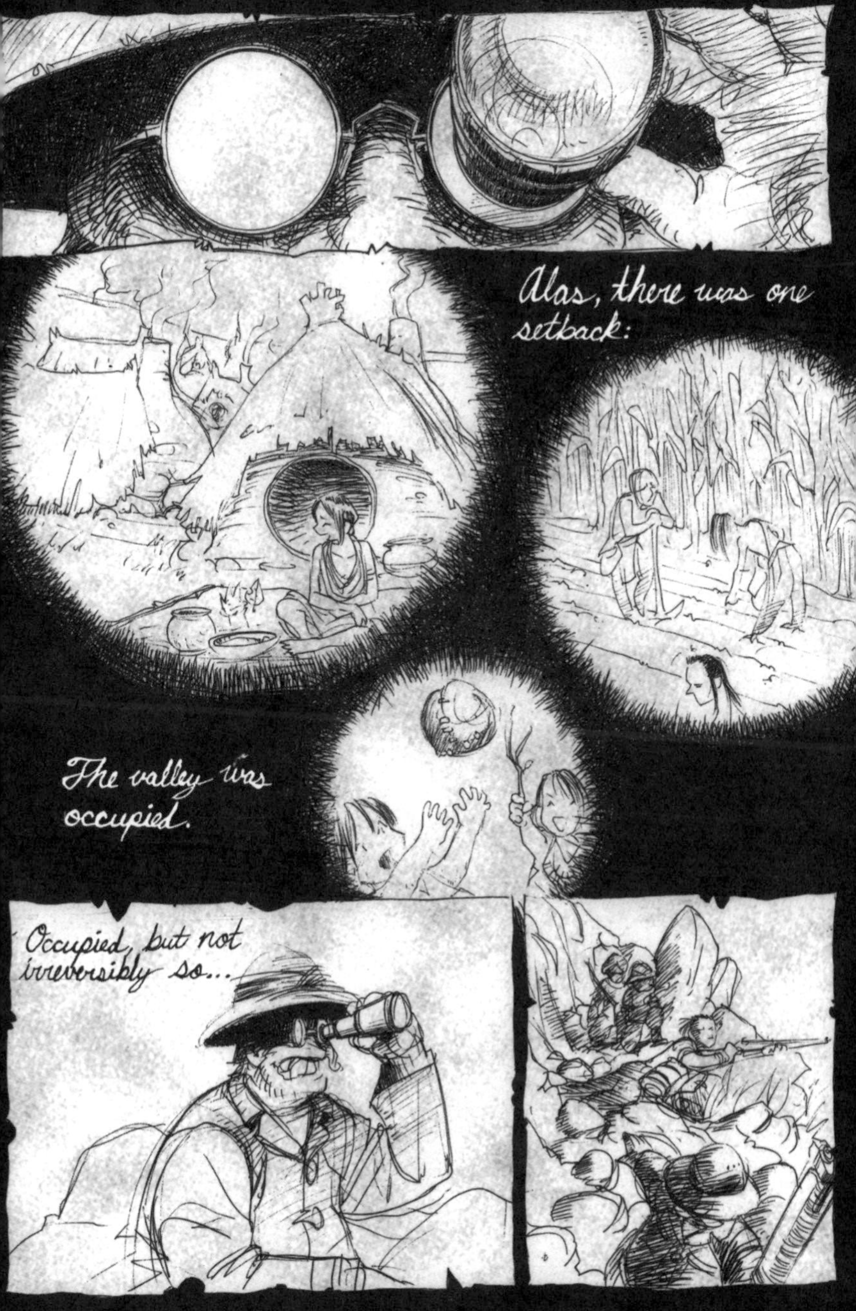

Alas, there was one setback:
The valley was occupied.
Occupied, but not irreversibly so...

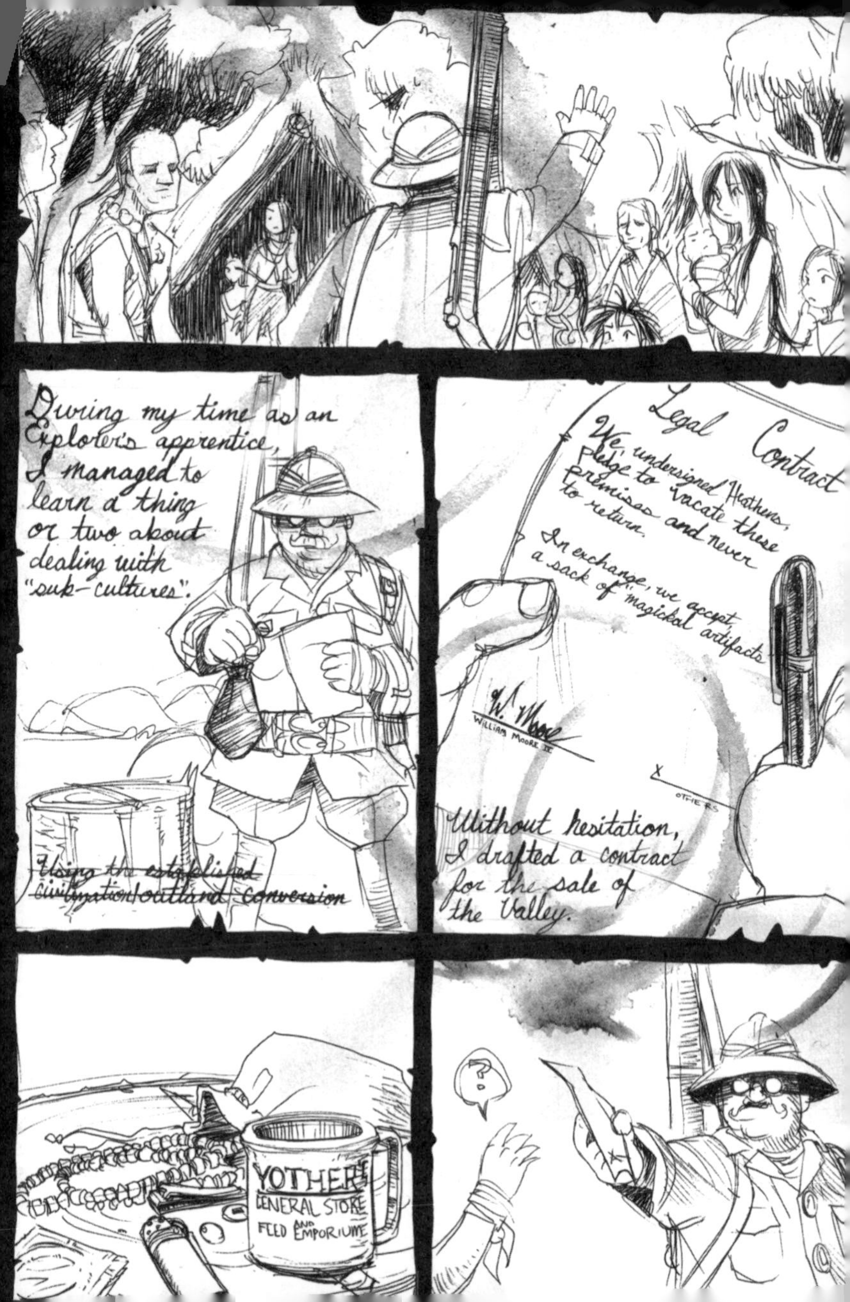
During my time as an Explorer's apprentice, I managed to learn a thing or two about dealing with "sub-cultures".
~~Using the established civilization/outland conversion~~
Legal Contract
We, undersigned Heathens, Pledge to vacate these premises and never to return.
In exchange, we accept, a sack of "magickal artifacts"
W. Moore
WILLIAM MOORE III
X
OTHERS
Without hesitation, I drafted a contract for the sale of the Valley.
YOTHER'S GENERAL STORE FEED AND EMPORIUM
?

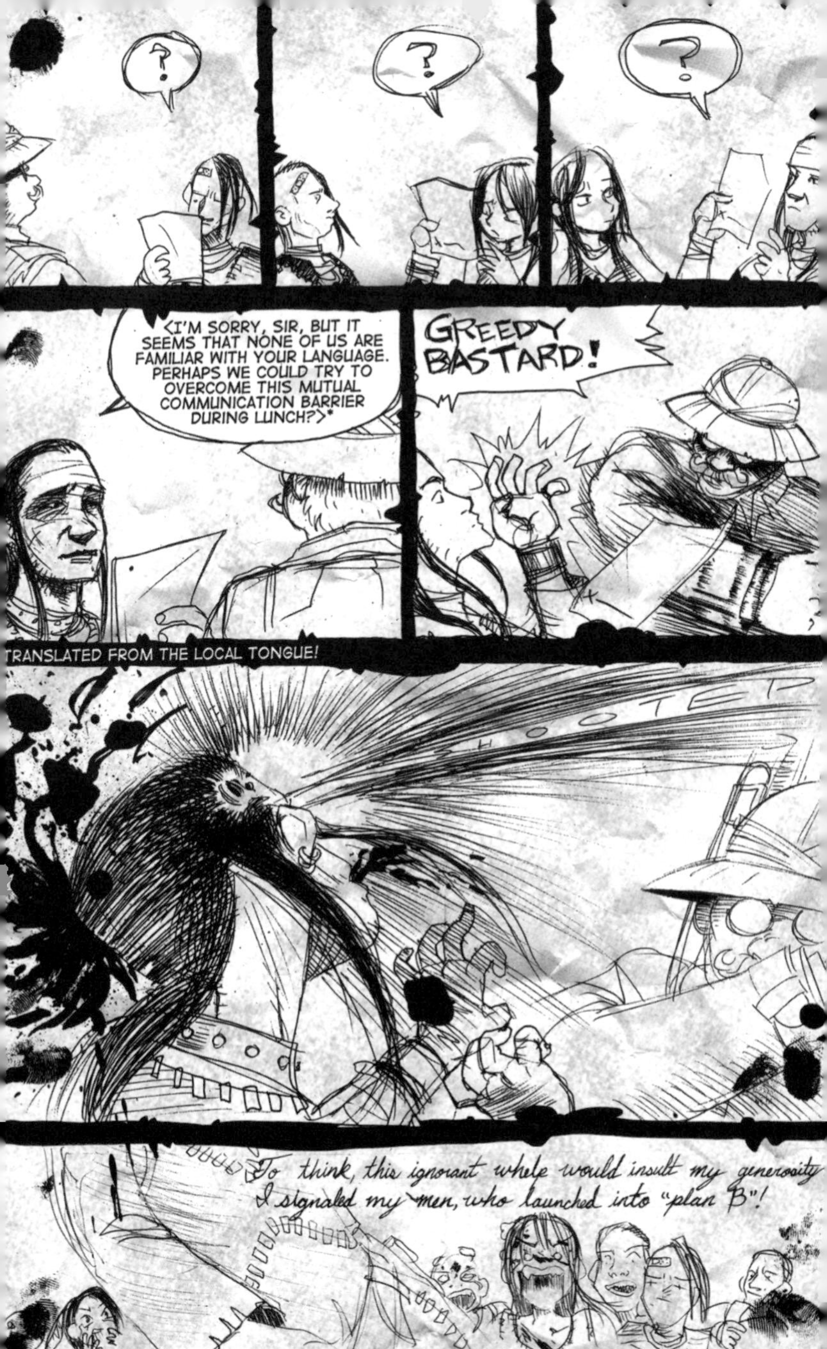
?
?
?
<I'M SORRY, SIR, BUT IT SEEMS THAT NONE OF US ARE FAMILIAR WITH YOUR LANGUAGE. PERHAPS WE COULD TRY TO OVERCOME THIS MUTUAL COMMUNICATION BARRIER DURING LUNCH?>*
GREEDY BASTARD!
*TRANSLATED FROM THE LOCAL TONGUE!
To think, this ignorant whelp would insult my generosity
I signaled my men, who launched into "plan B"!

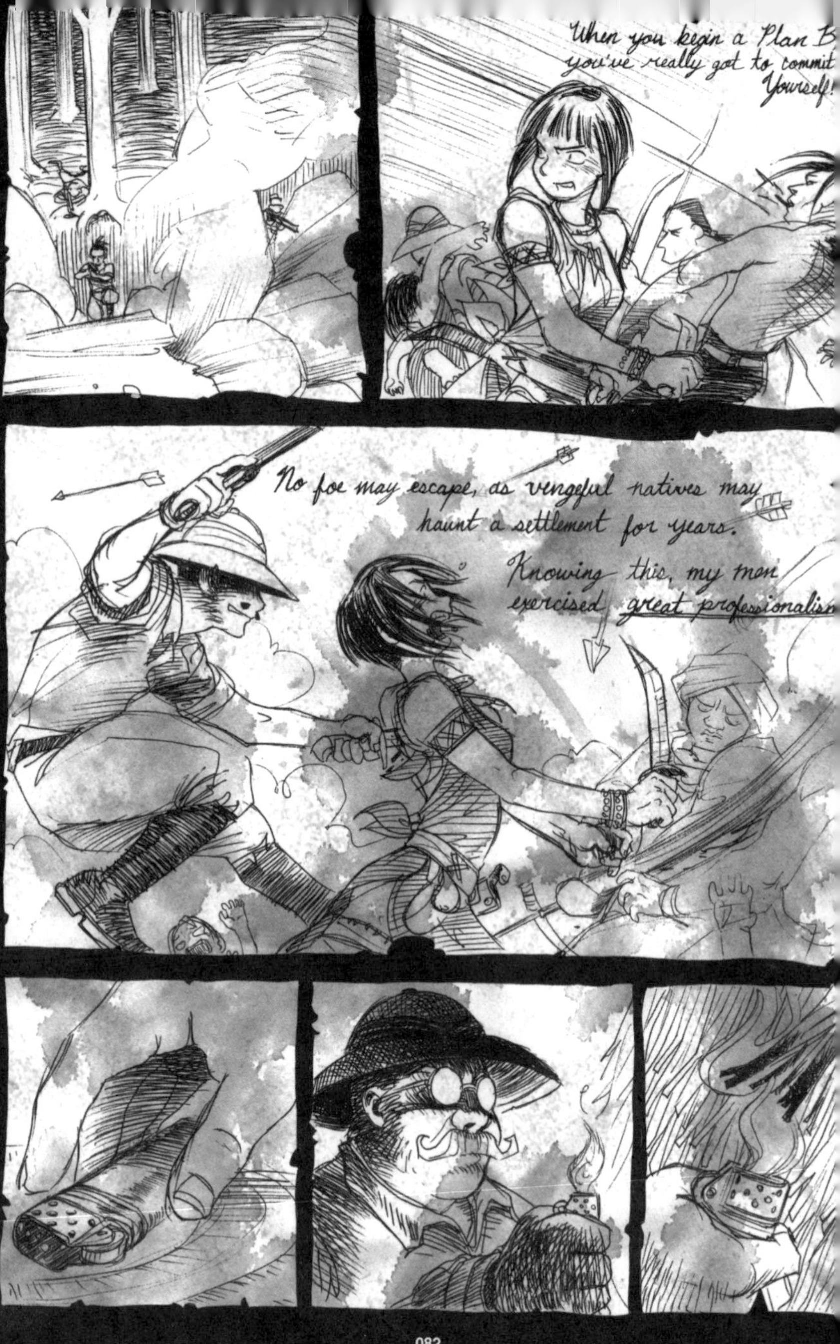
When you begin a Plan B you've really got to commit Yourself!
No foe may escape, as vengeful natives may haunt a settlement for years.
Knowing this, my men exercised great professionalism

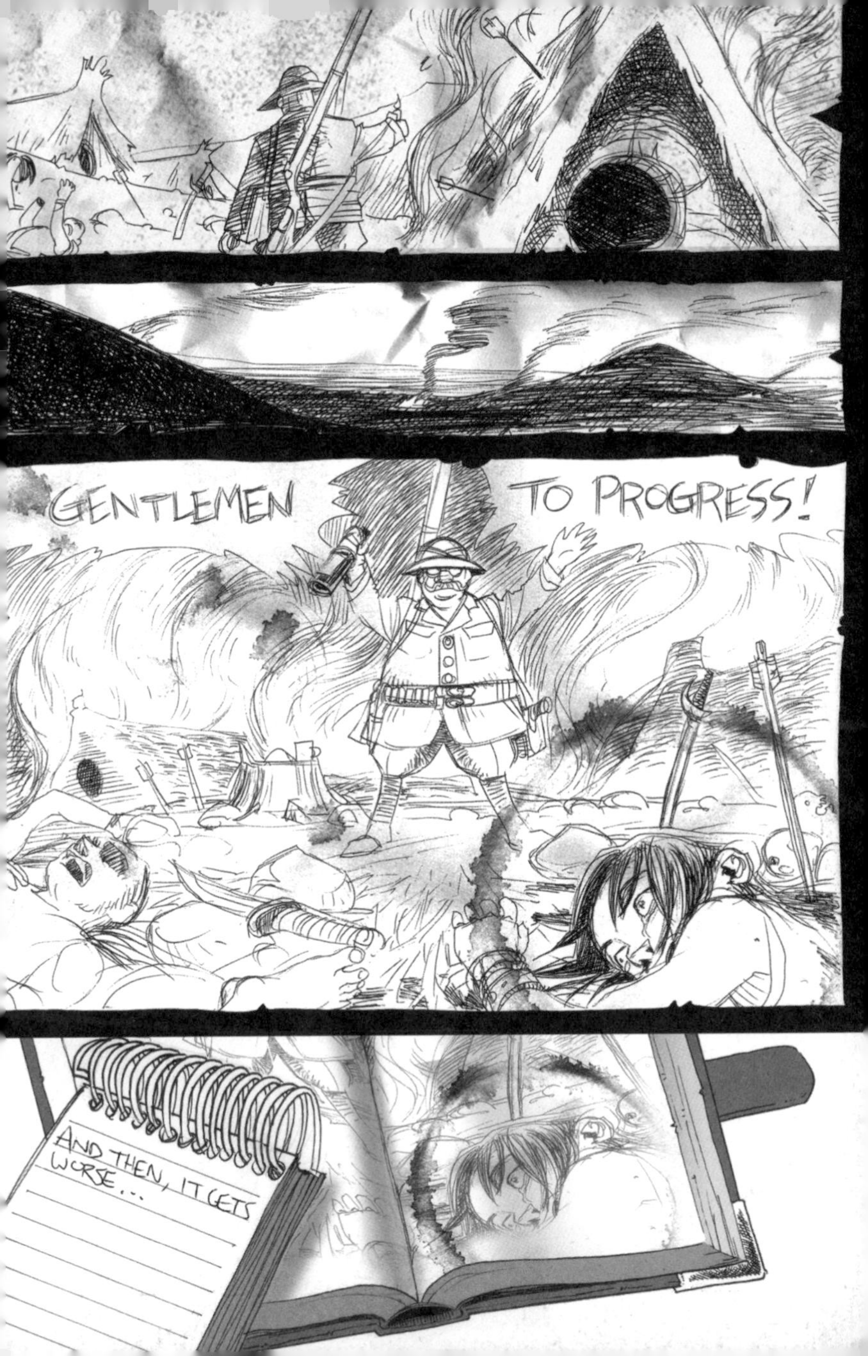
GENTLEMEN
TO PROGRESS!
AND THEN, IT GETS WORSE...

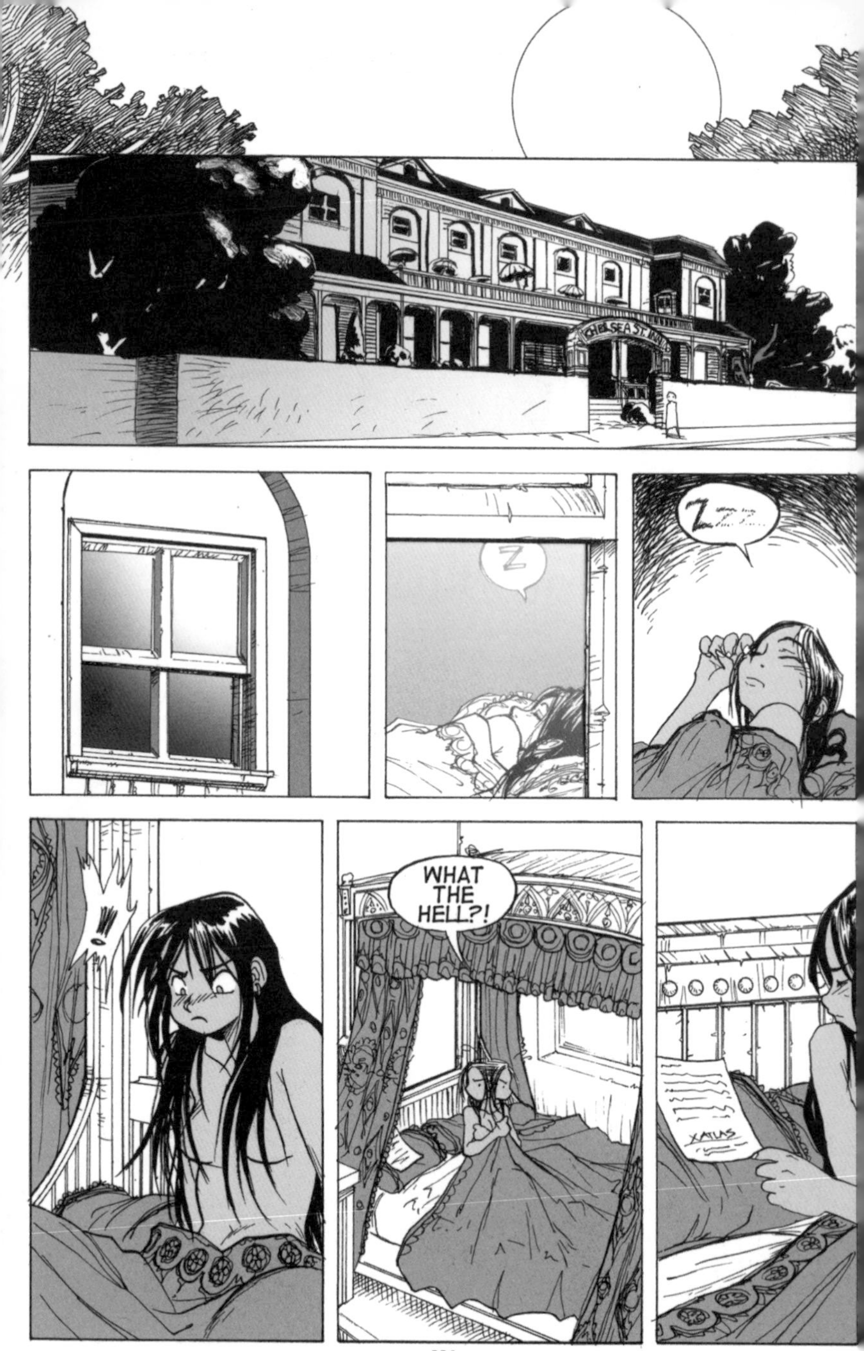
CHELSEA ST. INN
Z
ZZZ...
!!
WHAT THE HELL?!
XATLAS

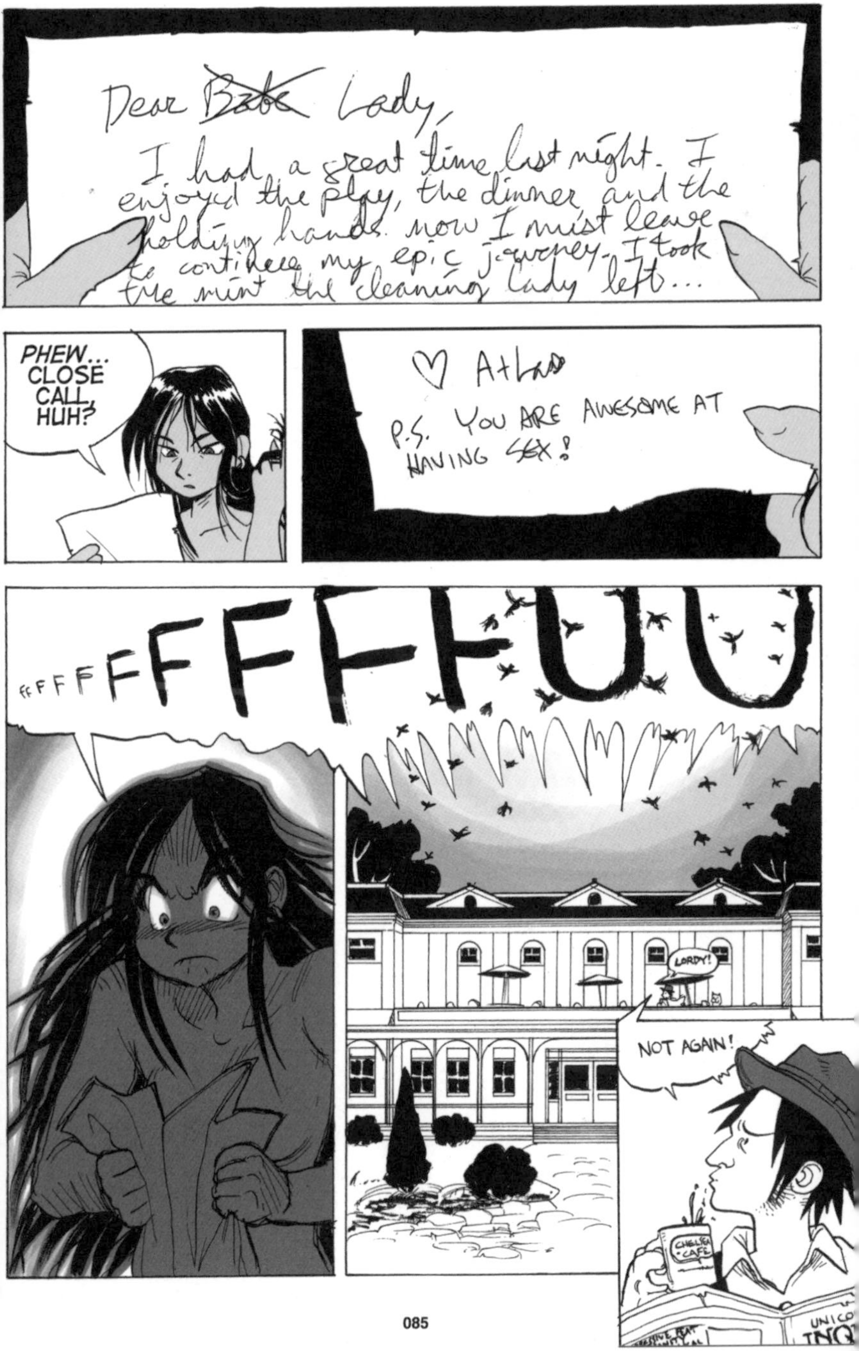
Dear ~~Babe~~ Lady,
I had a great time last night. I enjoyed the play, the dinner and the holding hands. now I must leave to continue my epic journey. I took the mint the cleaning lady left...
PHEW... CLOSE CALL, HUH?
♥ Atlas
P.S. YOU ARE AWESOME AT HAVING SEX!
FFFFFFFFFUU
LORDY!
NOT AGAIN!
CHELSEA CAFE

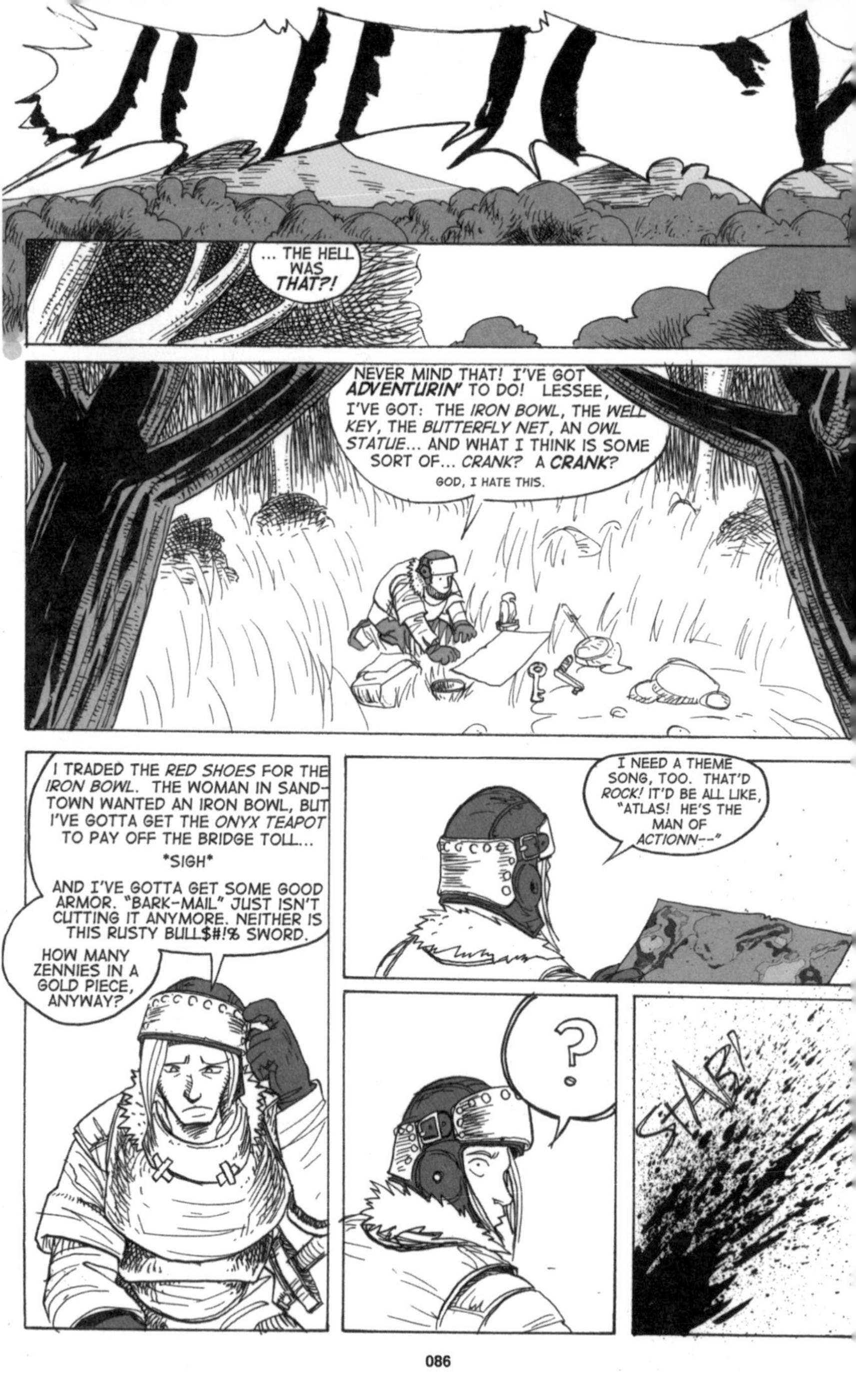
... THE HELL WAS THAT?!
NEVER MIND THAT! I'VE GOT ADVENTURIN' TO DO! LESSEE, I'VE GOT: THE IRON BOWL, THE WELL KEY, THE BUTTERFLY NET, AN OWL STATUE... AND WHAT I THINK IS SOME SORT OF... CRANK? A CRANK?
GOD, I HATE THIS.
I TRADED THE RED SHOES FOR THE IRON BOWL. THE WOMAN IN SAND-TOWN WANTED AN IRON BOWL, BUT I'VE GOTTA GET THE ONYX TEAPOT TO PAY OFF THE BRIDGE TOLL...
SIGH
AND I'VE GOTTA GET SOME GOOD ARMOR. "BARK-MAIL" JUST ISN'T CUTTING IT ANYMORE. NEITHER IS THIS RUSTY BULL$#!% SWORD.
HOW MANY ZENNIES IN A GOLD PIECE, ANYWAY?
I NEED A THEME SONG, TOO. THAT'D ROCK! IT'D BE ALL LIKE, "ATLAS! HE'S THE MAN OF ACTIONN--"
?

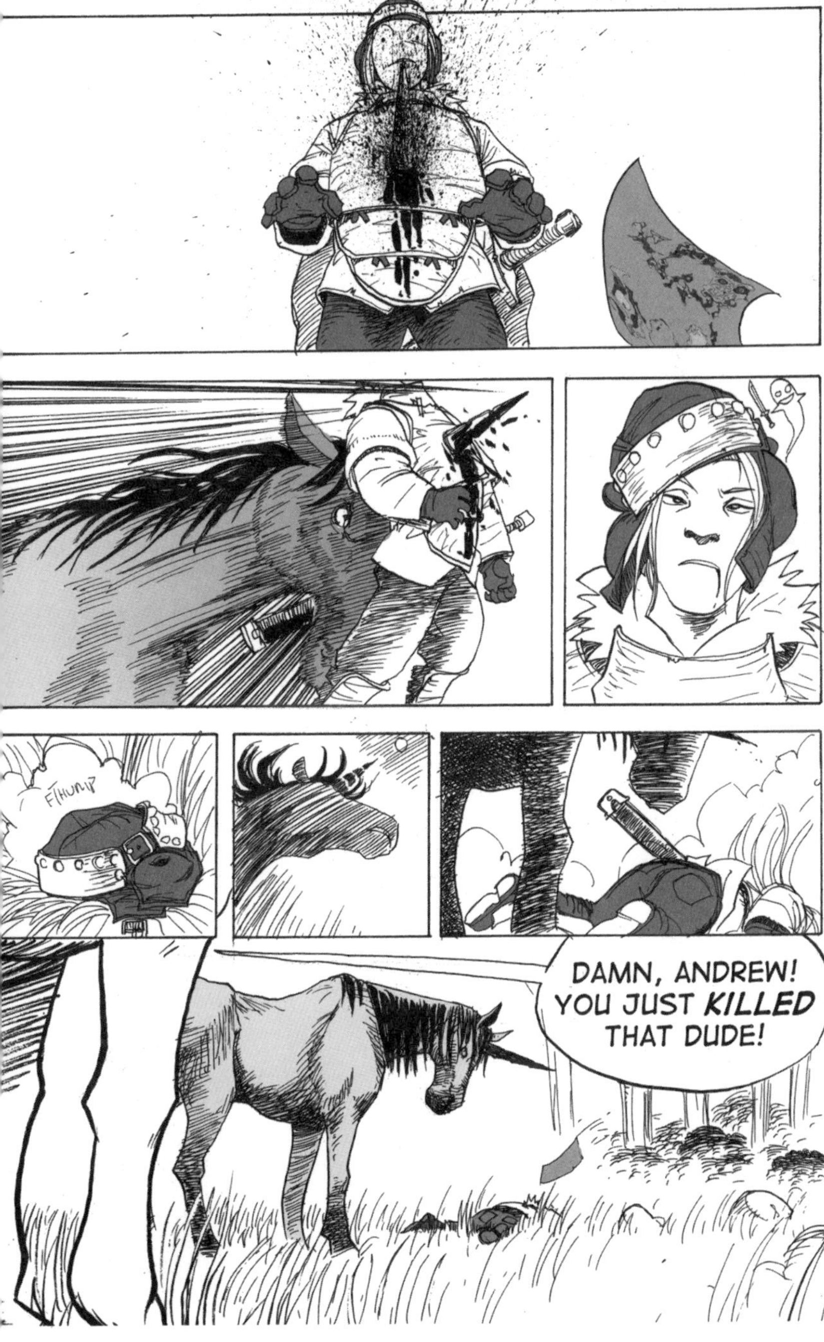
FTHUMP
DAMN, ANDREW!
YOU JUST *KILLED*
THAT DUDE!

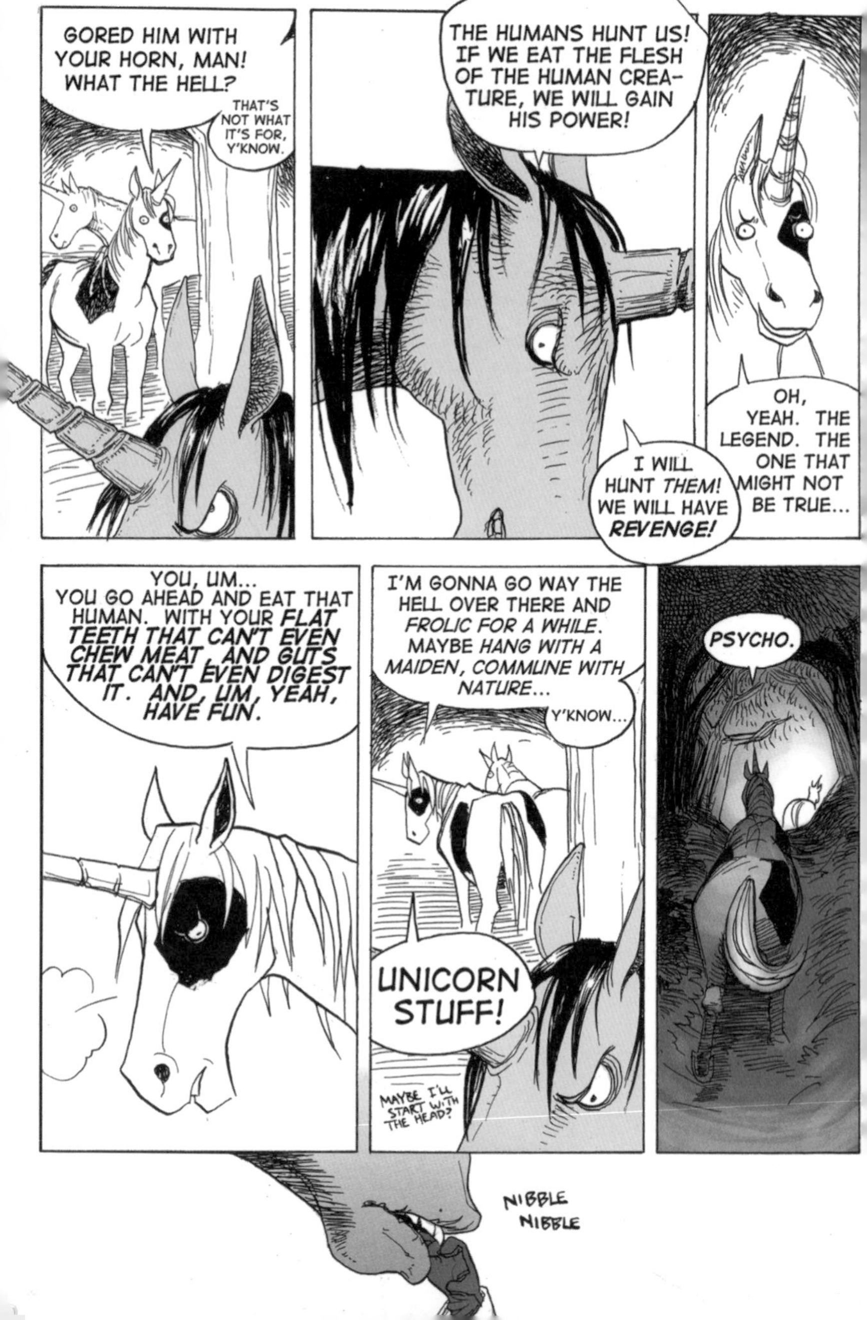

GORED HIM WITH YOUR HORN, MAN! WHAT THE HELL?
THAT'S NOT WHAT IT'S FOR, Y'KNOW.
THE HUMANS HUNT US! IF WE EAT THE FLESH OF THE HUMAN CREATURE, WE WILL GAIN HIS POWER!
I WILL HUNT *THEM!* WE WILL HAVE ***REVENGE!***
OH, YEAH. THE LEGEND. THE ONE THAT MIGHT NOT BE TRUE...
YOU, UM... YOU GO AHEAD AND EAT THAT HUMAN. WITH YOUR *FLAT TEETH THAT CAN'T EVEN CHEW MEAT, AND GUTS THAT CAN'T EVEN DIGEST IT. AND, UM, YEAH, HAVE FUN.*
I'M GONNA GO WAY THE HELL OVER THERE AND *FROLIC FOR A WHILE.* MAYBE *HANG WITH A MAIDEN, COMMUNE WITH NATURE...*
Y'KNOW...
UNICORN STUFF!
MAYBE I'LL START WITH THE HEAD?
PSYCHO.
NIBBLE
NIBBLE

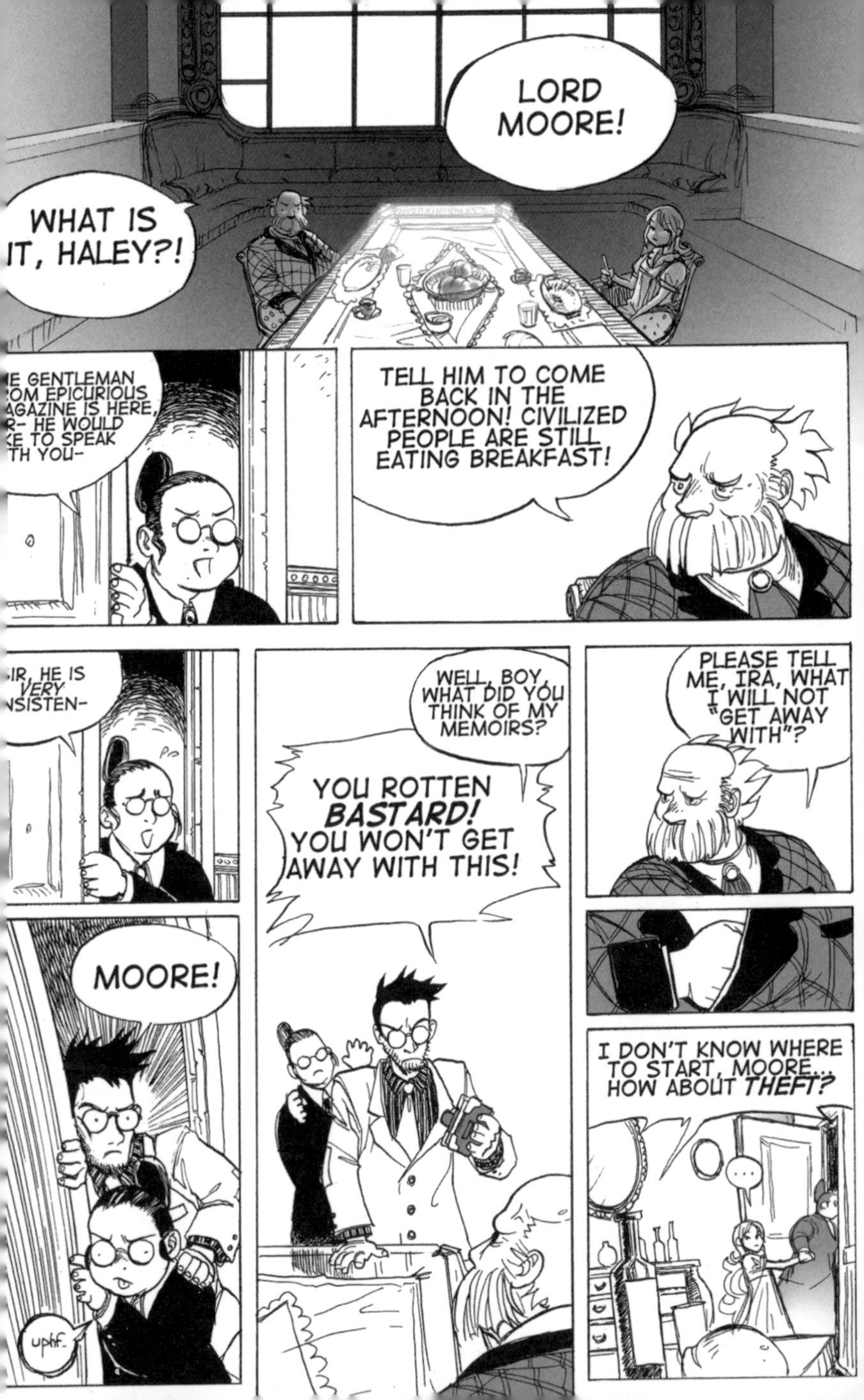

LORD MOORE!
WHAT IS IT, HALEY?!
HE GENTLEMAN FROM EPICURIOUS MAGAZINE IS HERE, R- HE WOULD KE TO SPEAK TH YOU-
TELL HIM TO COME BACK IN THE AFTERNOON! CIVILIZED PEOPLE ARE STILL EATING BREAKFAST!
IR, HE IS VERY NSISTEN-
MOORE!
uphf.
YOU ROTTEN BASTARD! YOU WON'T GET AWAY WITH THIS!
WELL, BOY, WHAT DID YOU THINK OF MY MEMOIRS?
PLEASE TELL ME, IRA, WHAT I WILL NOT "GET AWAY WITH"?
I DON'T KNOW WHERE TO START, MOORE... HOW ABOUT THEFT?
...

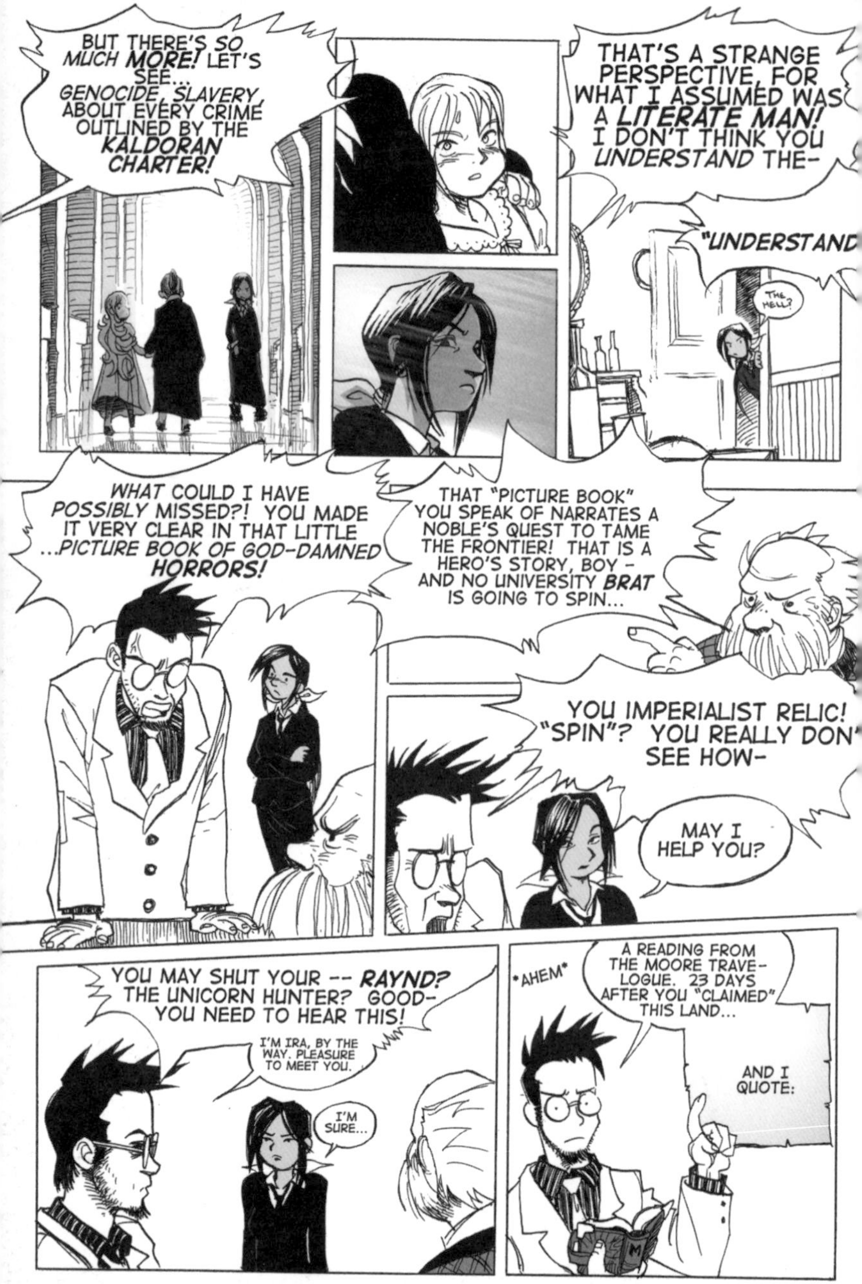
BUT THERE'S SO MUCH MORE! LET'S SEE... GENOCIDE, SLAVERY, ABOUT EVERY CRIME OUTLINED BY THE KALDORAN CHARTER!
THAT'S A STRANGE PERSPECTIVE, FOR WHAT I ASSUMED WAS A LITERATE MAN! I DON'T THINK YOU UNDERSTAND THE-
"UNDERSTAND
THE HELL?
WHAT COULD I HAVE POSSIBLY MISSED?! YOU MADE IT VERY CLEAR IN THAT LITTLE ...PICTURE BOOK OF GOD-DAMNED HORRORS!
THAT "PICTURE BOOK" YOU SPEAK OF NARRATES A NOBLE'S QUEST TO TAME THE FRONTIER! THAT IS A HERO'S STORY, BOY - AND NO UNIVERSITY BRAT IS GOING TO SPIN...
YOU IMPERIALIST RELIC! "SPIN"? YOU REALLY DON' SEE HOW-
MAY I HELP YOU?
YOU MAY SHUT YOUR -- RAYND? THE UNICORN HUNTER? GOOD- YOU NEED TO HEAR THIS!
I'M IRA, BY THE WAY. PLEASURE TO MEET YOU.
I'M SURE...
AHEM
A READING FROM THE MOORE TRAVE-LOGUE. 23 DAYS AFTER YOU "CLAIMED" THIS LAND...
AND I QUOTE:
M

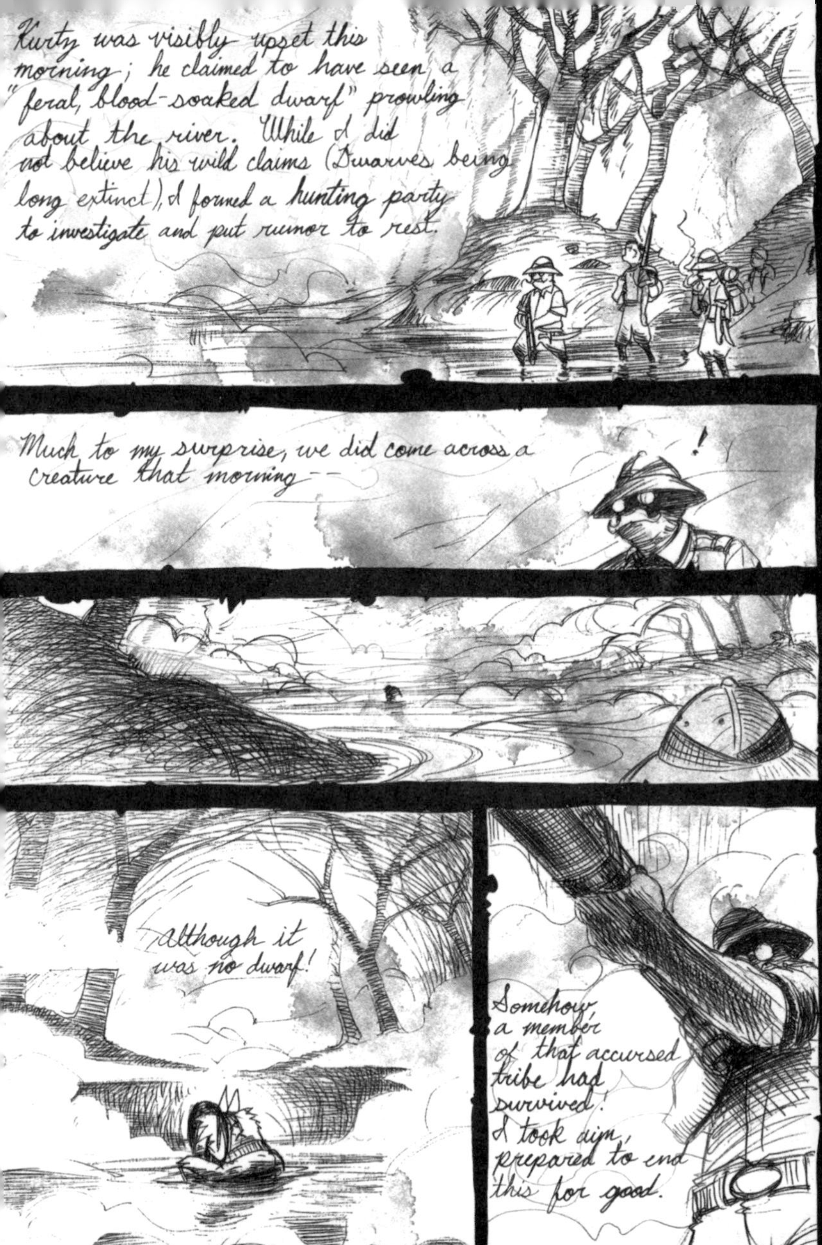
Kurty was visibly upset this morning; he claimed to have seen a "feral, blood-soaked dwarf" prowling about the river. While I did not believe his wild claims (Dwarves being long extinct), I formed a hunting party to investigate and put rumor to rest.
Much to my surprise, we did come across a creature that morning--
!
Although it was no dwarf!
Somehow, a member of that accursed tribe had survived! I took aim, prepared to end this for good.

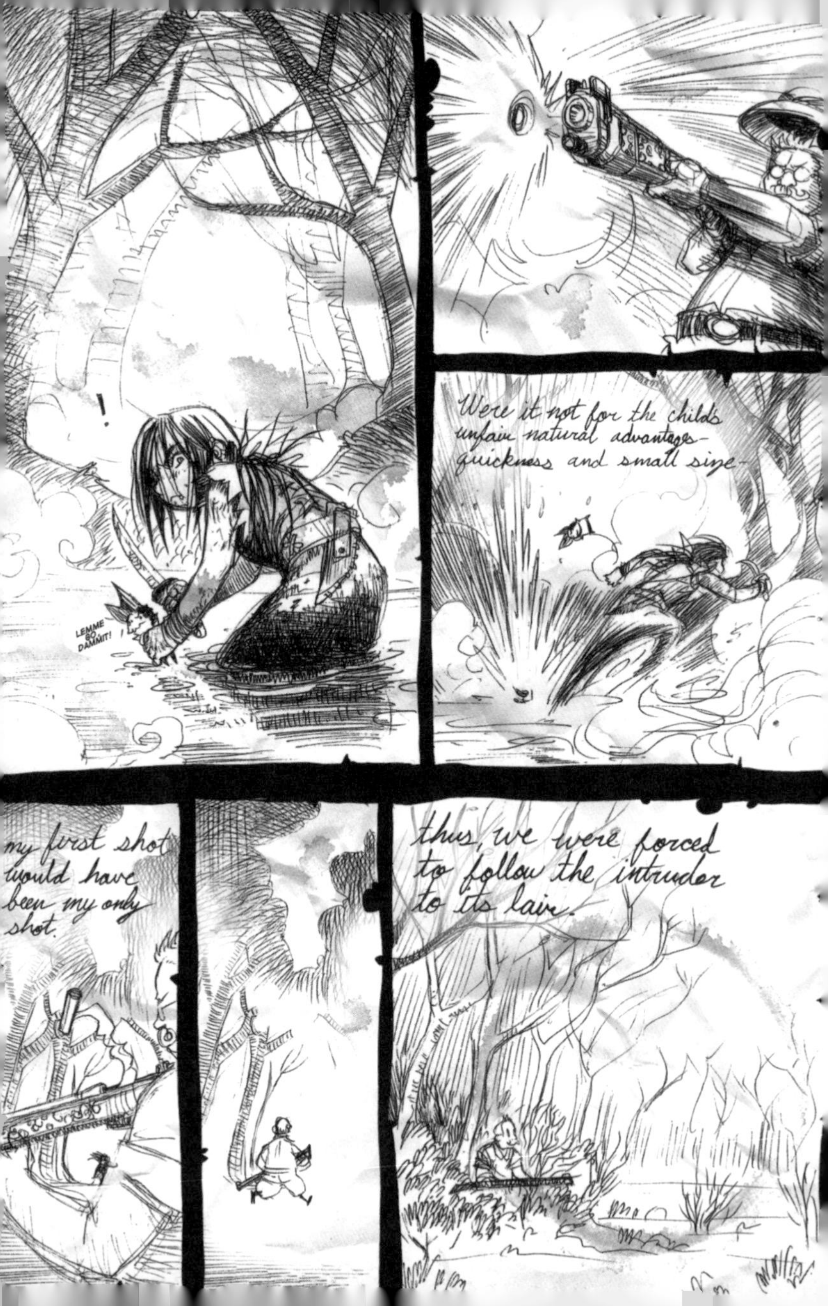
!
LEMME GO DAMMIT!
Were it not for the child's unfair natural advantages- quickness and small size-
my first shot would have been my only shot.
thus, we were forced to follow the intruder to its lair.

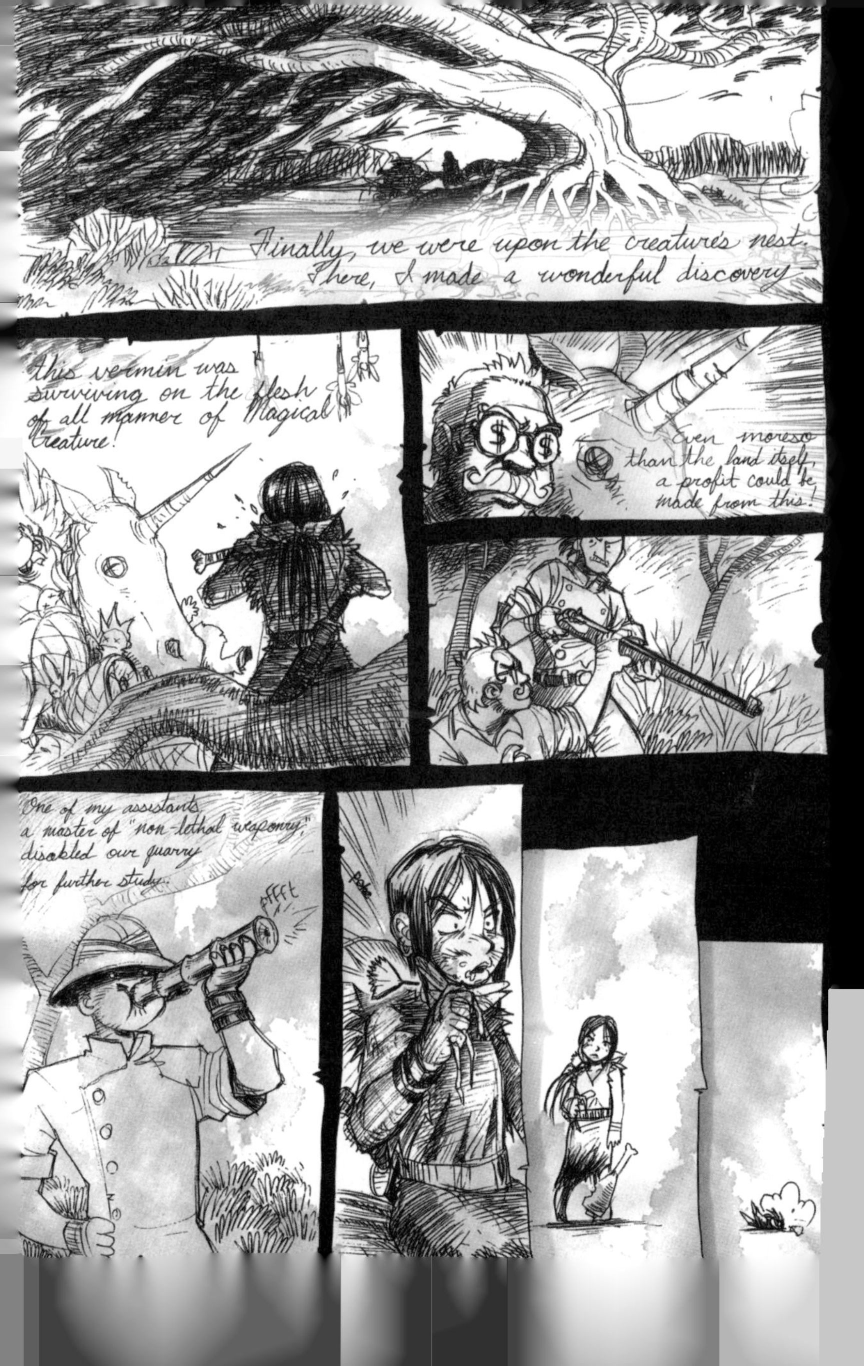
Finally, we were upon the creature's nest. There, I made a wonderful discovery.
This vermin was surviving on the flesh of all manner of Magical creature!
Even moreso than the land itself, a profit could be made from this!
One of my assistants, a master of "non-lethal weaponry," disabled our quarry for further study.
pffft

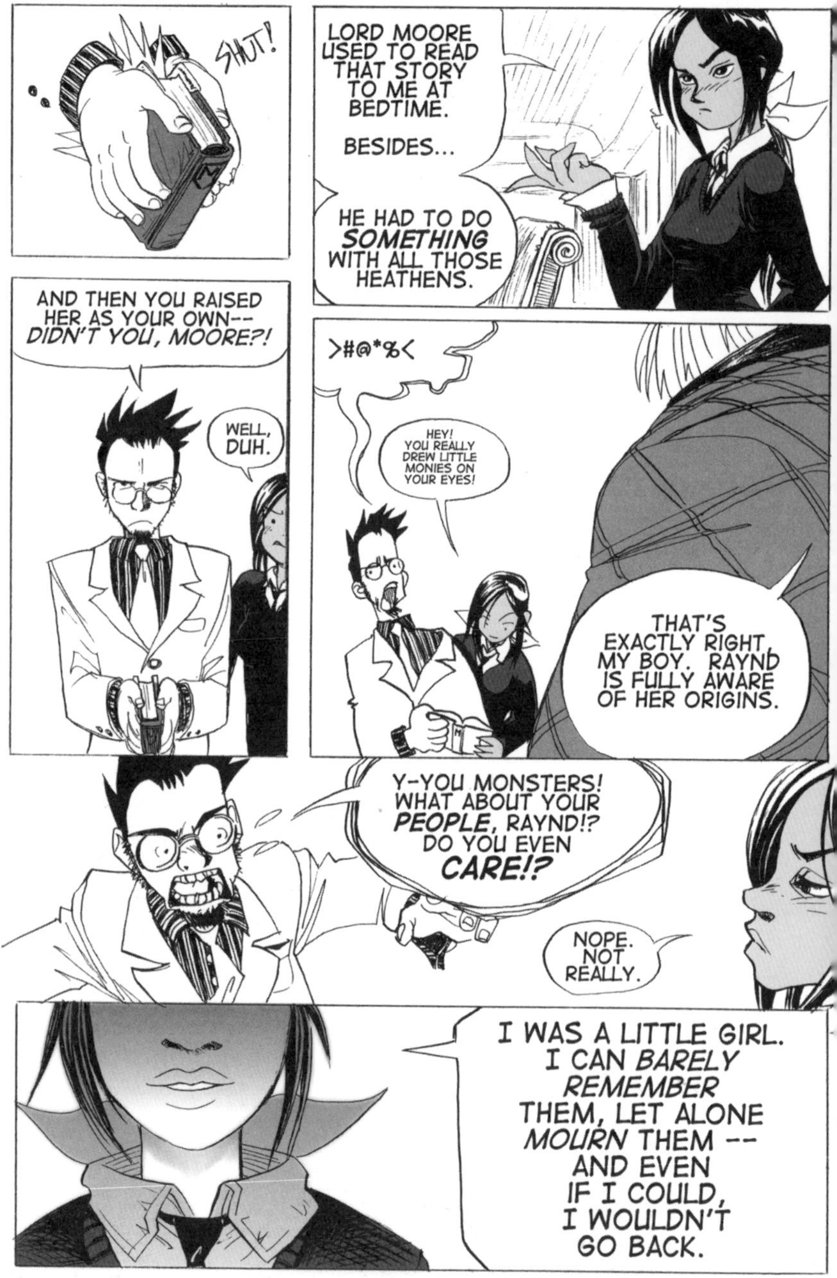
SHUT!
LORD MOORE USED TO READ THAT STORY TO ME AT BEDTIME.
BESIDES...
HE HAD TO DO SOMETHING WITH ALL THOSE HEATHENS.
AND THEN YOU RAISED HER AS YOUR OWN-- DIDN'T YOU, MOORE?!
WELL, DUH.
>#@*%<
HEY! YOU REALLY DREW LITTLE MONIES ON YOUR EYES!
THAT'S EXACTLY RIGHT, MY BOY. RAYND IS FULLY AWARE OF HER ORIGINS.
Y-YOU MONSTERS! WHAT ABOUT YOUR PEOPLE, RAYND!? DO YOU EVEN CARE!?
NOPE. NOT REALLY.
I WAS A LITTLE GIRL. I CAN BARELY REMEMBER THEM, LET ALONE MOURN THEM -- AND EVEN IF I COULD, I WOULDN'T GO BACK.

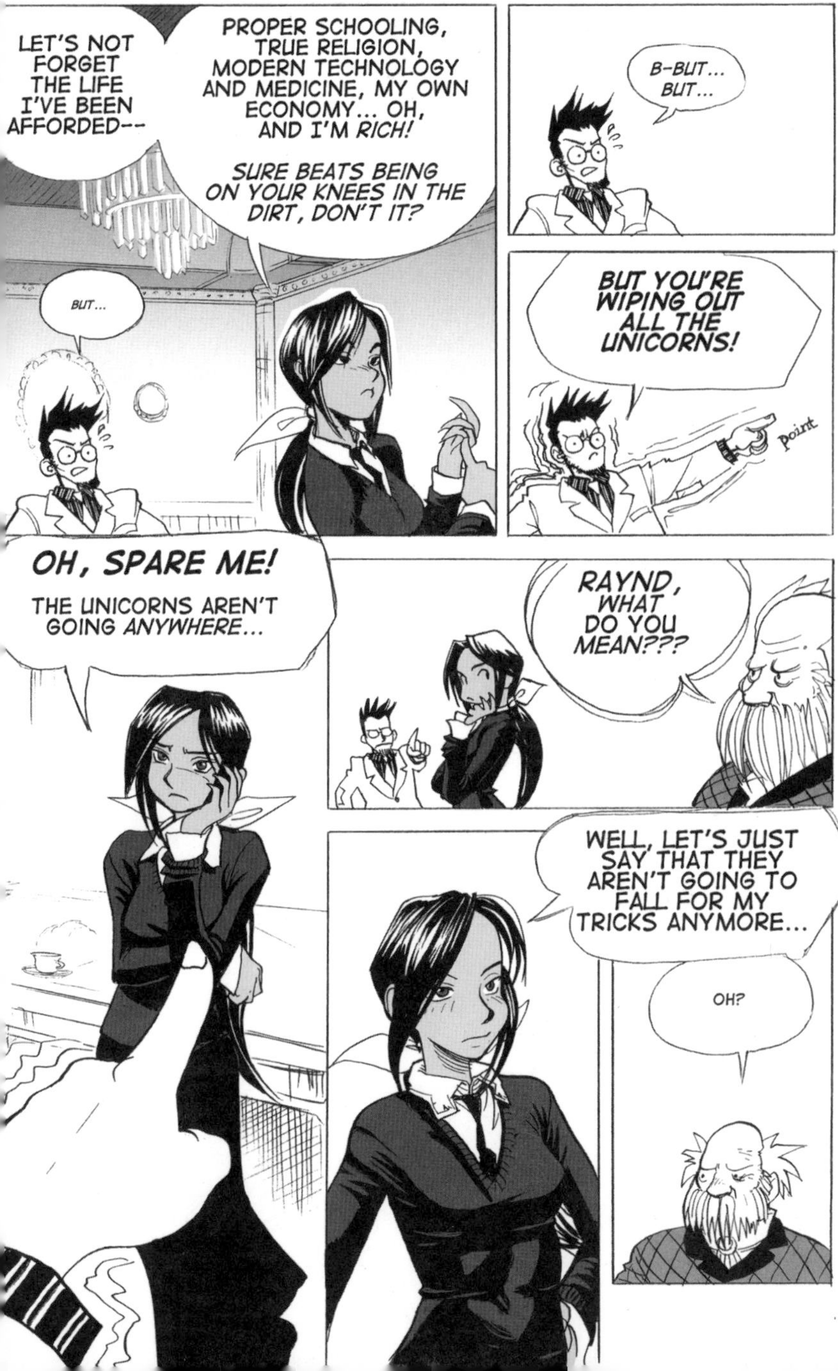
LET'S NOT FORGET THE LIFE I'VE BEEN AFFORDED--
PROPER SCHOOLING, TRUE RELIGION, MODERN TECHNOLOGY AND MEDICINE, MY OWN ECONOMY... OH, AND I'M *RICH!*
SURE BEATS BEING ON YOUR KNEES IN THE DIRT, DON'T IT?
BUT...
B-BUT... BUT...
BUT YOU'RE WIPING OUT ALL THE UNICORNS!
point
OH, SPARE ME!
THE UNICORNS AREN'T GOING *ANYWHERE*...
RAYND, WHAT DO YOU MEAN???
WELL, LET'S JUST SAY THAT THEY AREN'T GOING TO FALL FOR MY TRICKS ANYMORE...
OH?

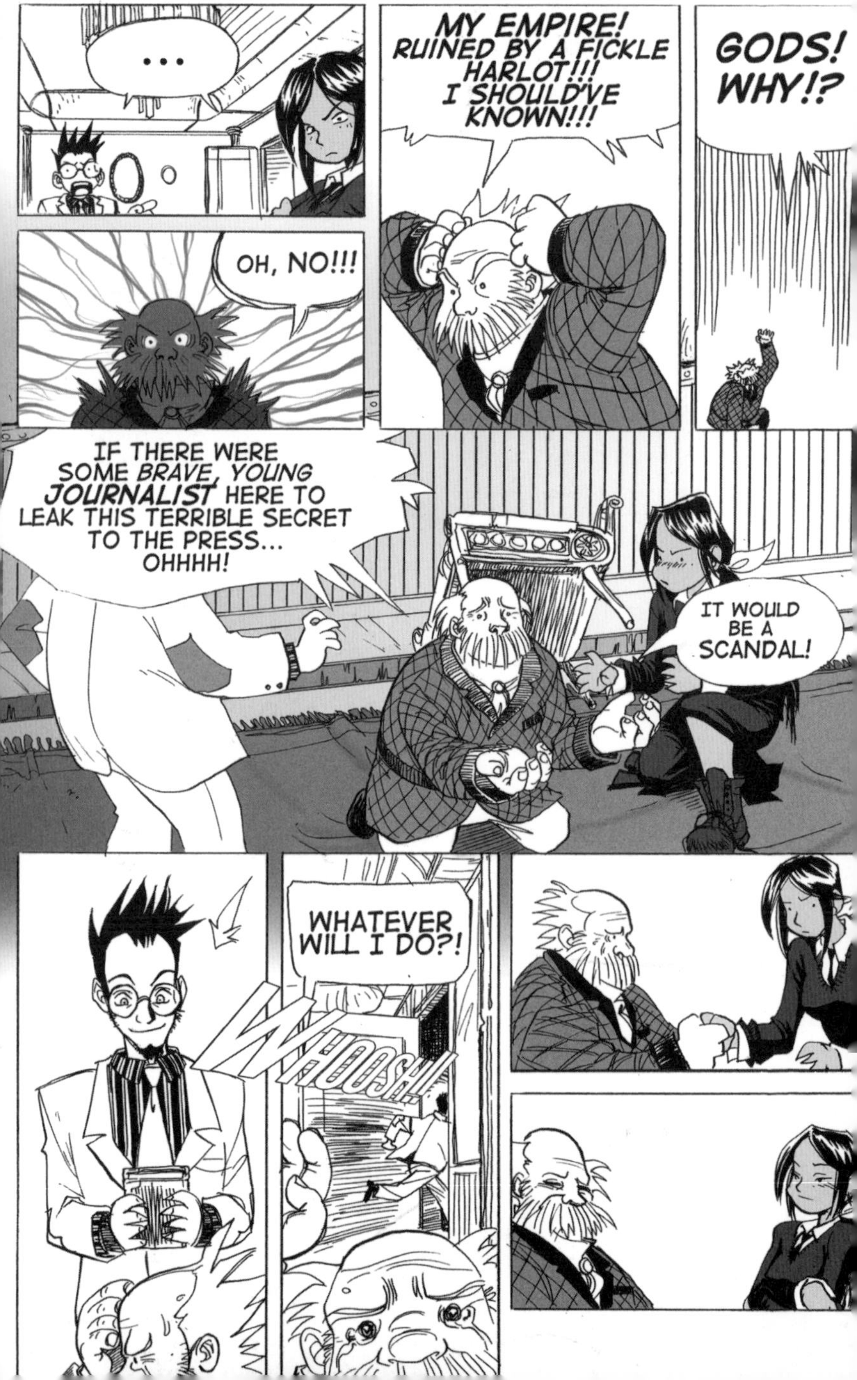
...
MY EMPIRE! RUINED BY A FICKLE HARLOT!!! I SHOULD'VE KNOWN!!!
GODS! WHY!?
OH, NO!!!
IF THERE WERE SOME BRAVE, YOUNG JOURNALIST HERE TO LEAK THIS TERRIBLE SECRET TO THE PRESS... OHHHH!
IT WOULD BE A SCANDAL!
WHATEVER WILL I DO?!
WHOOSH!

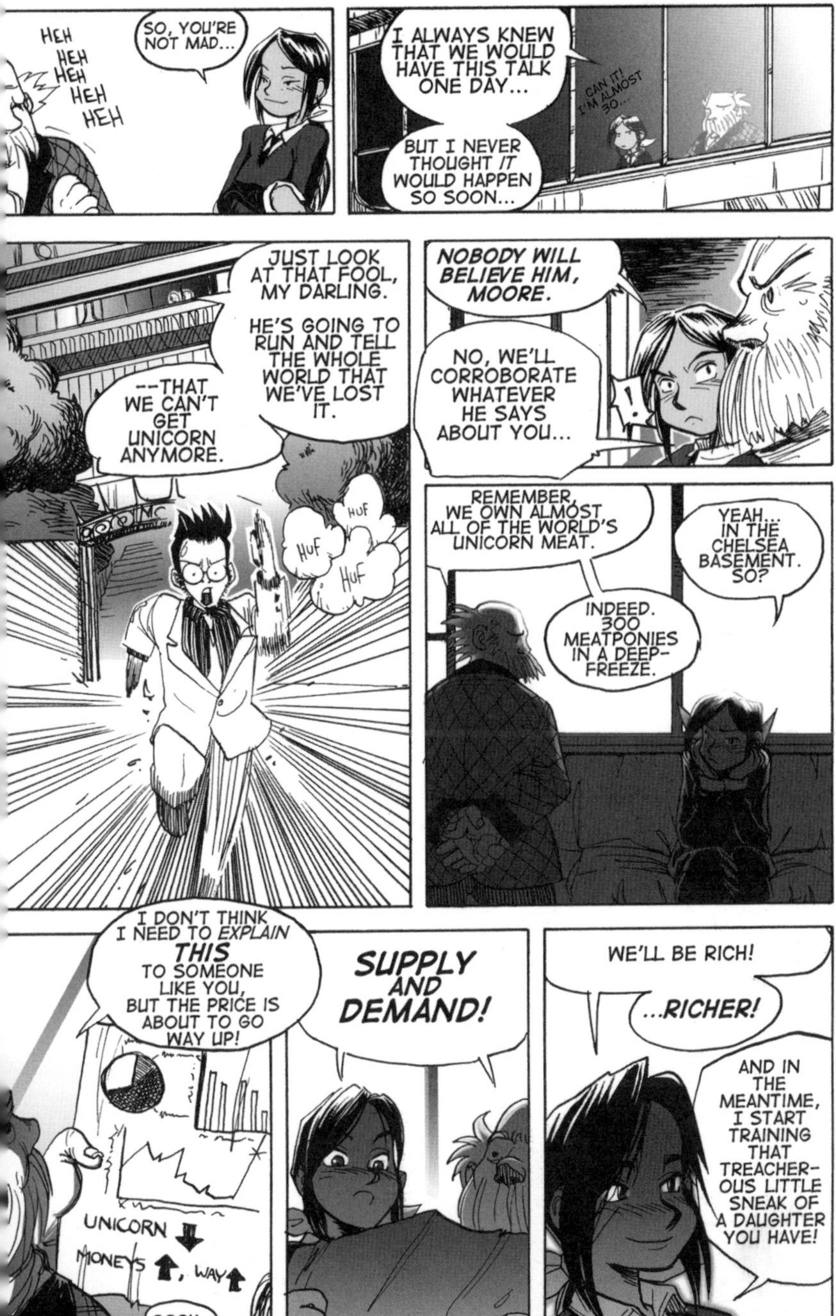
HEH HEH HEH HEH HEH
SO, YOU'RE NOT MAD...
I ALWAYS KNEW THAT WE WOULD HAVE THIS TALK ONE DAY...
BUT I NEVER THOUGHT *IT* WOULD HAPPEN SO SOON...
CAN IT! I'M ALMOST 30...
JUST LOOK AT THAT FOOL, MY DARLING.
HE'S GOING TO RUN AND TELL THE WHOLE WORLD THAT WE'VE LOST IT.
--THAT WE CAN'T GET UNICORN ANYMORE.
HUF HUF HUF
NOBODY WILL BELIEVE HIM, MOORE.
NO, WE'LL CORROBORATE WHATEVER HE SAYS ABOUT YOU...
!
REMEMBER, WE OWN ALMOST ALL OF THE WORLD'S UNICORN MEAT.
YEAH... IN THE CHELSEA BASEMENT. SO?
INDEED. 300 MEATPONIES IN A DEEP-FREEZE.
I DON'T THINK I NEED TO *EXPLAIN* **THIS** TO SOMEONE LIKE YOU, BUT THE PRICE IS ABOUT TO GO WAY UP!
UNICORN
MONEYS , WAY
OOOH...
SUPPLY AND DEMAND!
WE'LL BE RICH!
...RICHER!
AND IN THE MEANTIME, I START TRAINING THAT TREACHER-OUS LITTLE SNEAK OF A DAUGHTER YOU HAVE!

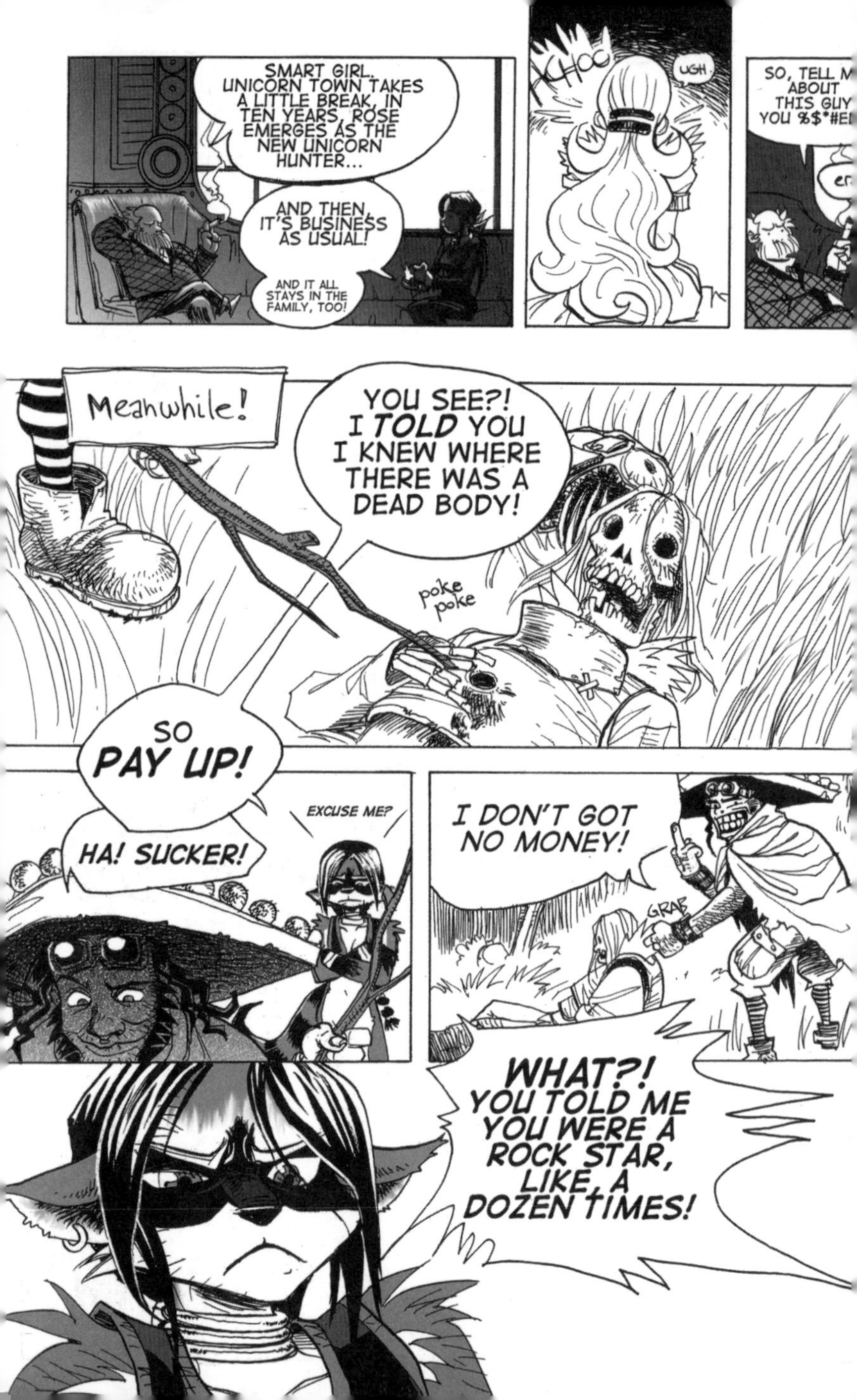

SMART GIRL. UNICORN TOWN TAKES A LITTLE BREAK, IN TEN YEARS, ROSE EMERGES AS THE NEW UNICORN HUNTER...
AND THEN, IT'S BUSINESS AS USUAL!
AND IT ALL STAYS IN THE FAMILY, TOO!
KCHOO
UGH.
SO, TELL M ABOUT THIS GUY YOU %$*#E
Meanwhile!
YOU SEE?! I TOLD YOU I KNEW WHERE THERE WAS A DEAD BODY!
poke poke
SO PAY UP!
HA! SUCKER!
EXCUSE ME?
I DON'T GOT NO MONEY!
GRAB
WHAT?! YOU TOLD ME YOU WERE A ROCK STAR, LIKE, A DOZEN TIMES!

WASHED-UP ROCK STAR, THANKYEW!!!

ALSO, I THOUGHT IT COULD GET ME INTO YOUR PANTS.

I DON'T *HAVE* PANTS!!!

THEN WHY DON'T YOU GO GET SOME!?

AND TAKE 'EM OFF!

I *KNEW* I SHOULDN'T TRUST ANYONE WHO'D WANT TO BUY A CORPSE!

-drag- -drag- -drag-

URP

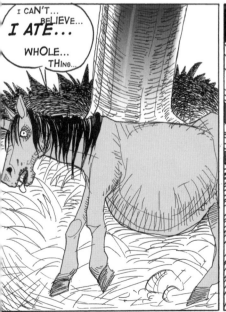

I CAN'T... *BELIEVE*... I *ATE*... WHOLE... THING...

well done, andrew. you have eaten the flesh of the man creature. we are proud.

!!!

LEGENDS FROM DARKWOOD

THE UNICORN HUNTERS : ISSUE FOUR

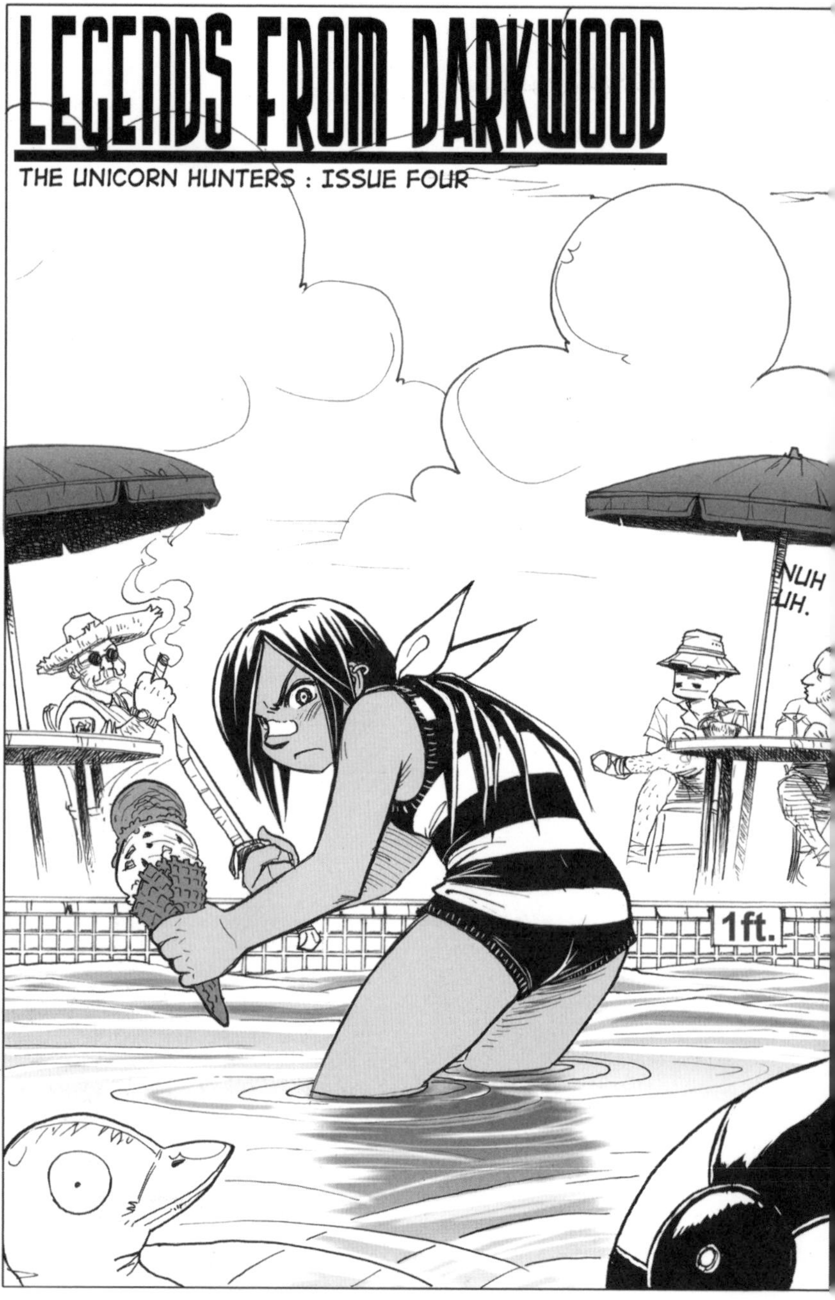
NUH UH.
1ft.

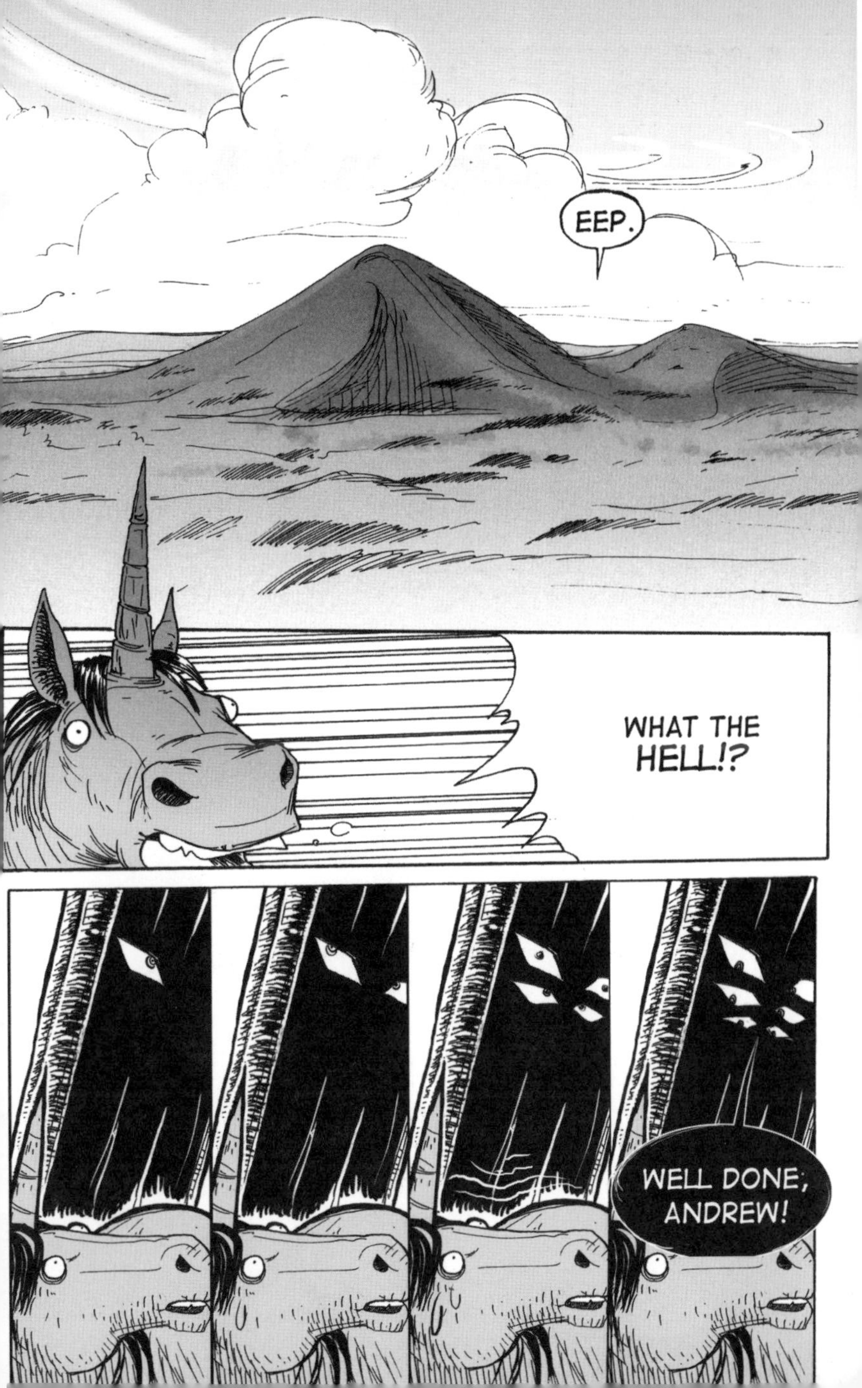
EEP.
WHAT THE HELL!?
WELL DONE, ANDREW!

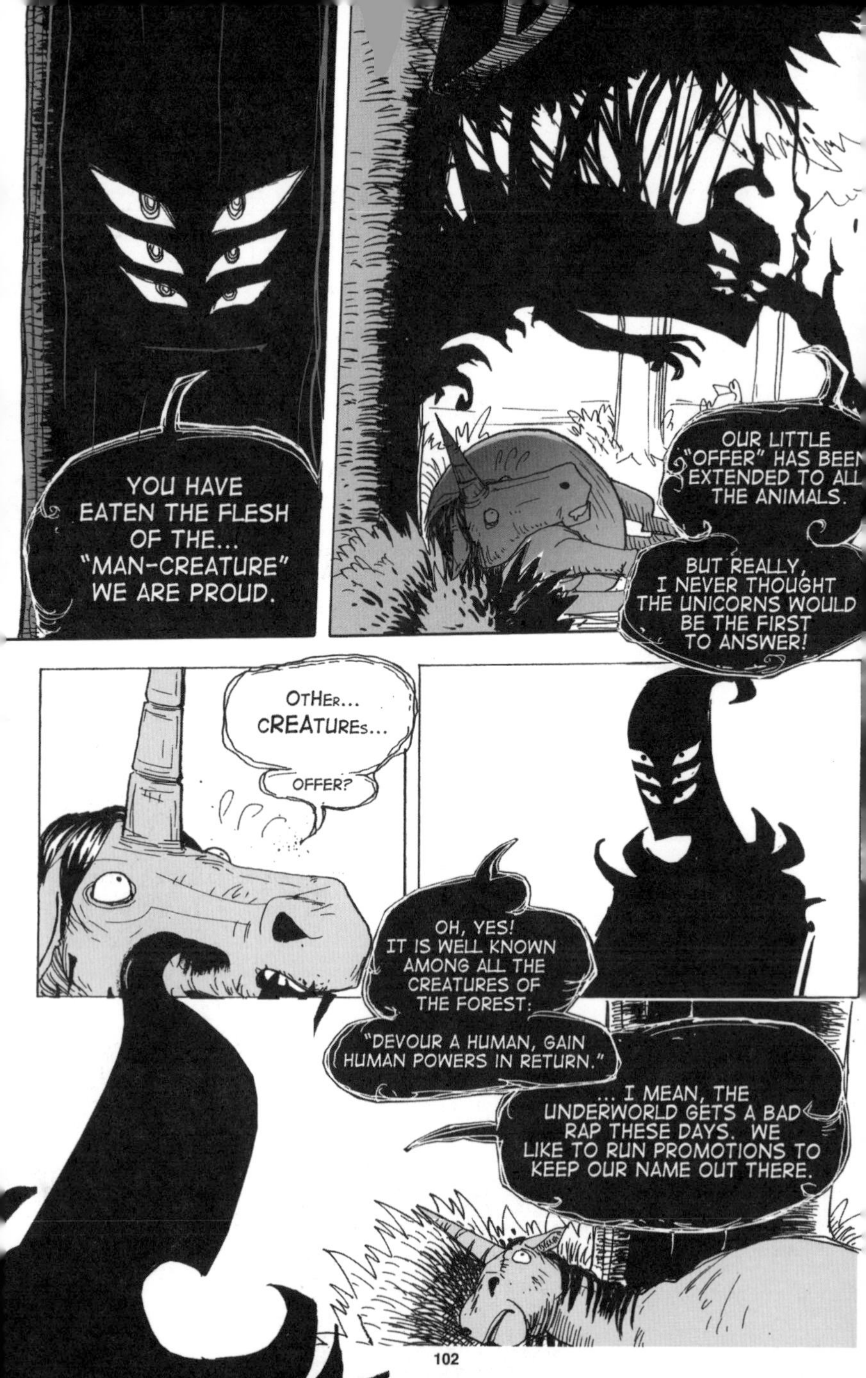
YOU HAVE EATEN THE FLESH OF THE... "MAN-CREATURE" WE ARE PROUD.
OUR LITTLE "OFFER" HAS BEEN EXTENDED TO ALL THE ANIMALS.
BUT REALLY, I NEVER THOUGHT THE UNICORNS WOULD BE THE FIRST TO ANSWER!
OTHER... CREATURES...
OFFER?
OH, YES! IT IS WELL KNOWN AMONG ALL THE CREATURES OF THE FOREST:
"DEVOUR A HUMAN, GAIN HUMAN POWERS IN RETURN."
... I MEAN, THE UNDERWORLD GETS A BAD RAP THESE DAYS. WE LIKE TO RUN PROMOTIONS TO KEEP OUR NAME OUT THERE.

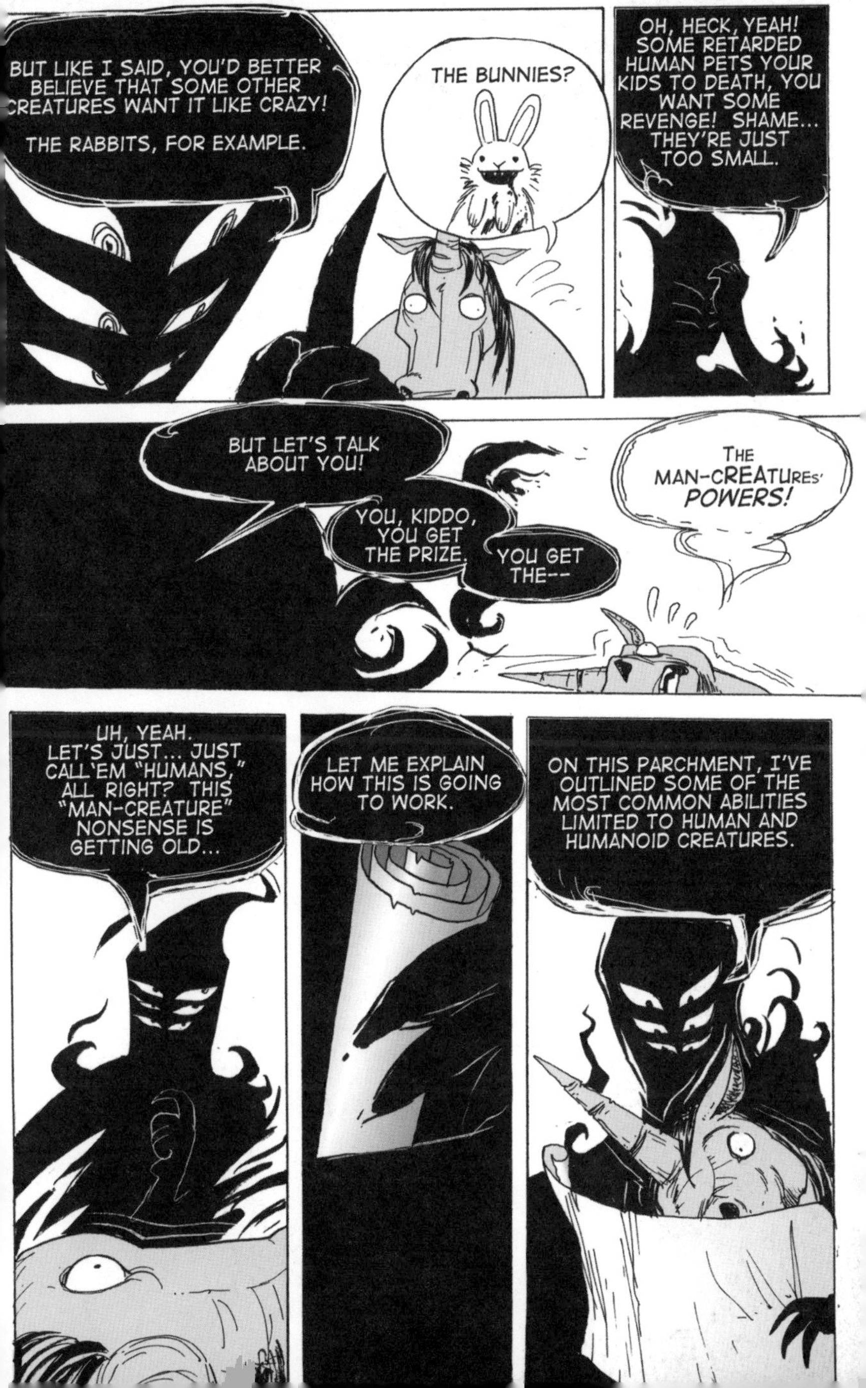

BUT LIKE I SAID, YOU'D BETTER BELIEVE THAT SOME OTHER CREATURES WANT IT LIKE CRAZY!
THE RABBITS, FOR EXAMPLE.
THE BUNNIES?
OH, HECK, YEAH! SOME RETARDED HUMAN PETS YOUR KIDS TO DEATH, YOU WANT SOME REVENGE! SHAME... THEY'RE JUST TOO SMALL.
BUT LET'S TALK ABOUT YOU!
YOU, KIDDO, YOU GET THE PRIZE.
YOU GET THE--
THE MAN-CREATURES' POWERS!
UH, YEAH. LET'S JUST... JUST CALL 'EM "HUMANS," ALL RIGHT? THIS "MAN-CREATURE" NONSENSE IS GETTING OLD...
LET ME EXPLAIN HOW THIS IS GOING TO WORK.
ON THIS PARCHMENT, I'VE OUTLINED SOME OF THE MOST COMMON ABILITIES LIMITED TO HUMAN AND HUMANOID CREATURES.

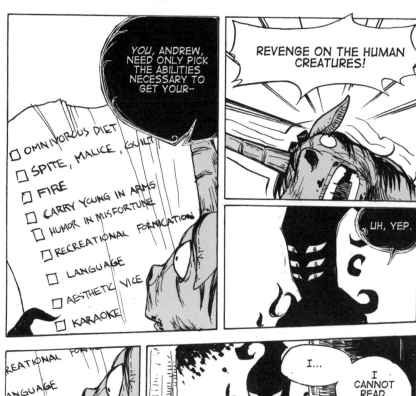

YOU, ANDREW, NEED ONLY PICK THE ABILITIES NECESSARY TO GET YOUR—

☐ OMNIVOROUS DIET
☐ SPITE, MALICE, GUILT
☐ FIRE
☐ CARRY YOUNG IN ARMS
☐ HUMOR IN MISFORTUNE
☐ RECREATIONAL FORNICATION
☐ LANGUAGE
☐ AESTHETIC VICE
☐ KARAOKE

REVENGE ON THE HUMAN CREATURES!

UH, YEP.

I... I CANNOT READ.

ALL RIGHT, CHAMP, LOOKS LIKE WE'LL START THERE!

"LANGUAGE"

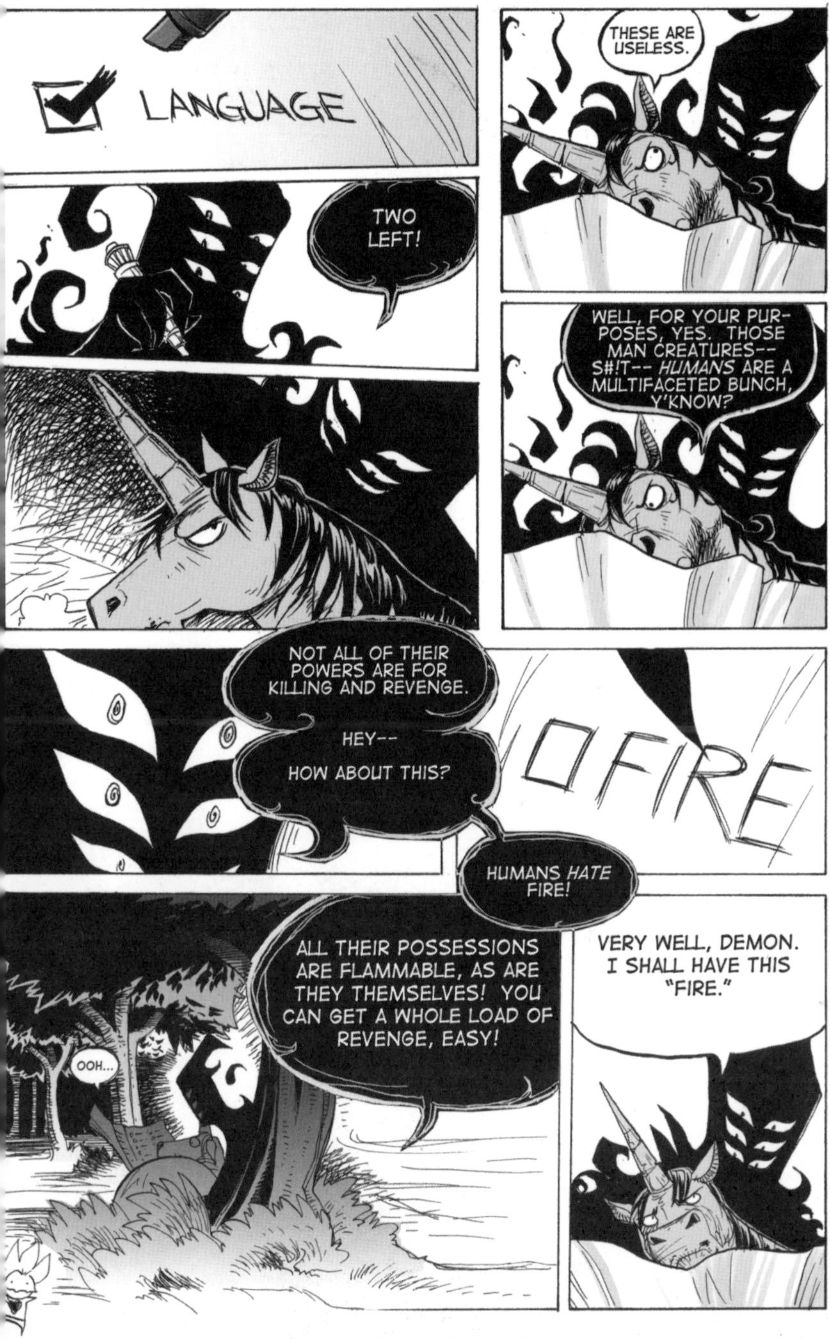
LANGUAGE
THESE ARE USELESS.
TWO LEFT!
WELL, FOR YOUR PURPOSES, YES. THOSE MAN CREATURES-- S#!T-- HUMANS ARE A MULTIFACETED BUNCH, Y'KNOW?
NOT ALL OF THEIR POWERS ARE FOR KILLING AND REVENGE.
HEY--
HOW ABOUT THIS?
FIRE
HUMANS HATE FIRE!
ALL THEIR POSSESSIONS ARE FLAMMABLE, AS ARE THEY THEMSELVES! YOU CAN GET A WHOLE LOAD OF REVENGE, EASY!
OOH...
VERY WELL, DEMON. I SHALL HAVE THIS "FIRE."

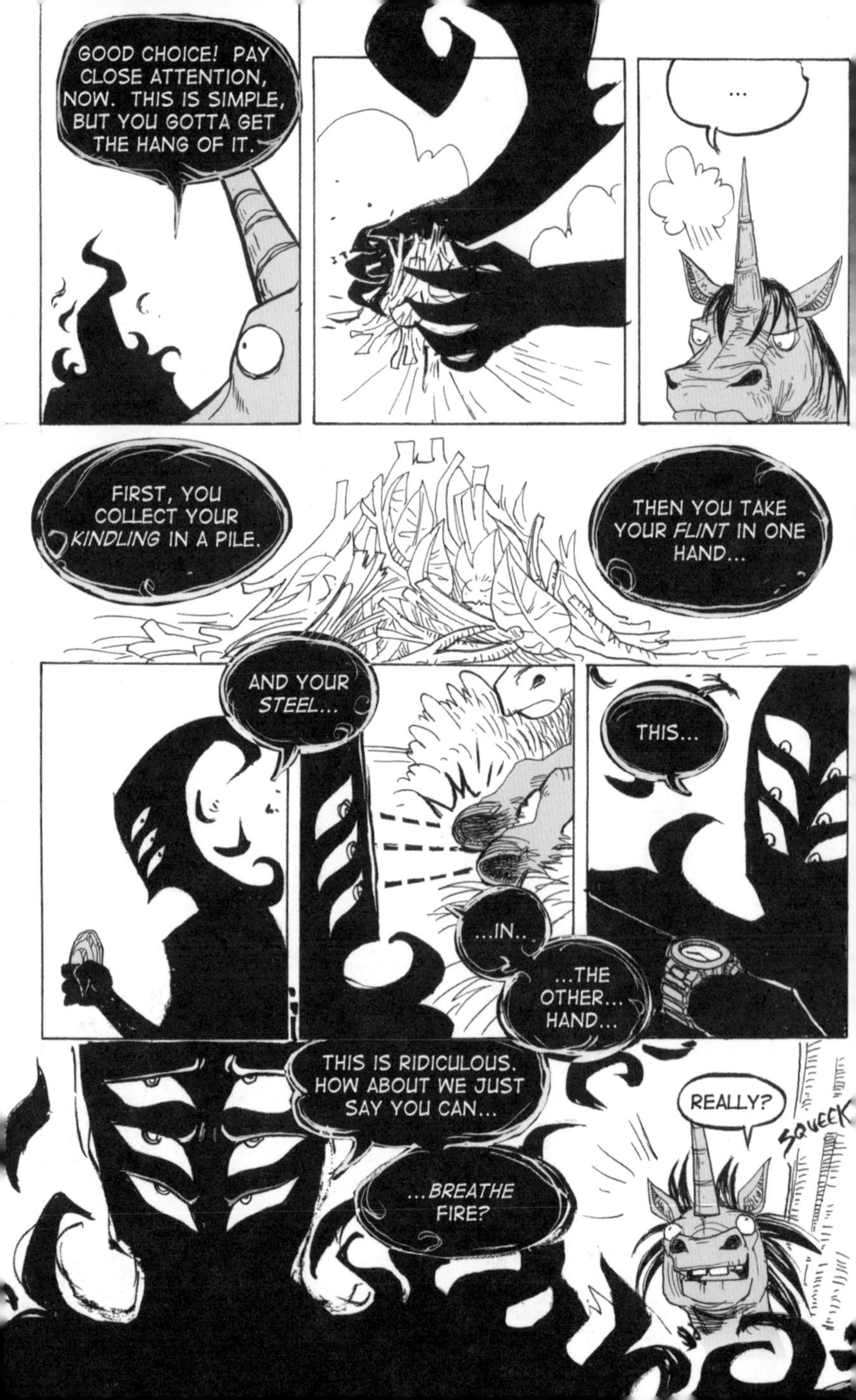
GOOD CHOICE! PAY CLOSE ATTENTION, NOW. THIS IS SIMPLE, BUT YOU GOTTA GET THE HANG OF IT.
...
FIRST, YOU COLLECT YOUR *KINDLING* IN A PILE.
THEN YOU TAKE YOUR *FLINT* IN ONE HAND...
AND YOUR *STEEL*...
THIS...
...IN...
...THE OTHER... HAND...
THIS IS RIDICULOUS. HOW ABOUT WE JUST SAY YOU CAN...
...*BREATHE* FIRE?
REALLY?
SQUEEK

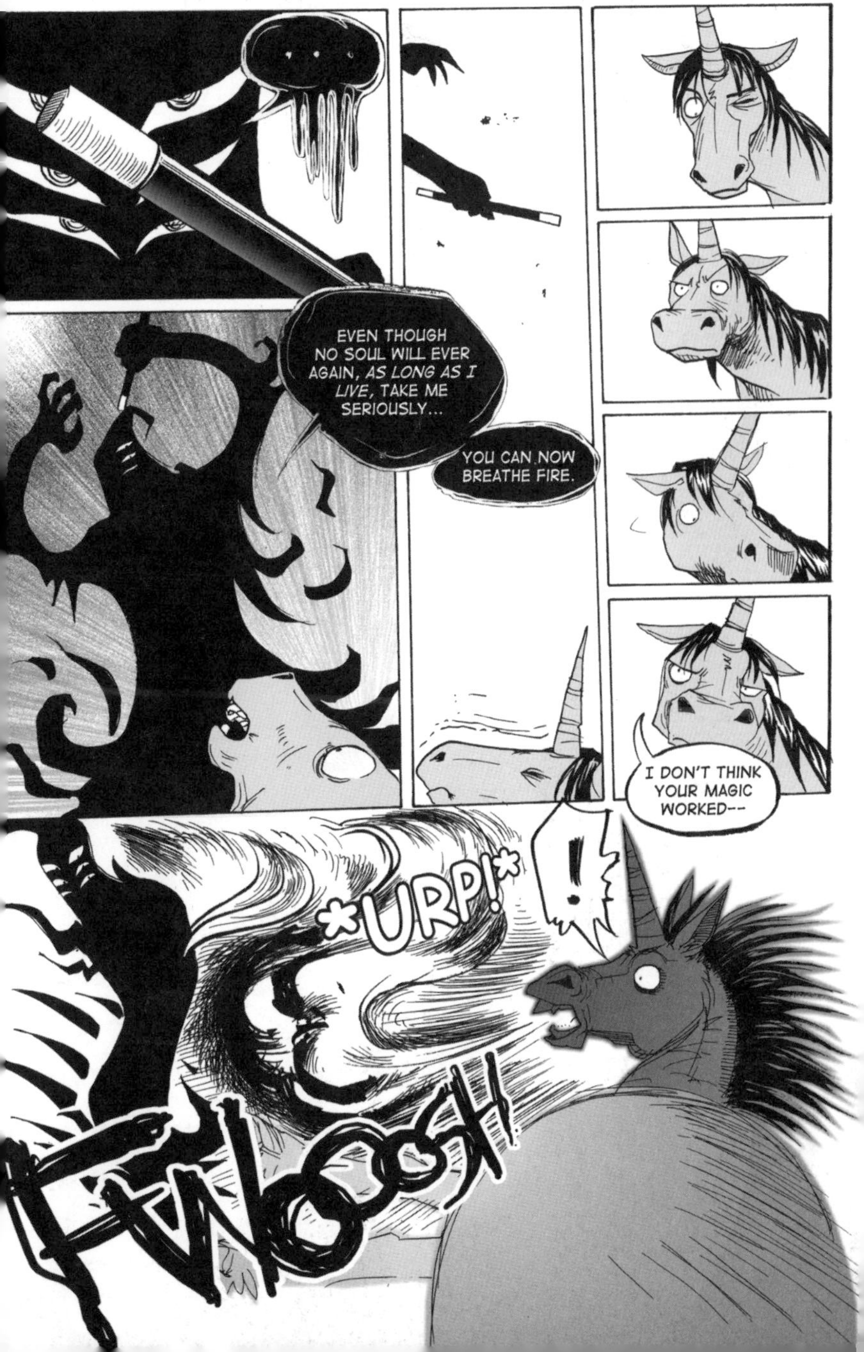
EVEN THOUGH NO SOUL WILL EVER AGAIN, *AS LONG AS I LIVE*, TAKE ME SERIOUSLY...
YOU CAN NOW BREATHE FIRE.
I DON'T THINK YOUR MAGIC WORKED--
URP!
!
FWOOOSH!

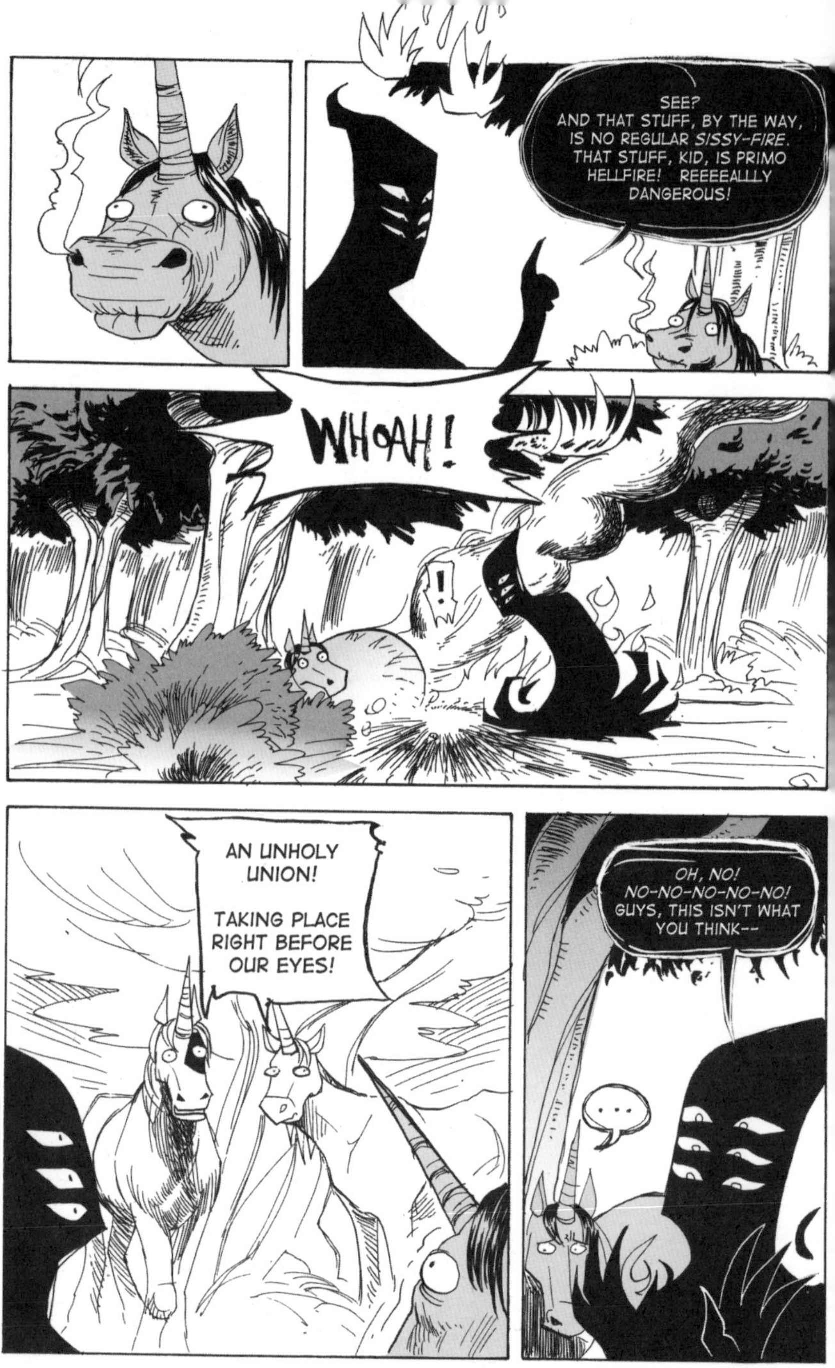
SEE? AND THAT STUFF, BY THE WAY, IS NO REGULAR *SISSY-FIRE*. THAT STUFF, KID, IS PRIMO HELLFIRE! REEEEALLLY DANGEROUS!
WHOAH!
!
AN UNHOLY UNION! TAKING PLACE RIGHT BEFORE OUR EYES!
OH, NO! NO-NO-NO-NO-NO! GUYS, THIS ISN'T WHAT YOU THINK--
...

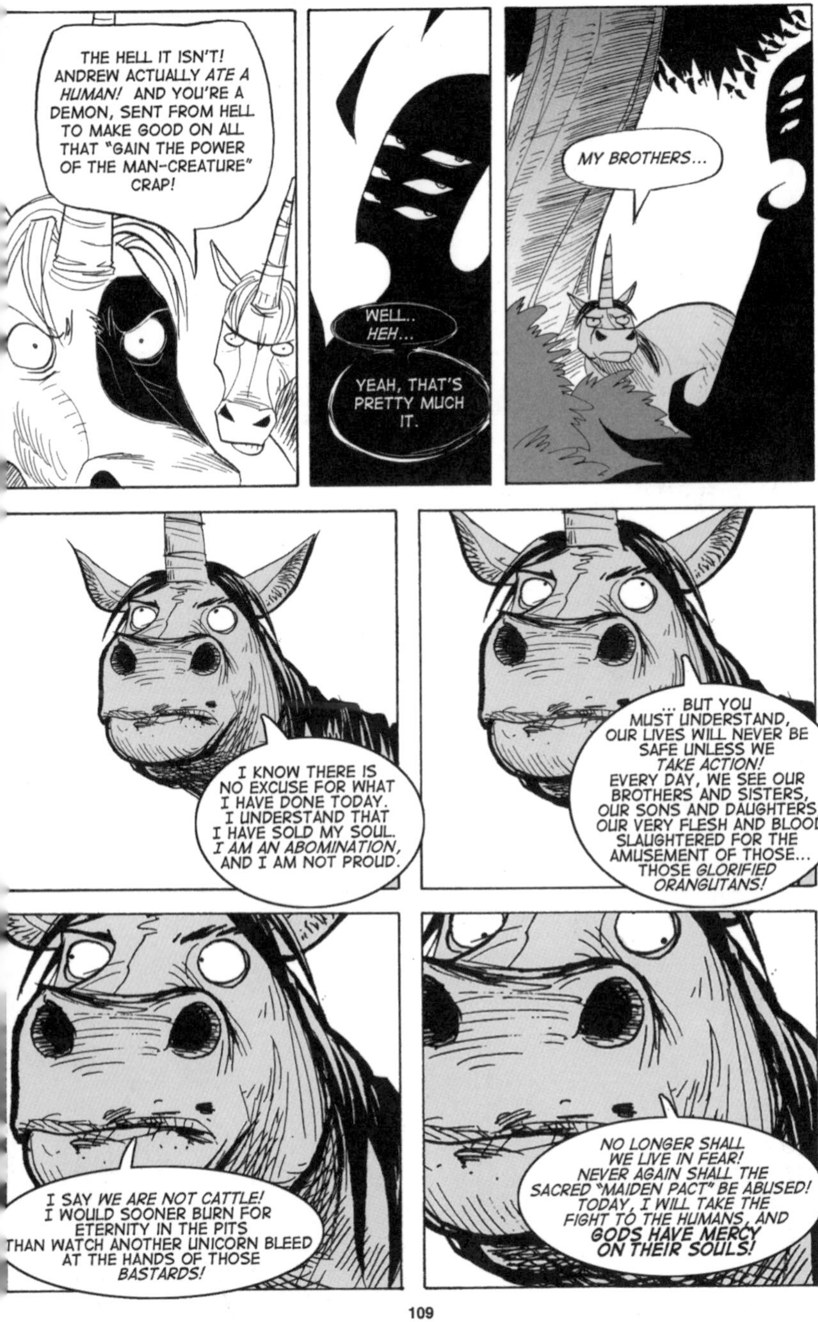
THE HELL IT ISN'T! ANDREW ACTUALLY *ATE A HUMAN!* AND YOU'RE A DEMON, SENT FROM HELL TO MAKE GOOD ON ALL THAT "GAIN THE POWER OF THE MAN-CREATURE" CRAP!
WELL.. *HEH...*
YEAH, THAT'S PRETTY MUCH IT.
MY BROTHERS...
I KNOW THERE IS NO EXCUSE FOR WHAT I HAVE DONE TODAY. I UNDERSTAND THAT I HAVE SOLD MY SOUL. *I AM AN ABOMINATION,* AND I AM NOT PROUD.
... BUT YOU MUST UNDERSTAND, OUR LIVES WILL NEVER BE SAFE UNLESS WE *TAKE ACTION!* EVERY DAY, WE SEE OUR BROTHERS AND SISTERS, OUR SONS AND DAUGHTERS, OUR VERY FLESH AND BLOOD SLAUGHTERED FOR THE AMUSEMENT OF THOSE... THOSE *GLORIFIED ORANGUTANS!*
I SAY *WE ARE NOT CATTLE!* I WOULD SOONER BURN FOR ETERNITY IN THE PITS THAN WATCH ANOTHER UNICORN BLEED AT THE HANDS OF THOSE *BASTARDS!*
NO LONGER SHALL WE LIVE IN FEAR! NEVER AGAIN SHALL THE SACRED "MAIDEN PACT" BE ABUSED! TODAY, I WILL TAKE THE FIGHT TO THE HUMANS, AND ***GODS HAVE MERCY ON THEIR SOULS!***

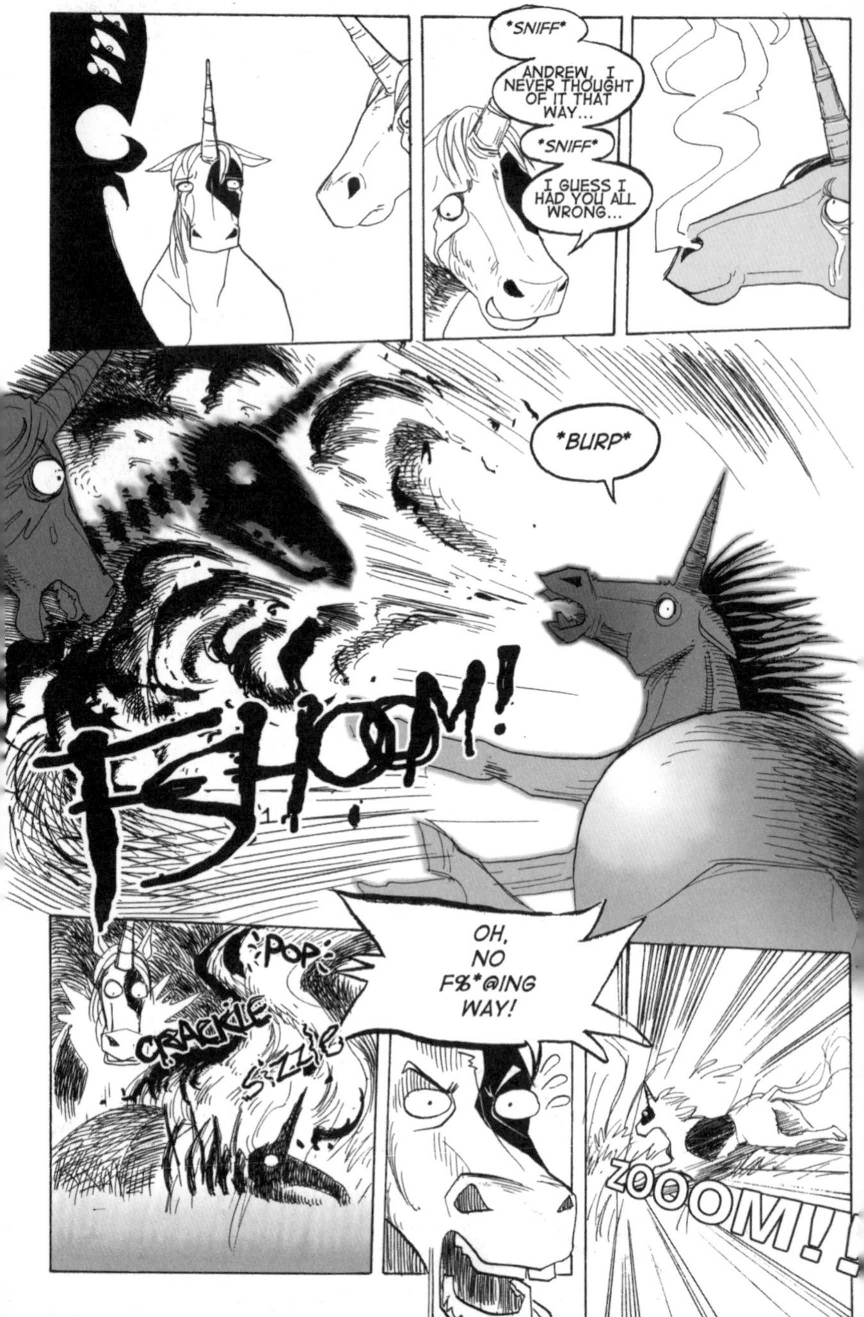
SNIFF
ANDREW, I NEVER THOUGHT OF IT THAT WAY...
SNIFF
I GUESS I HAD YOU ALL WRONG...
BURP
FSHOOM!
POP
CRACKLE
SIZZLE
OH, NO F%*@ING WAY!
ZOOOM!!

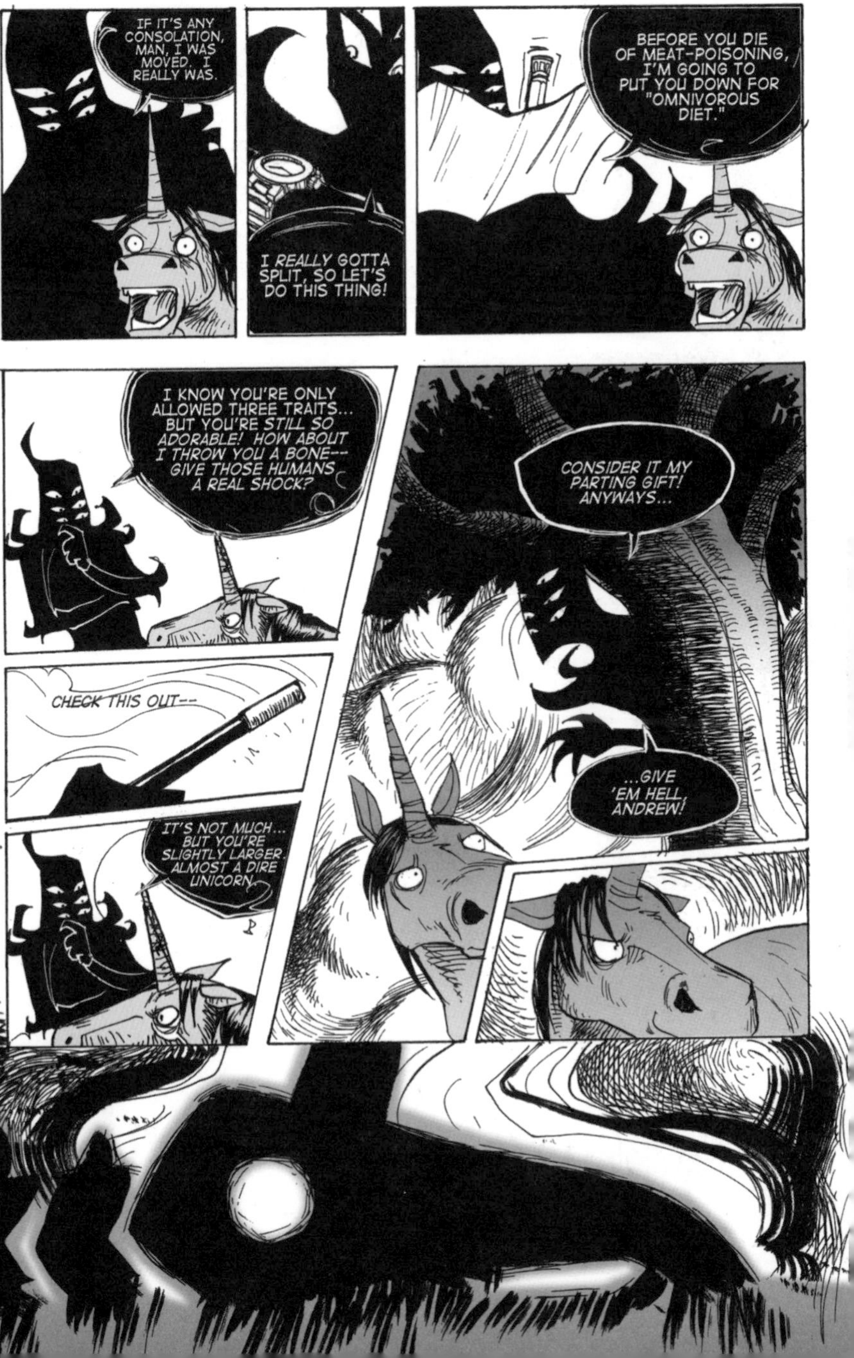
IF IT'S ANY CONSOLATION, MAN, I WAS MOVED. I REALLY WAS.
I REALLY GOTTA SPLIT, SO LET'S DO THIS THING!
BEFORE YOU DIE OF MEAT-POISONING, I'M GOING TO PUT YOU DOWN FOR "OMNIVOROUS DIET."
I KNOW YOU'RE ONLY ALLOWED THREE TRAITS... BUT YOU'RE STILL SO ADORABLE! HOW ABOUT I THROW YOU A BONE-- GIVE THOSE HUMANS A REAL SHOCK?
CHECK THIS OUT--
IT'S NOT MUCH... BUT YOU'RE SLIGHTLY LARGER. ALMOST A DIRE UNICORN.
CONSIDER IT MY PARTING GIFT! ANYWAYS...
...GIVE 'EM HELL, ANDREW!

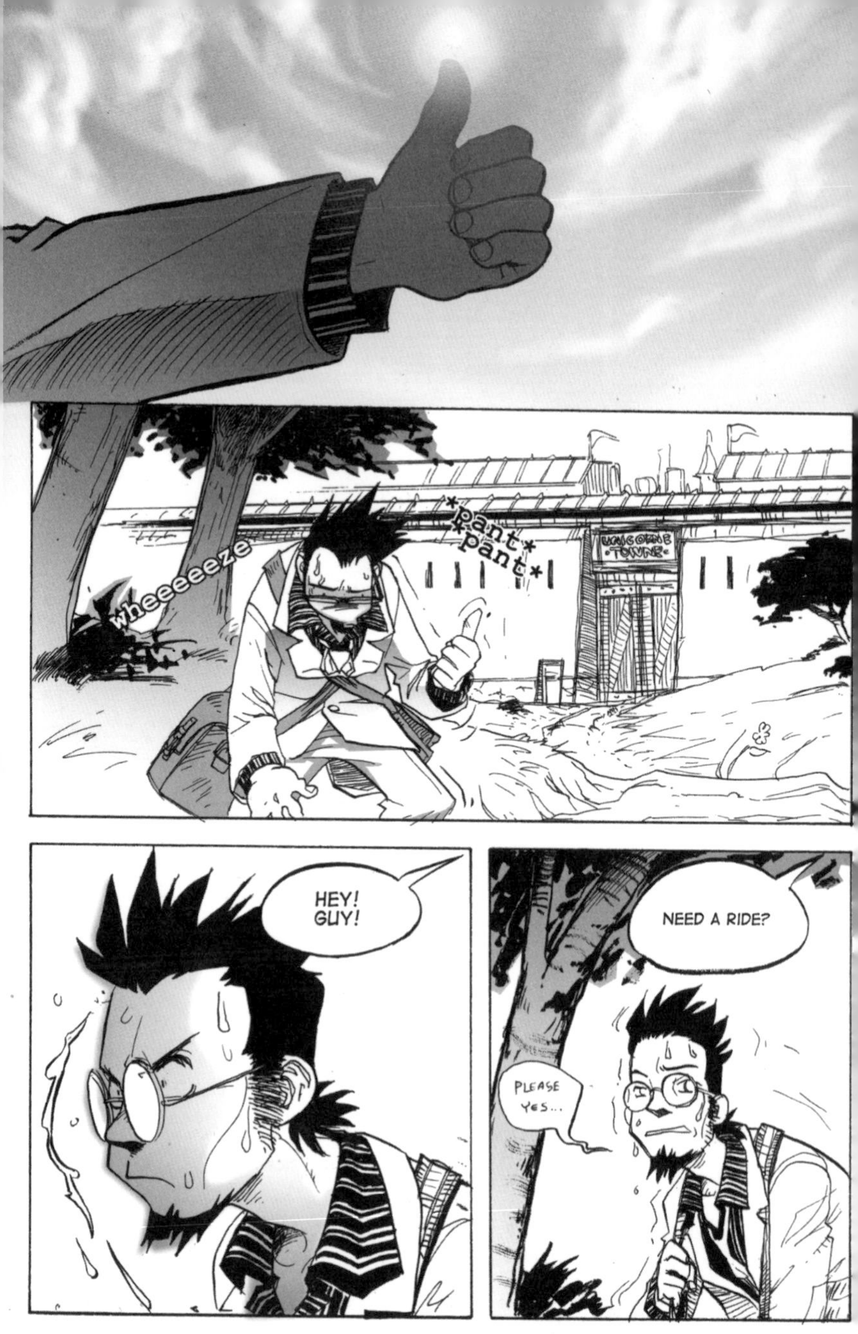
wheeeeeeze
pant *pant*
HEY! GUY!
NEED A RIDE?
PLEASE YES...

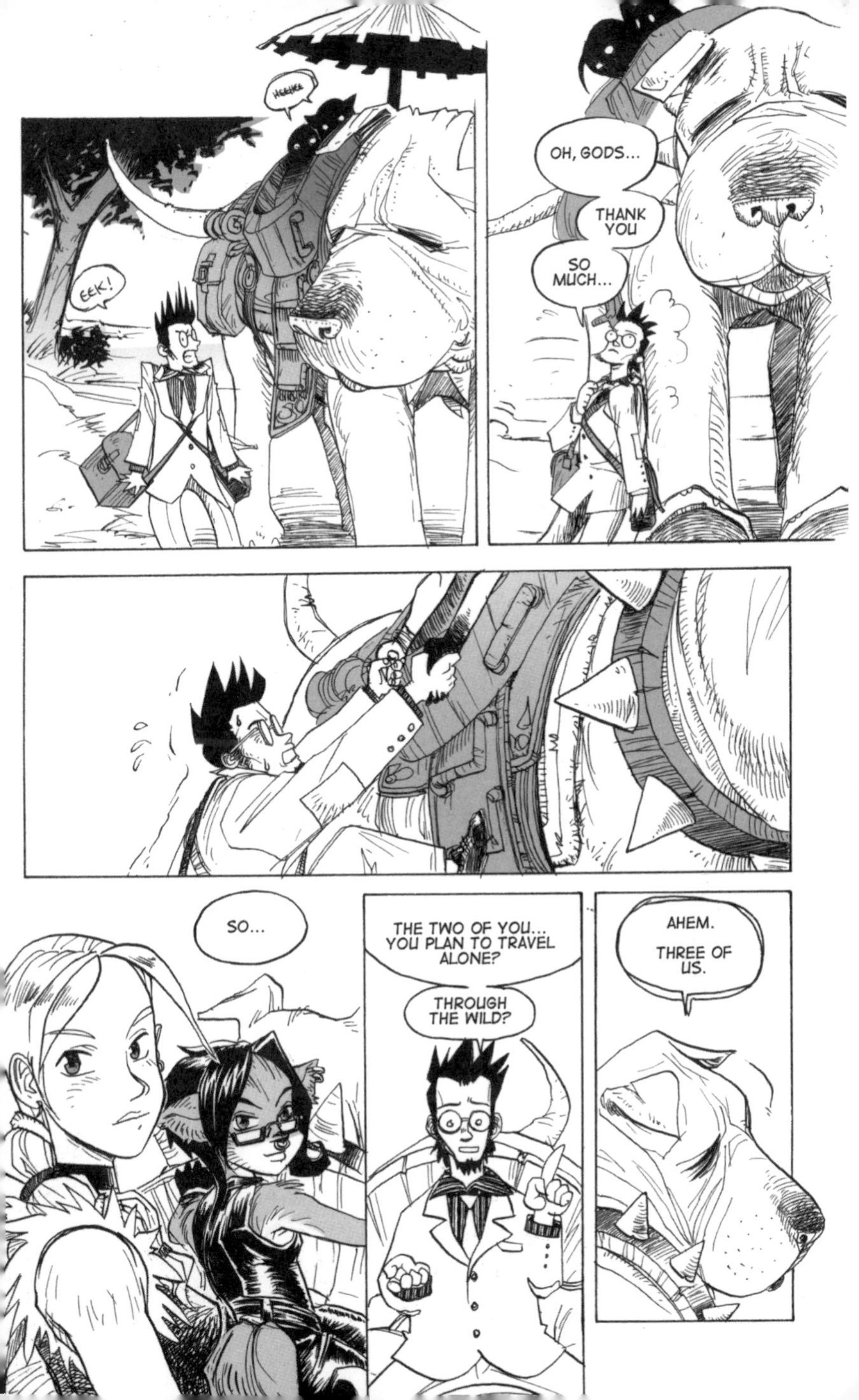
HEEHEE
EEK!
OH, GODS...
THANK YOU
SO MUCH...
SO...
THE TWO OF YOU... YOU PLAN TO TRAVEL ALONE?
THROUGH THE WILD?
AHEM.
THREE OF US.

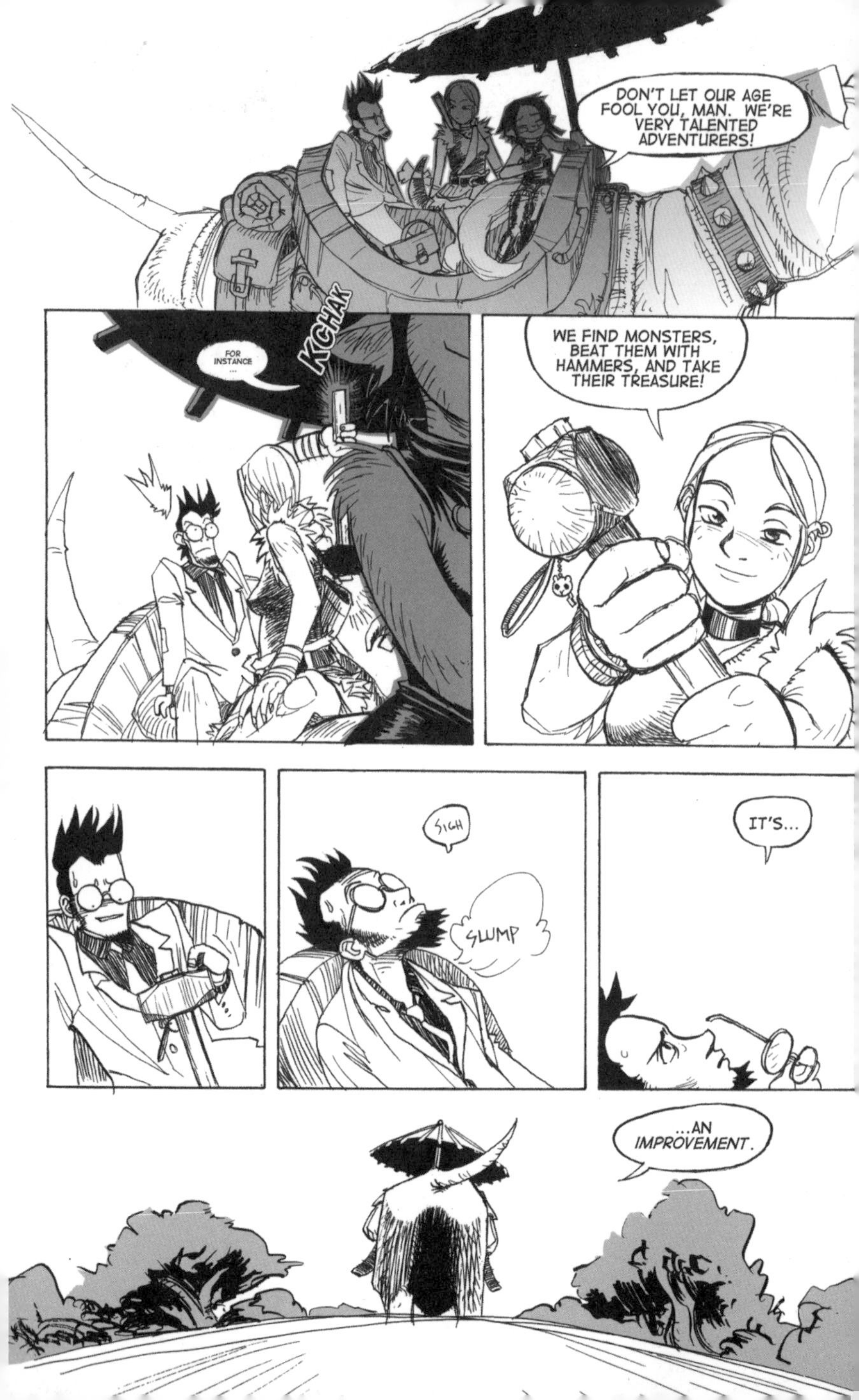
DON'T LET OUR AGE FOOL YOU, MAN. WE'RE VERY TALENTED ADVENTURERS!
FOR INSTANCE ...
KCHAK
WE FIND MONSTERS, BEAT THEM WITH HAMMERS, AND TAKE THEIR TREASURE!
SIGH
SLUMP
IT'S...
...AN IMPROVEMENT.

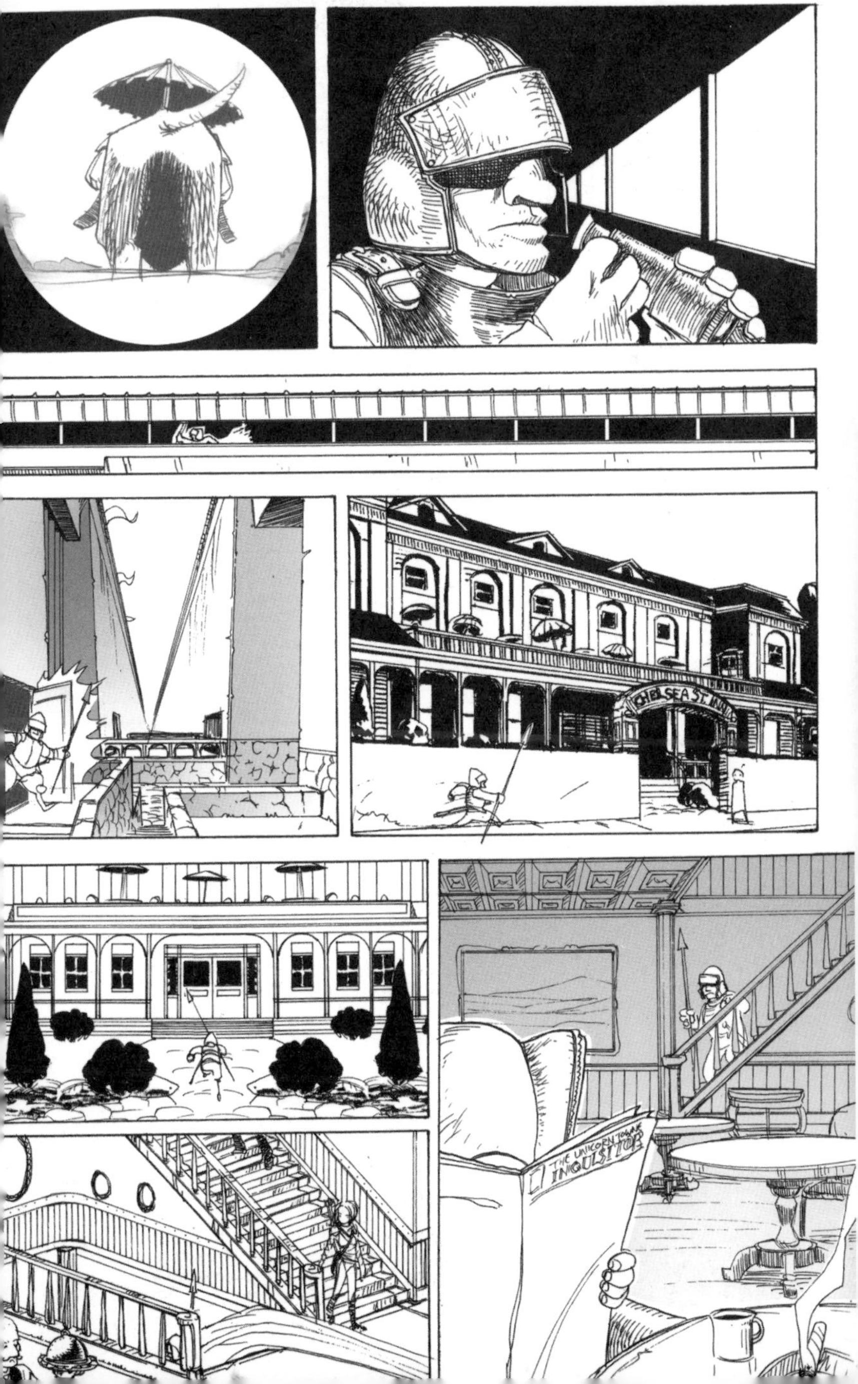
CHELSEA ST. INN
THE UNICORN
INQUISITOR

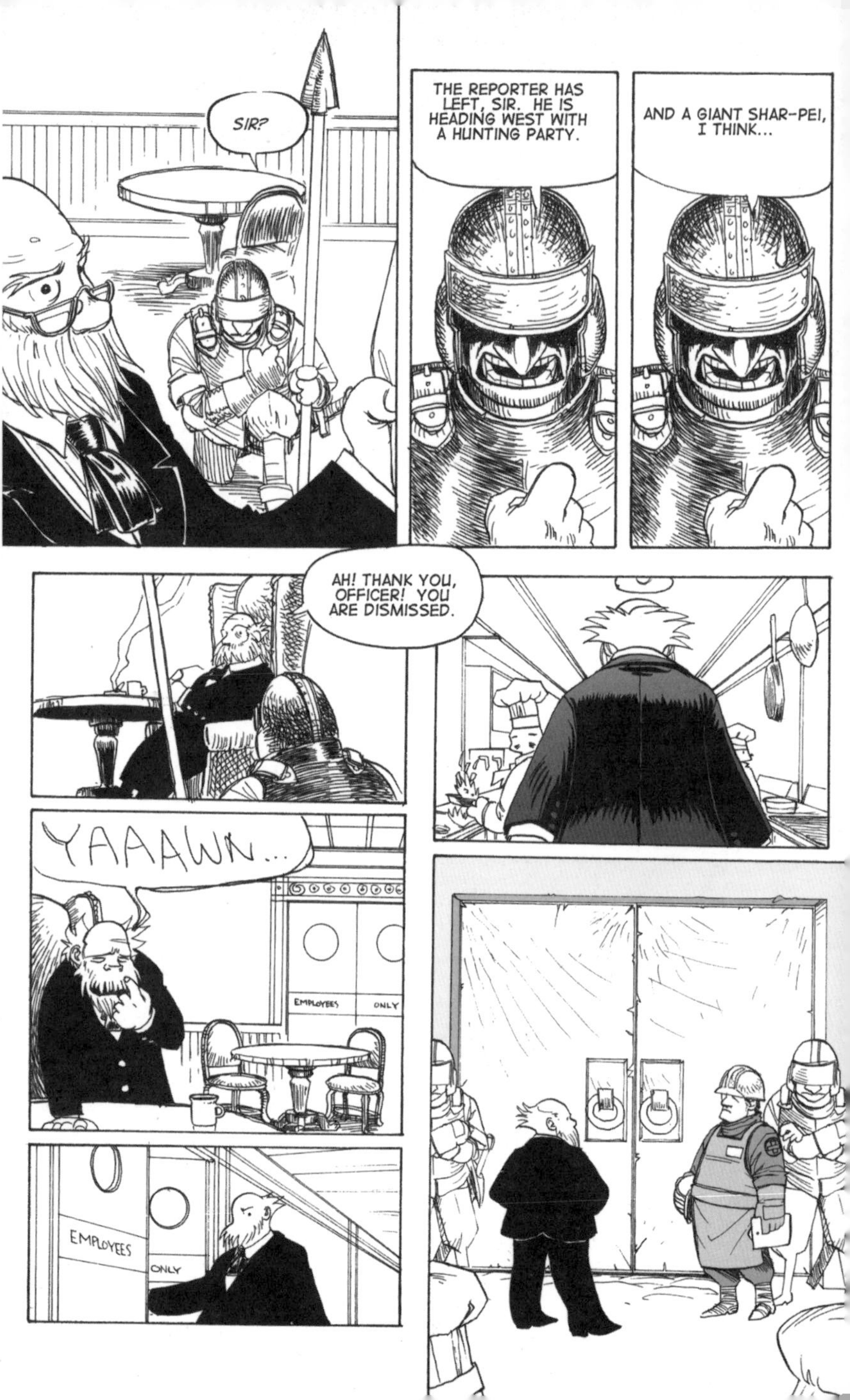
SIR?
THE REPORTER HAS LEFT, SIR. HE IS HEADING WEST WITH A HUNTING PARTY.
AND A GIANT SHAR-PEI, I THINK...
AH! THANK YOU, OFFICER! YOU ARE DISMISSED.
YAAAWN...
EMPLOYEES ONLY
EMPLOYEES
ONLY

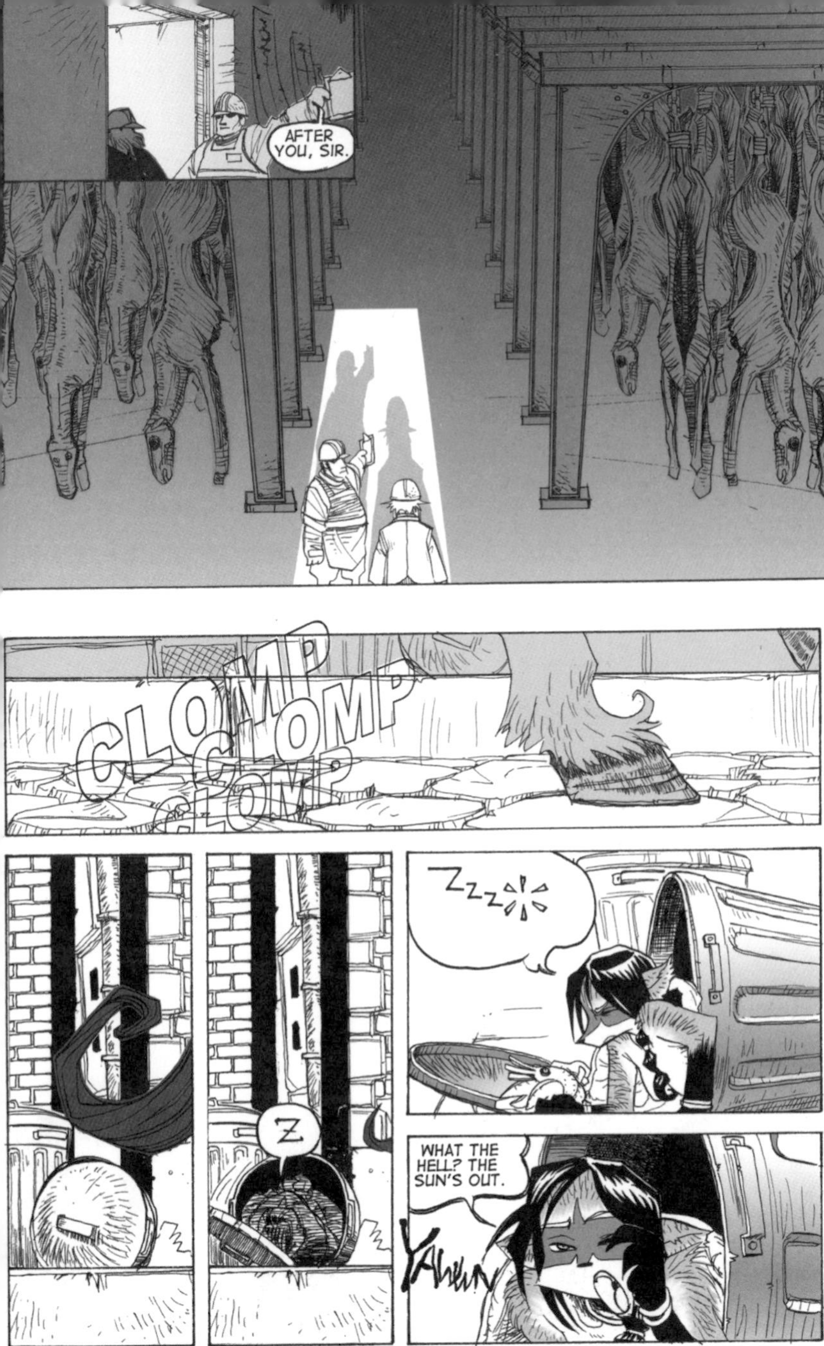
AFTER YOU, SIR.
CLOMP CLOMP CLOMP CLOMP
Z
ZZZ
WHAT THE HELL? THE SUN'S OUT.
YAWN

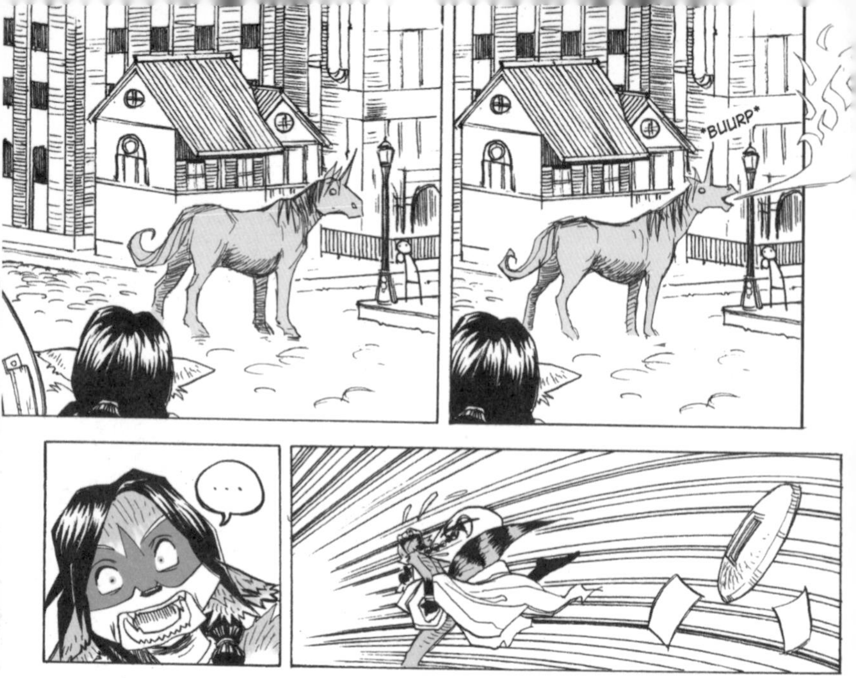
BUURP
...

LATER AT THE "OLD MAN WITH MAP"

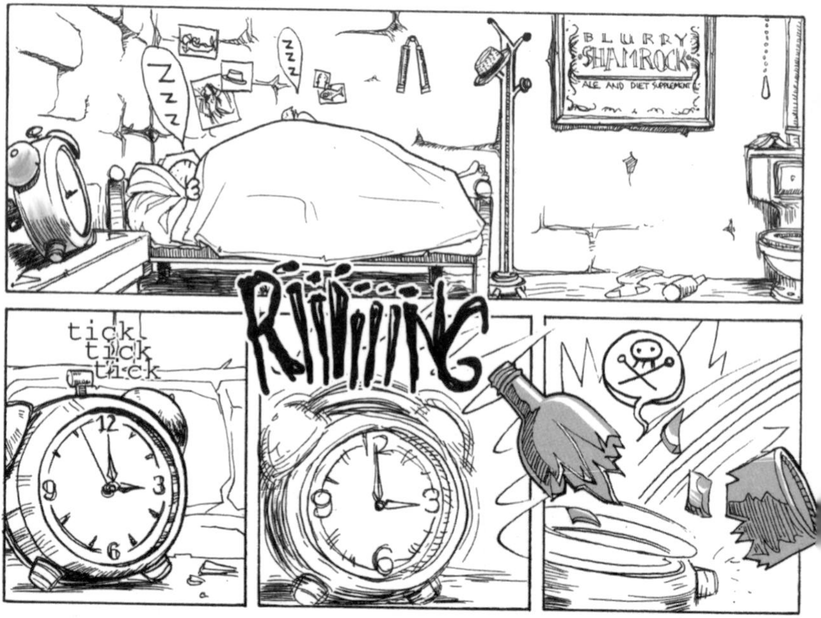
ZZZ
ZZZ
BLURRY
SHAMROCK
ALE AND DIET SUPPLEMENT
tick
tick
tick
RIIIIING

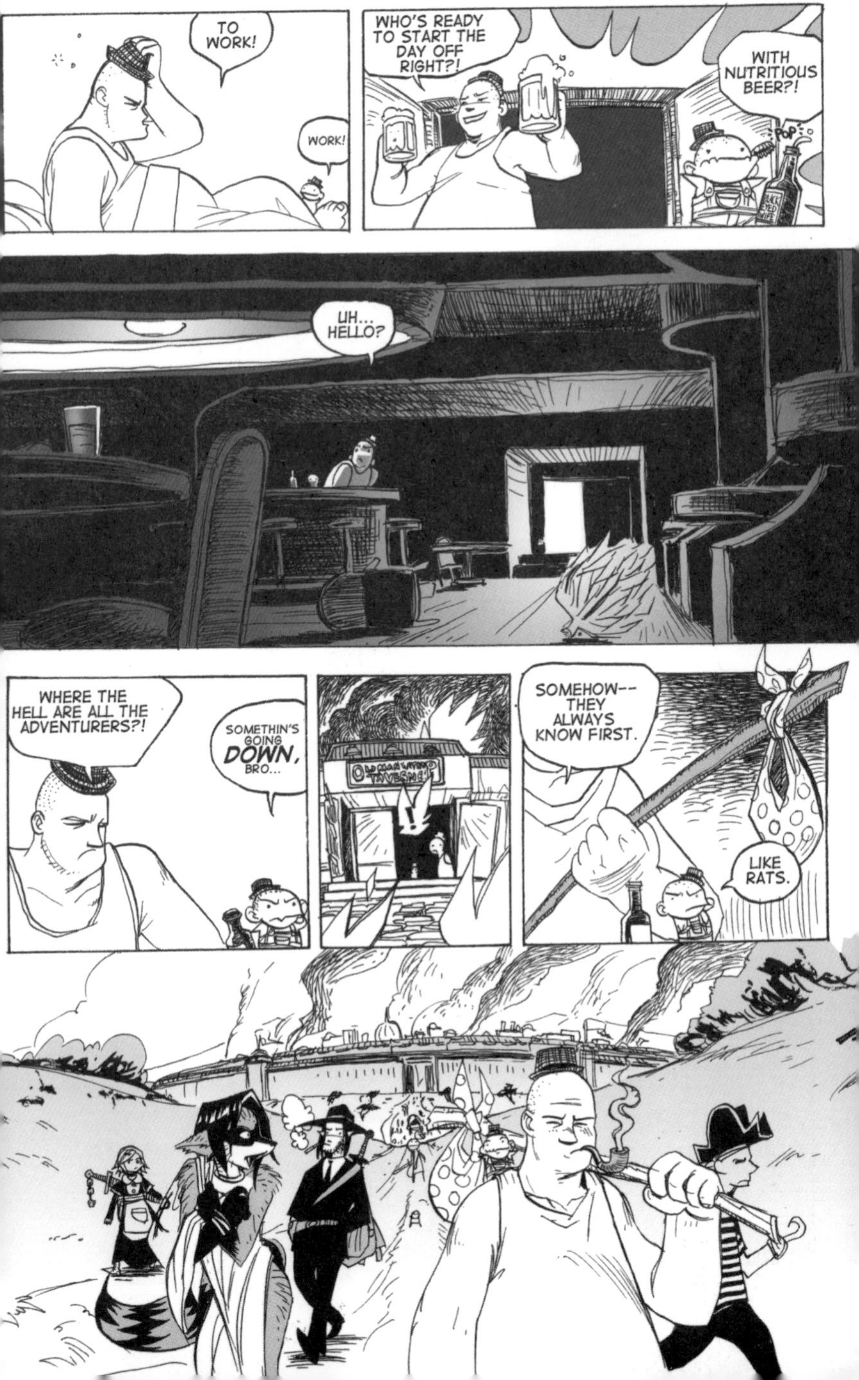
TO WORK!
WORK!
WHO'S READY TO START THE DAY OFF RIGHT?!
WITH NUTRITIOUS BEER?!
POP
UH... HELLO?
WHERE THE HELL ARE ALL THE ADVENTURERS?!
SOMETHIN'S GOING DOWN, BRO...
SOMEHOW-- THEY ALWAYS KNOW FIRST.
LIKE RATS.

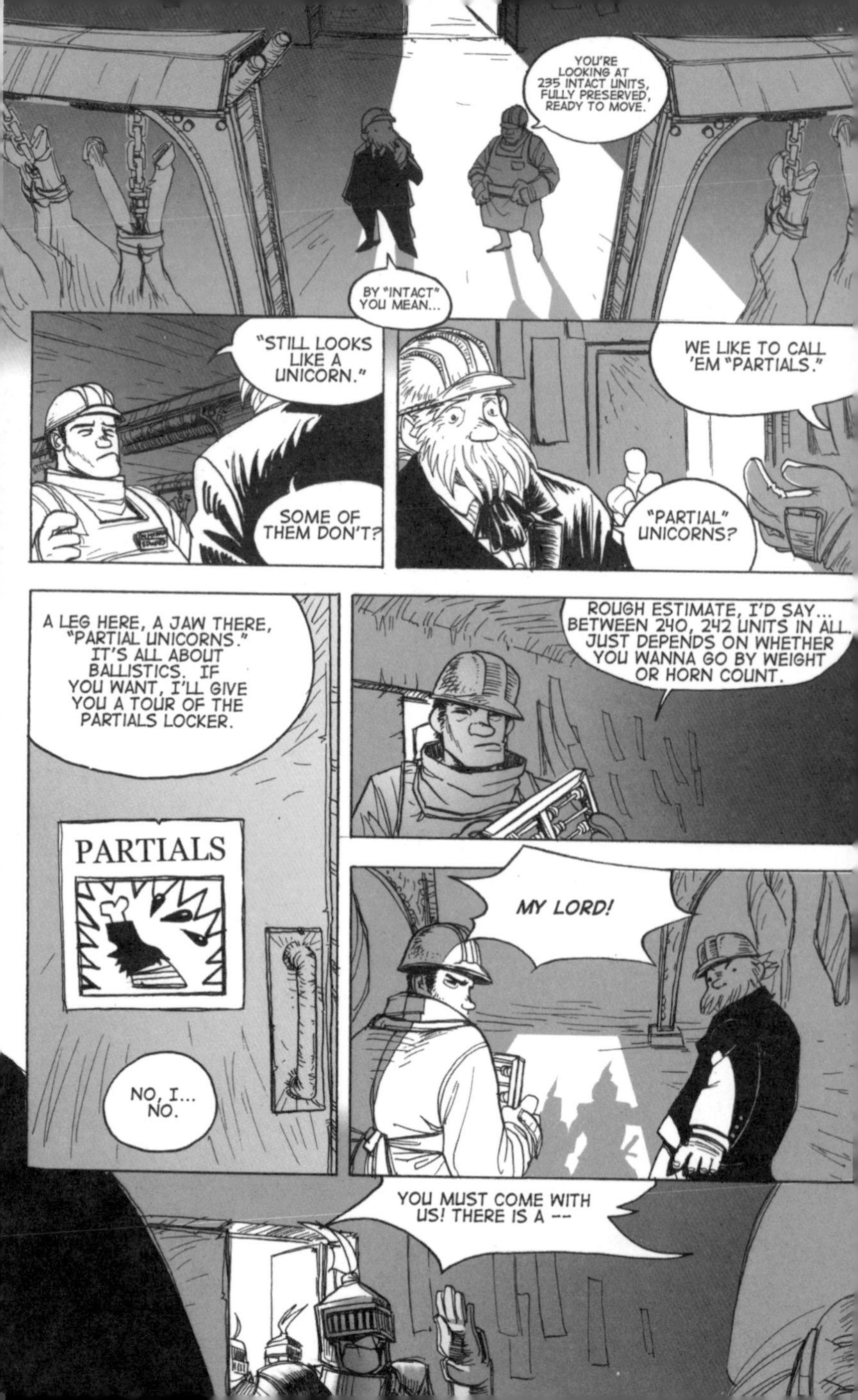
YOU'RE LOOKING AT 235 INTACT UNITS, FULLY PRESERVED, READY TO MOVE.
BY "INTACT" YOU MEAN...
"STILL LOOKS LIKE A UNICORN."
SOME OF THEM DON'T?
WE LIKE TO CALL 'EM "PARTIALS."
"PARTIAL" UNICORNS?
A LEG HERE, A JAW THERE, "PARTIAL UNICORNS." IT'S ALL ABOUT BALLISTICS. IF YOU WANT, I'LL GIVE YOU A TOUR OF THE PARTIALS LOCKER.
PARTIALS
NO, I... NO.
ROUGH ESTIMATE, I'D SAY... BETWEEN 240, 242 UNITS IN ALL. JUST DEPENDS ON WHETHER YOU WANNA GO BY WEIGHT OR HORN COUNT.
MY LORD!
YOU MUST COME WITH US! THERE IS A --

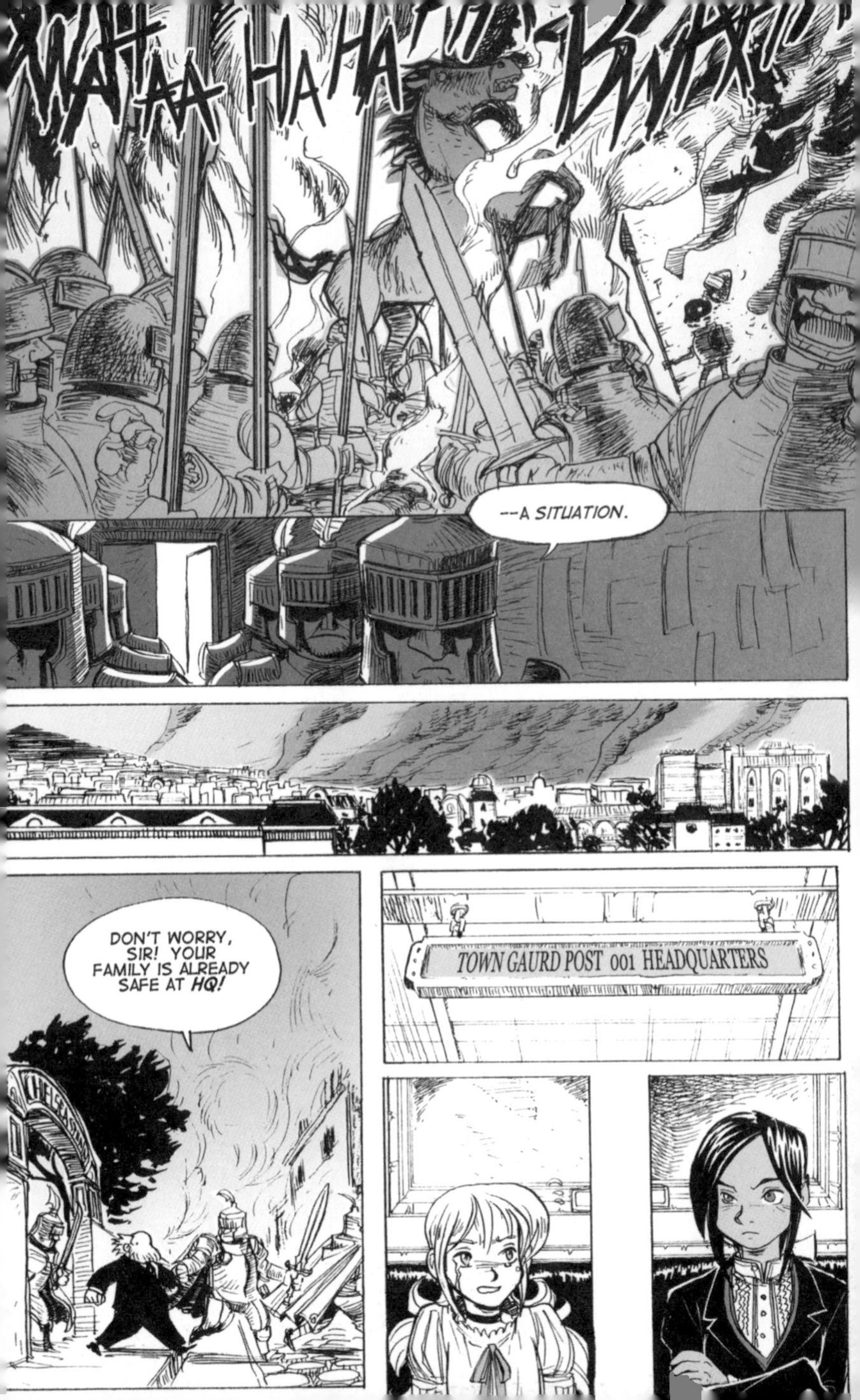
WAHAAHAHA
KWAX
--A SITUATION.
DON'T WORRY, SIR! YOUR FAMILY IS ALREADY SAFE AT HQ!
TOWN GAURD POST 001 HEADQUARTERS

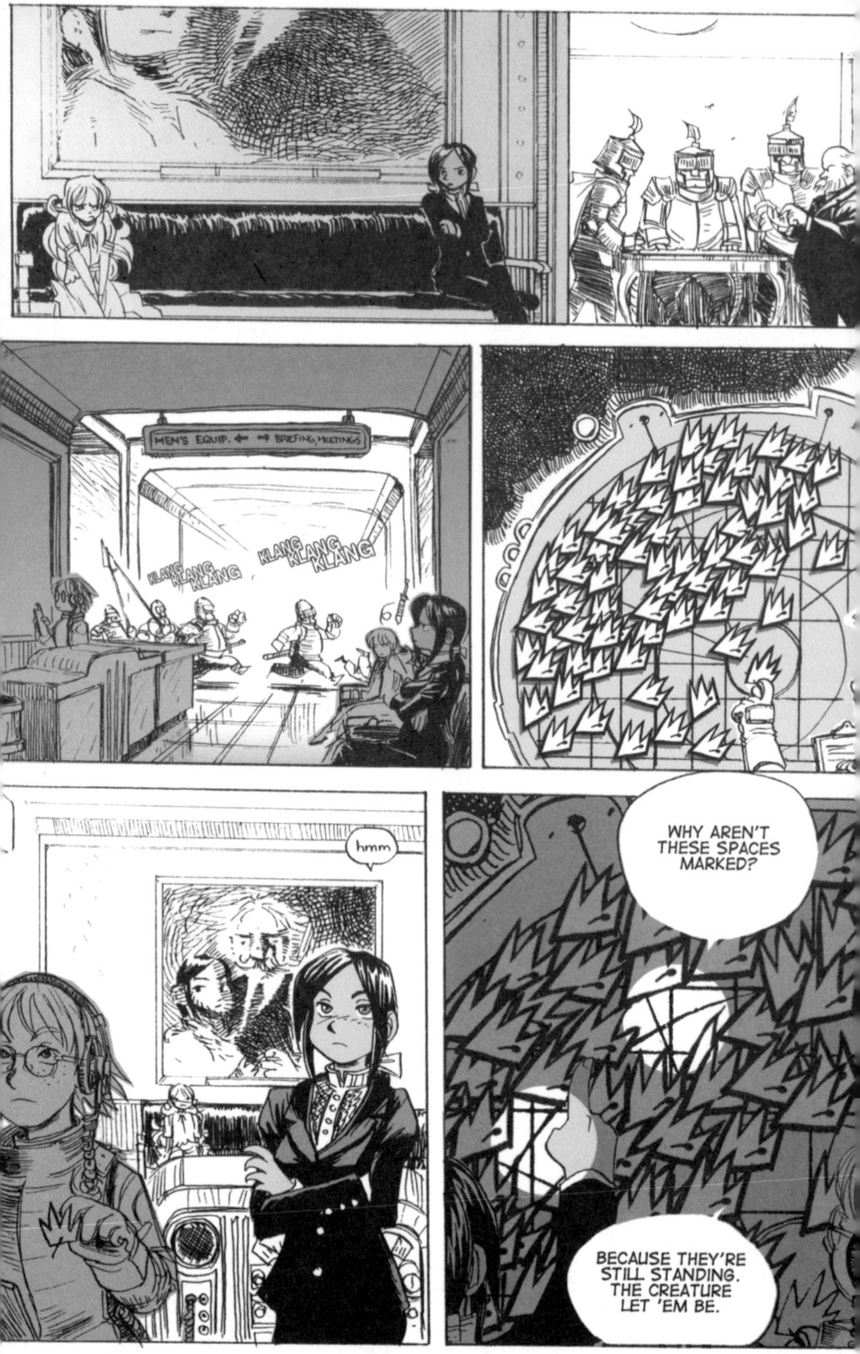
MEN'S EQUIP. ← → BRIEFING, MEETINGS
KLANG KLANG KLANG
KLANG KLANG KLANG
hmm
WHY AREN'T THESE SPACES MARKED?
BECAUSE THEY'RE STILL STANDING. THE CREATURE LET 'EM BE.

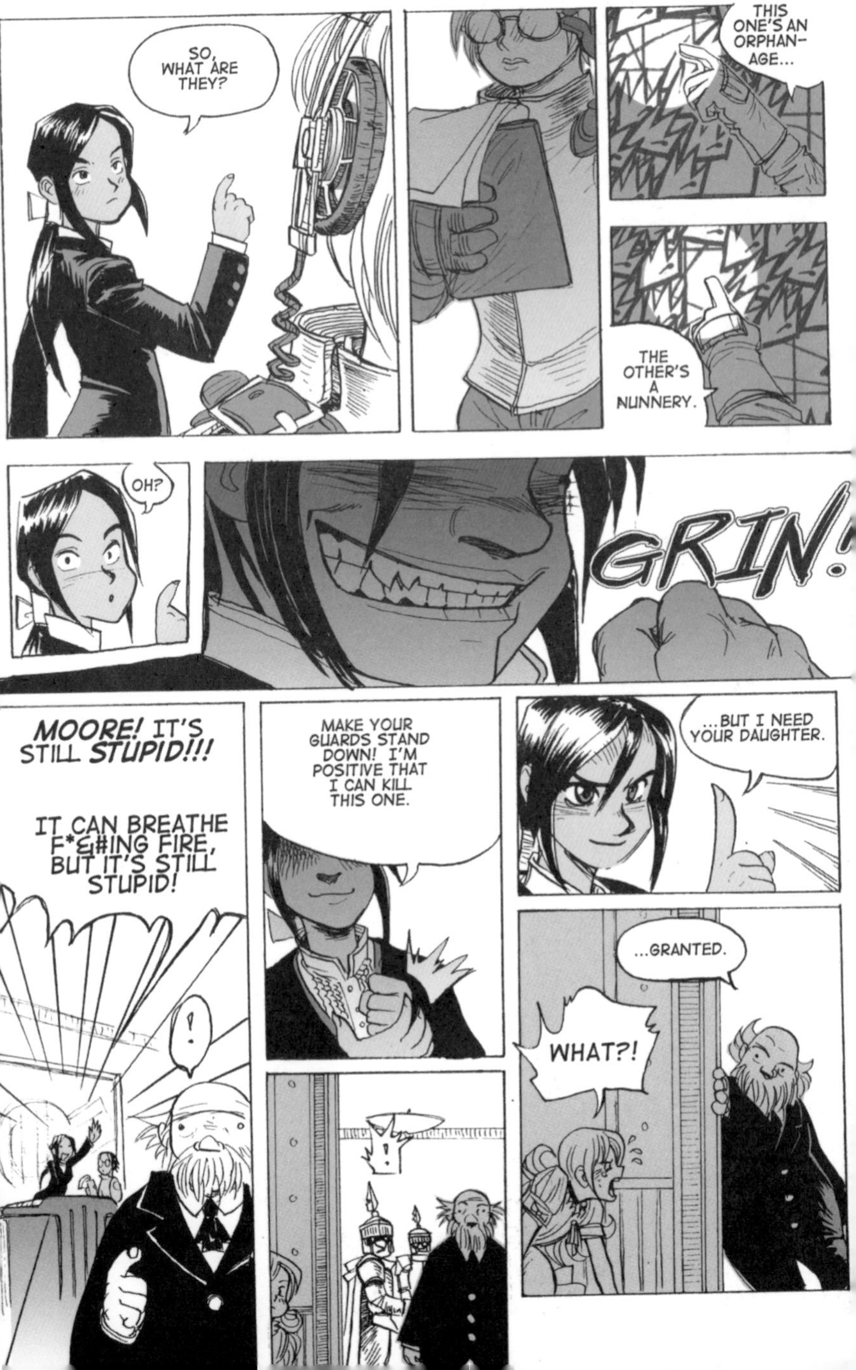

SO, WHAT ARE THEY?
THIS ONE'S AN ORPHAN-AGE...
THE OTHER'S A NUNNERY.
OH?
GRIN!
MOORE! IT'S STILL STUPID!!!
IT CAN BREATHE F*&#ING FIRE, BUT IT'S STILL STUPID!
!
MAKE YOUR GUARDS STAND DOWN! I'M POSITIVE THAT I CAN KILL THIS ONE.
!
...BUT I NEED YOUR DAUGHTER.
...GRANTED.
WHAT?!

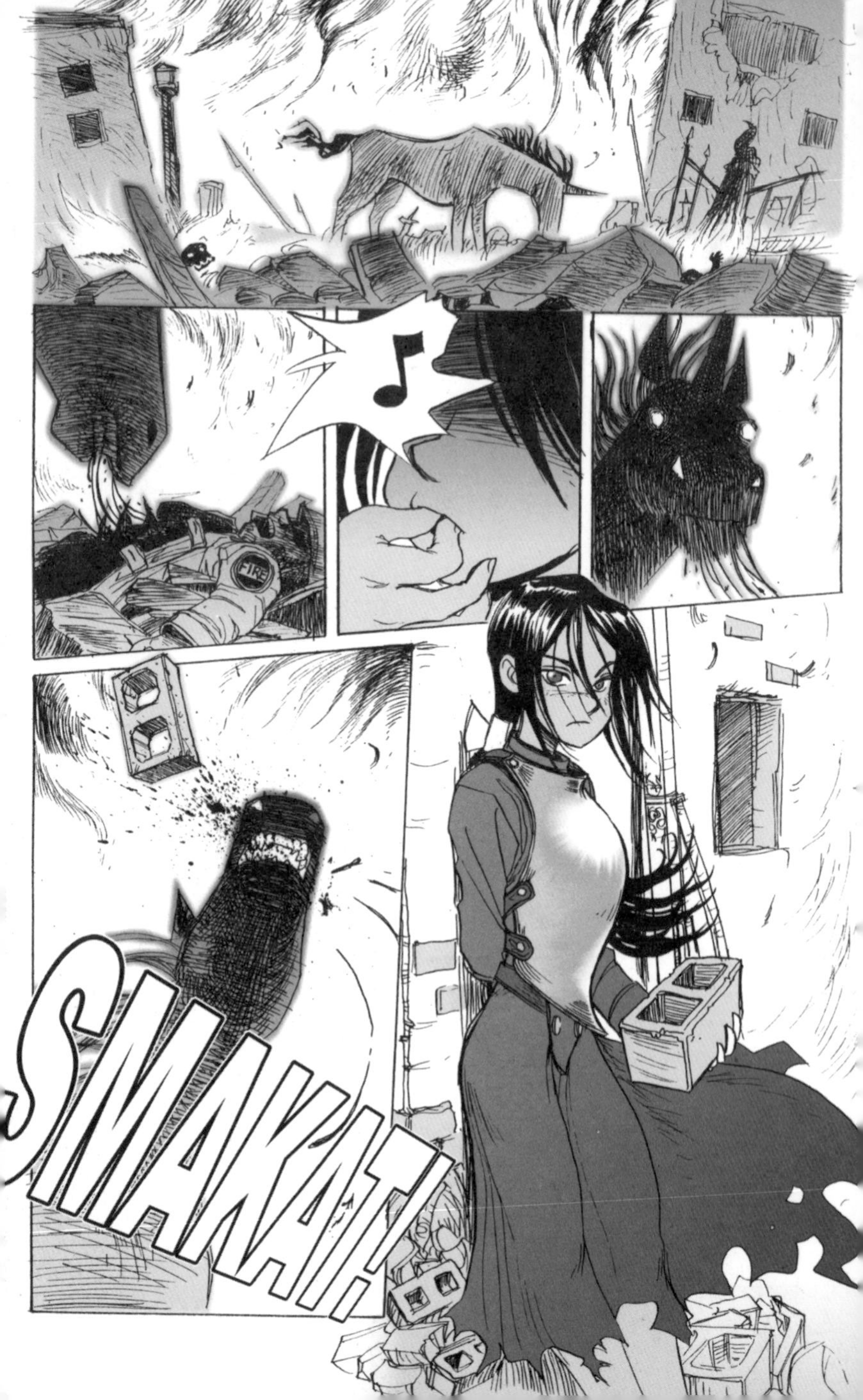
SMAKA!!

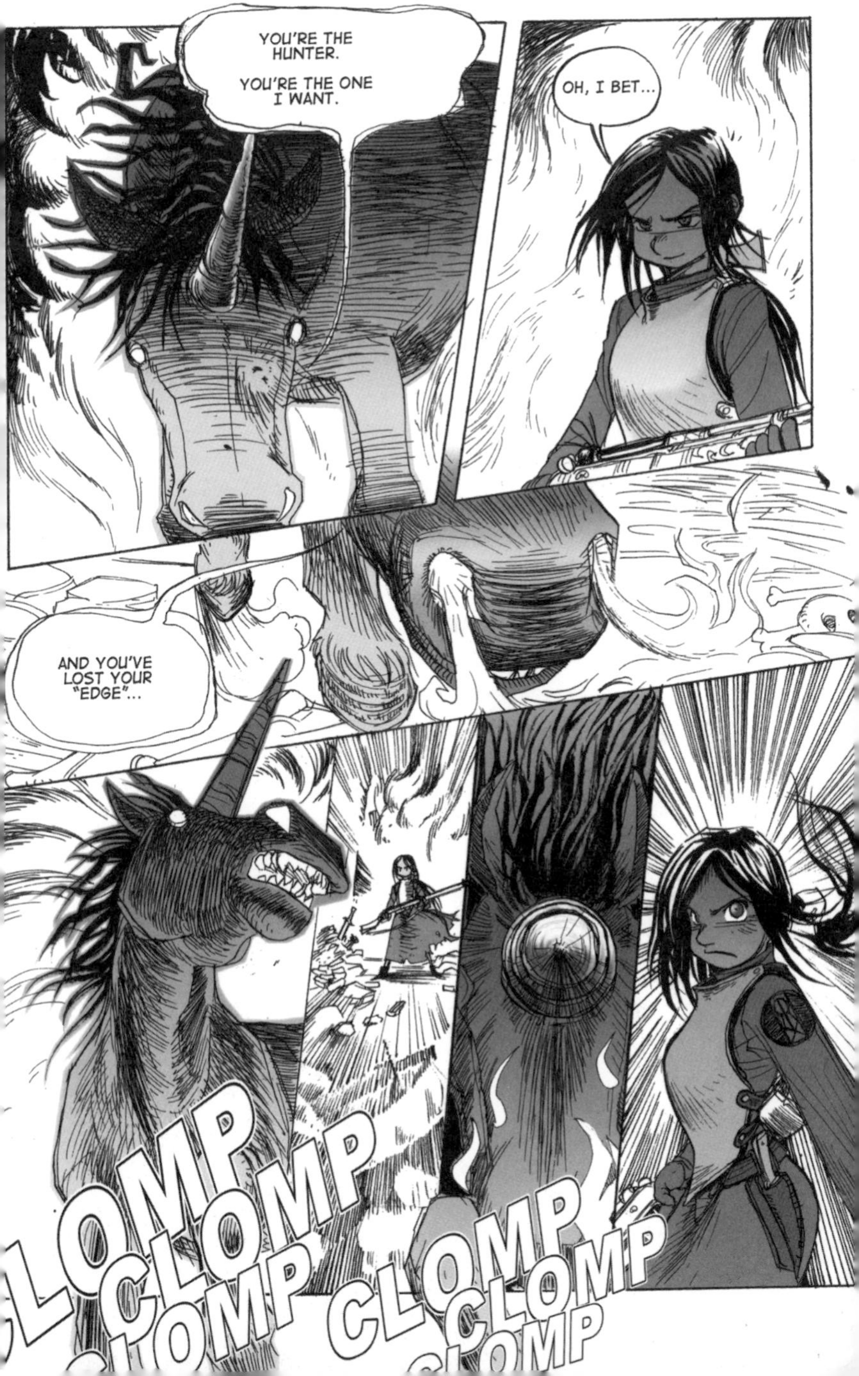
YOU'RE THE HUNTER.
YOU'RE THE ONE I WANT.
OH, I BET...
AND YOU'VE LOST YOUR "EDGE"...
CLOMP
CLOMP
CLOMP
CLOMP
CLOMP
CLOMP

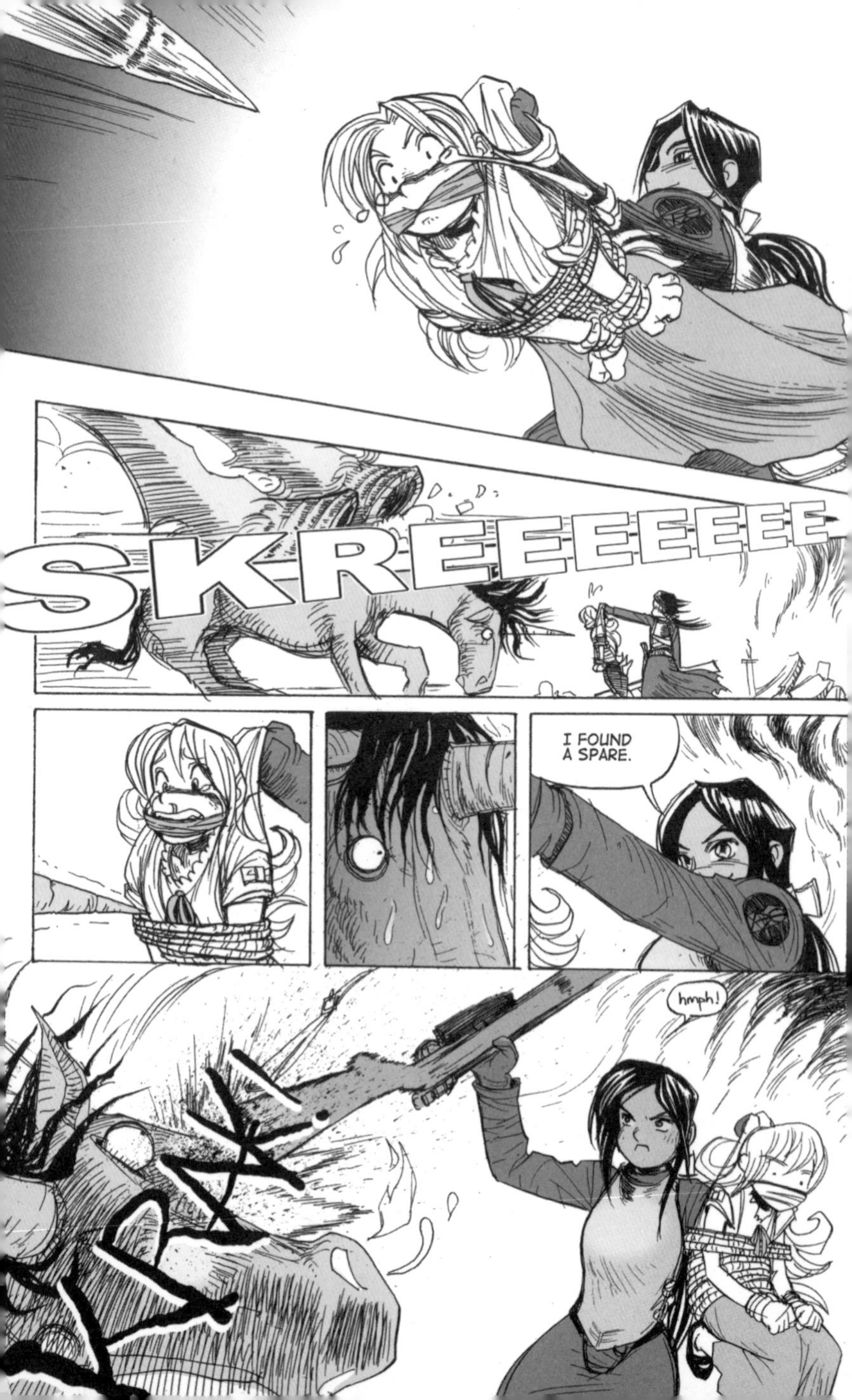
SKREEEEEEEE
I FOUND A SPARE.
hmph!

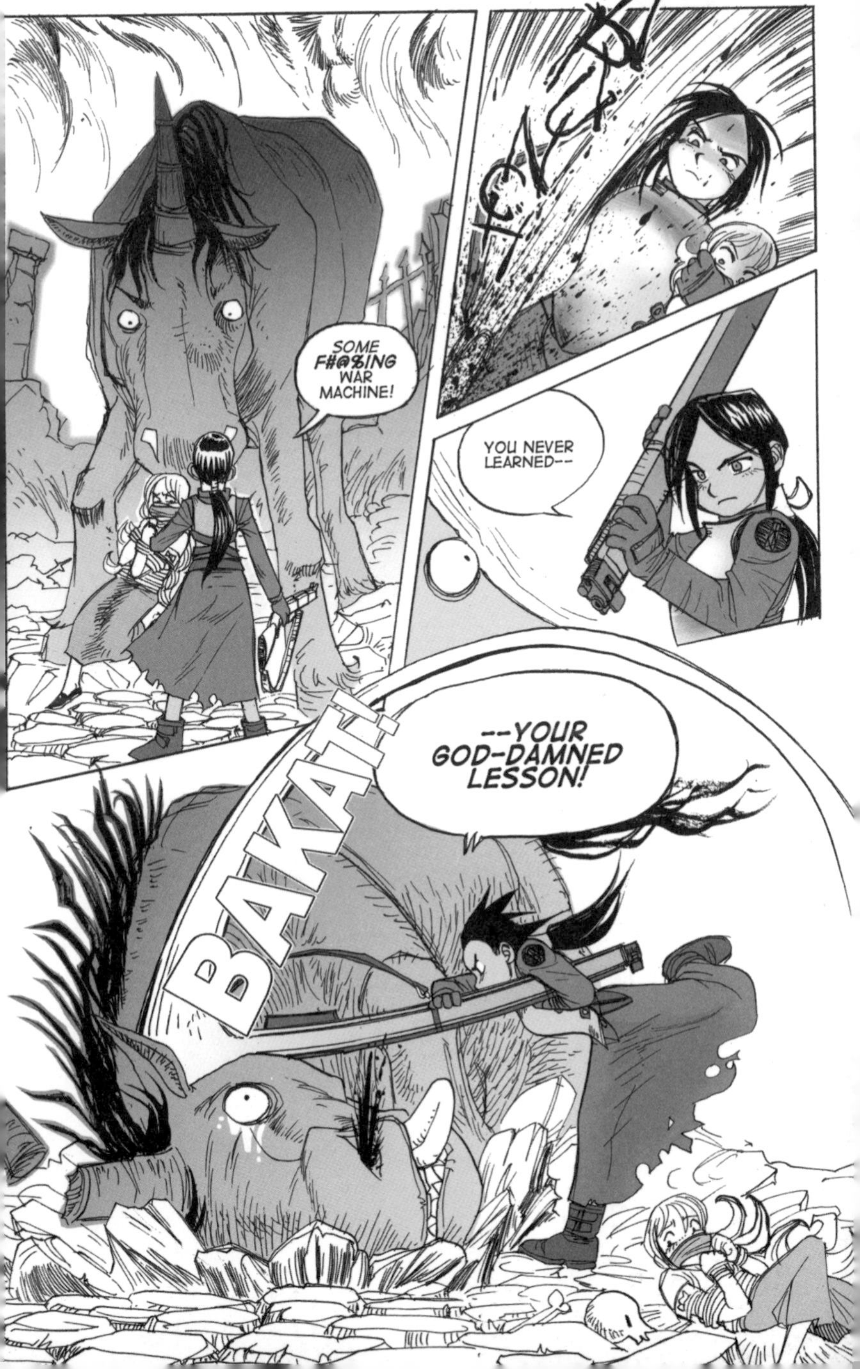

SOME F#@%ING WAR MACHINE!
YOU NEVER LEARNED--
BAKA!!
--YOUR GOD-DAMNED LESSON!

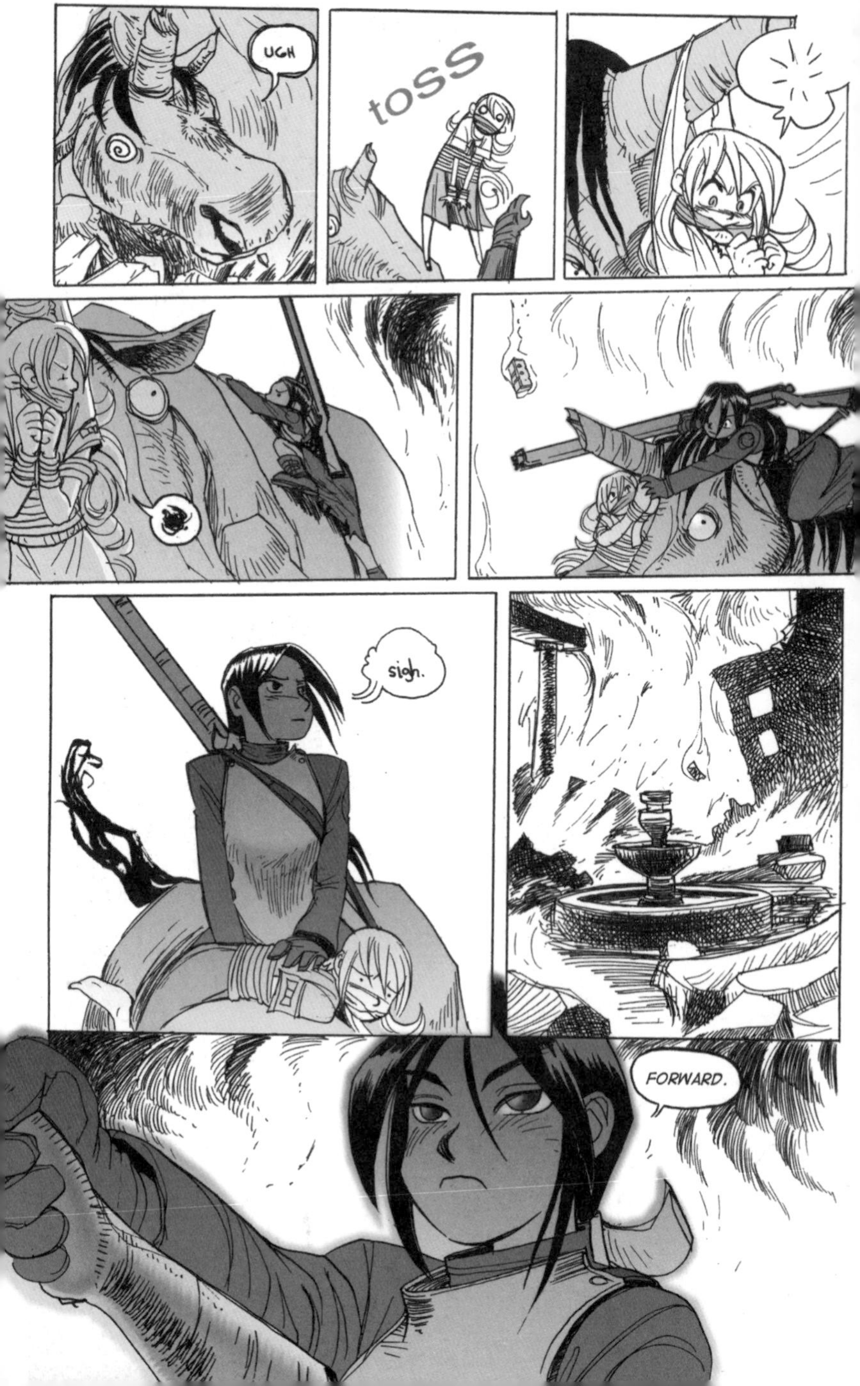
UGH
toss
sigh.
FORWARD.

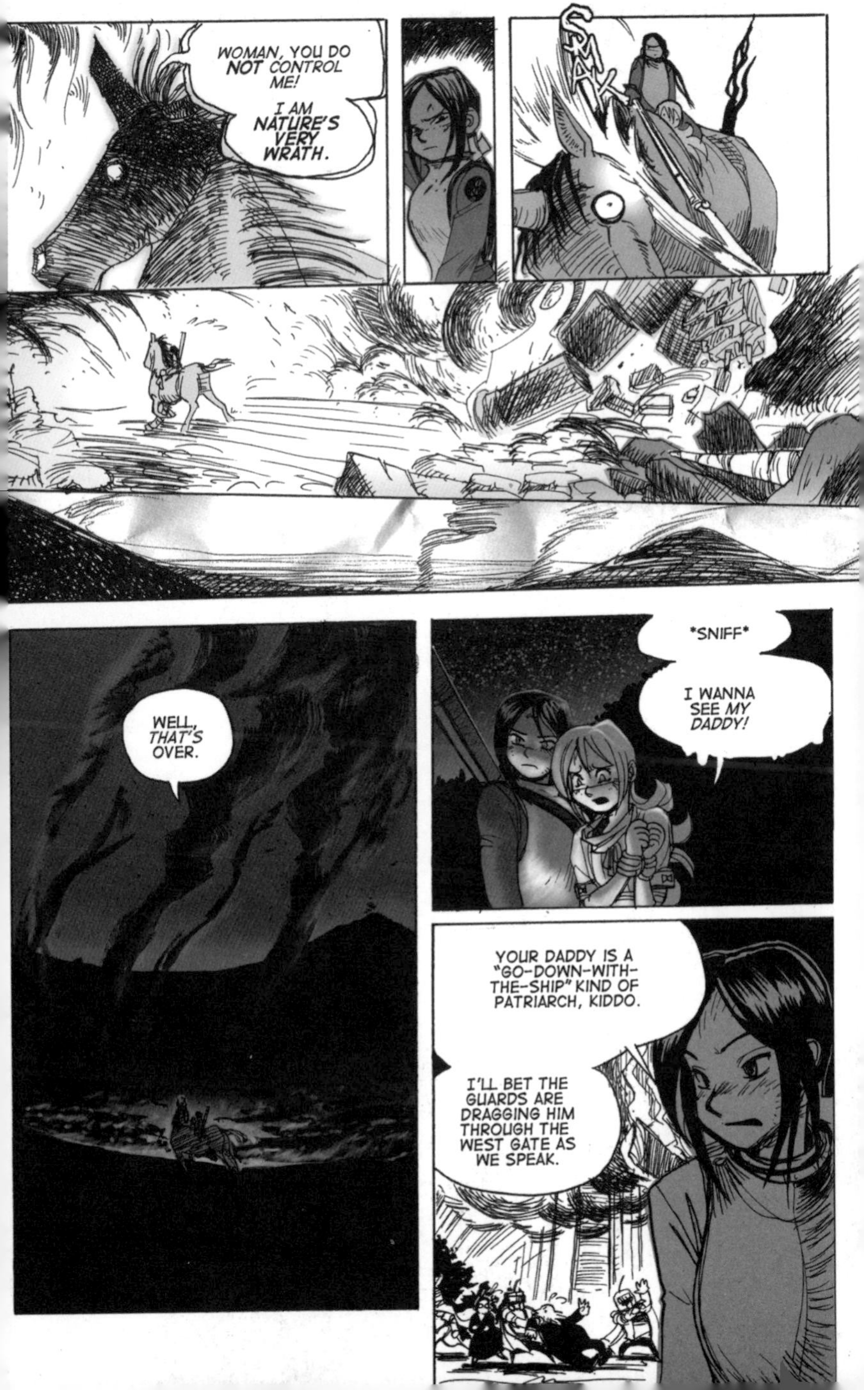
WOMAN, YOU DO NOT CONTROL ME!
I AM NATURE'S VERY WRATH.
SMAK
WELL, THAT'S OVER.
SNIFF
I WANNA SEE MY DADDY!
YOUR DADDY IS A "GO-DOWN-WITH-THE-SHIP" KIND OF PATRIARCH, KIDDO.
I'LL BET THE GUARDS ARE DRAGGING HIM THROUGH THE WEST GATE AS WE SPEAK.

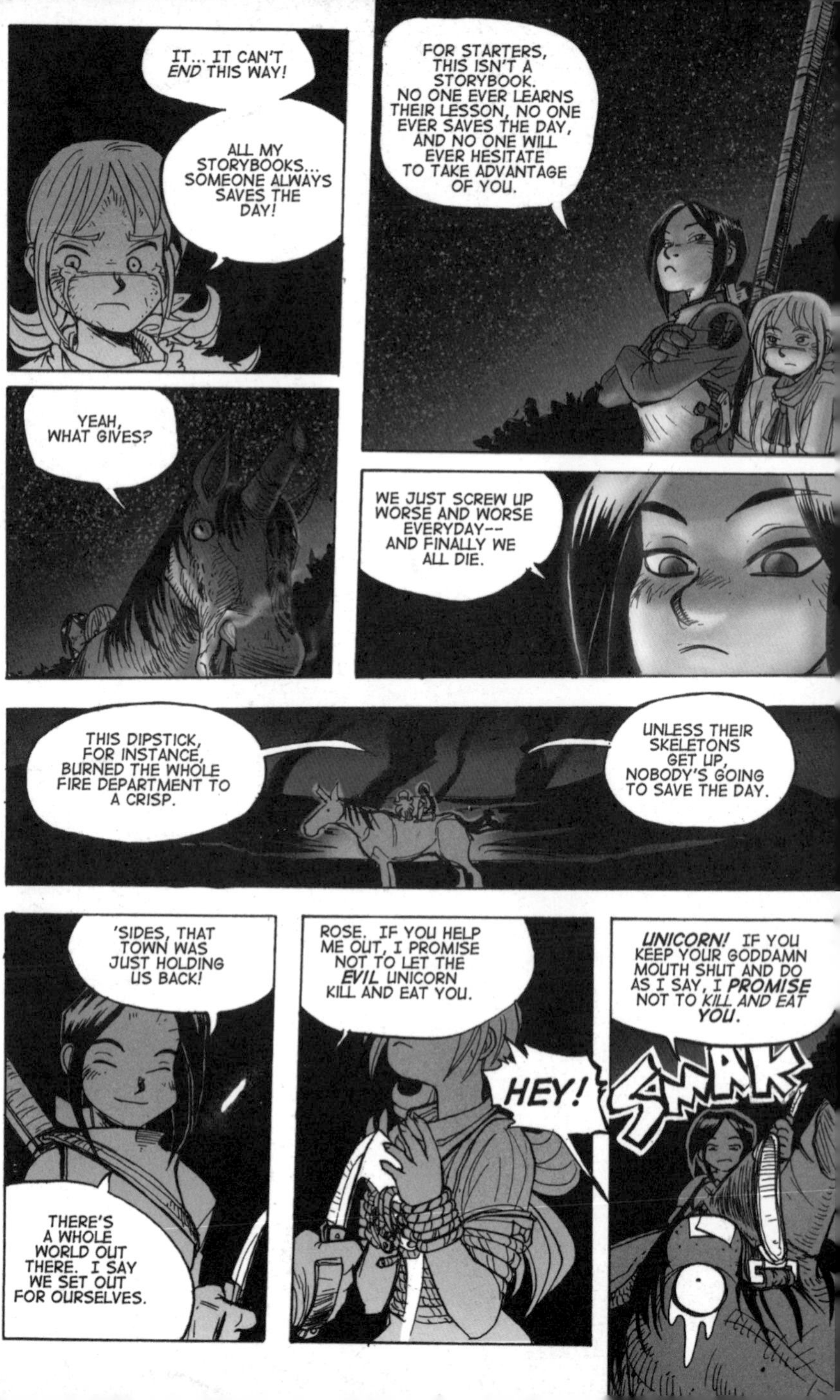
IT... IT CAN'T *END* THIS WAY!
ALL MY STORYBOOKS... SOMEONE ALWAYS SAVES THE DAY!
FOR STARTERS, THIS ISN'T A STORYBOOK. NO ONE EVER LEARNS THEIR LESSON, NO ONE EVER SAVES THE DAY, AND NO ONE WILL EVER HESITATE TO TAKE ADVANTAGE OF YOU.
YEAH, WHAT GIVES?
WE JUST SCREW UP WORSE AND WORSE EVERYDAY-- AND FINALLY WE ALL DIE.
THIS DIPSTICK, FOR INSTANCE, BURNED THE WHOLE FIRE DEPARTMENT TO A CRISP.
UNLESS THEIR SKELETONS GET UP, NOBODY'S GOING TO SAVE THE DAY.
'SIDES, THAT TOWN WAS JUST HOLDING US BACK!
THERE'S A WHOLE WORLD OUT THERE. I SAY WE SET OUT FOR OURSELVES.
ROSE. IF YOU HELP ME OUT, I PROMISE NOT TO LET THE *EVIL* UNICORN KILL AND EAT YOU.
HEY!
UNICORN! IF YOU KEEP YOUR GODDAMN MOUTH SHUT AND DO AS I SAY, I *PROMISE* NOT TO *KILL AND EAT YOU*.
SMAK

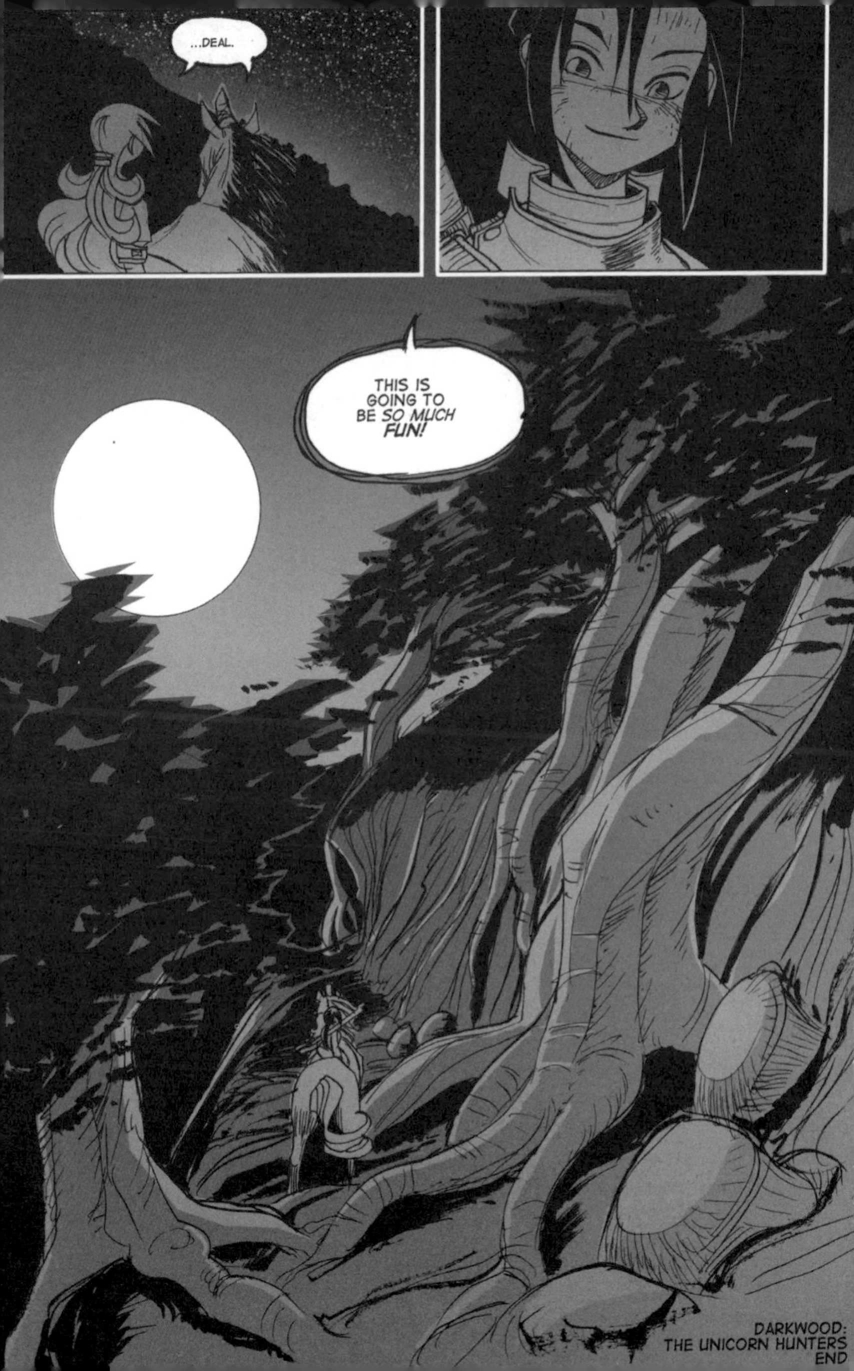
...DEAL.
THIS IS GOING TO BE SO MUCH FUN!
DARKWOOD: THE UNICORN HUNTERS END

NEXT TIME!

WE JOIN TRAVELING JOURNALIST IRA IN ISSUE FIVE OF DARKWOOD AS HE ADVENTURES ON AND FIGHTS EVIL IN THE ONLY WAY HE KNOWS HOW: BY RUNNING FOR HIS LIFE!

KIDS! BE LOOKING FOR LEGENDS FROM DARKWOOD ISSUE FIVE THIS FALL AT YOUR LOCAL COMICS RETAILER!

SHOCK! *FURRIES!* *HORROR!*

GOBLINS!

DECENCY LAWS!

WHATEVER WILL HE DO?

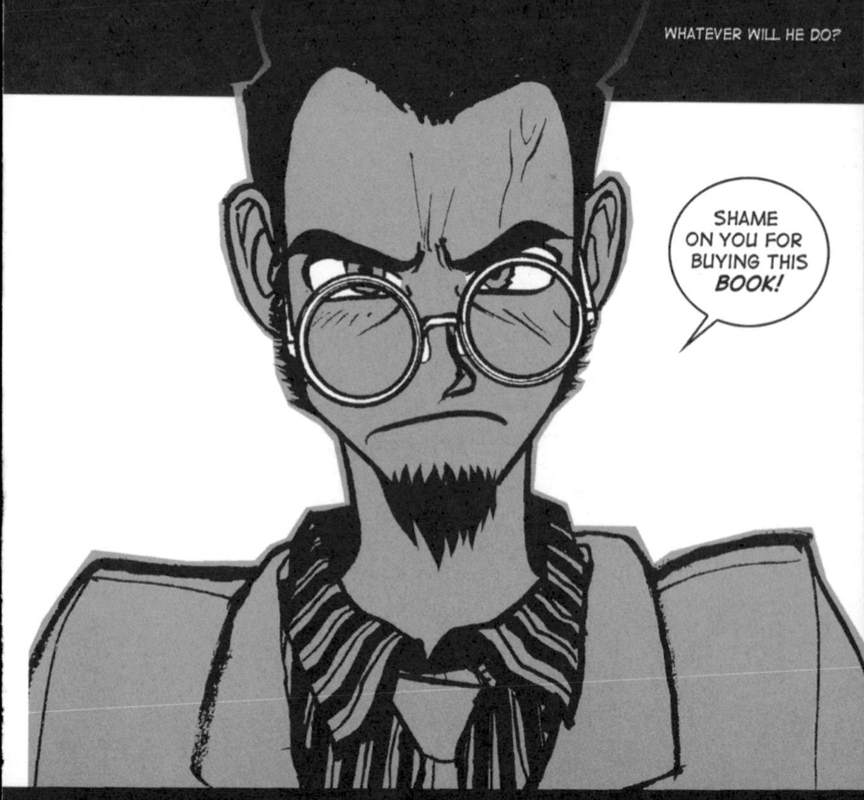
SHAME ON YOU FOR BUYING THIS *BOOK!*

BE SURE NOT TO MISS *LEGENDS FROM DARKWOOD: IRA AND THE EYE*

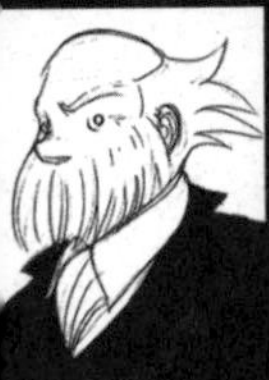

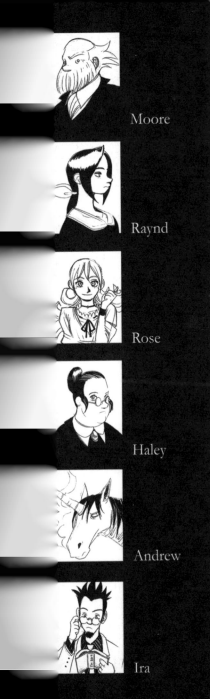

Moore

The mastermind behind Unicorntown, Moore is equal parts explorer, conqueror, and entrepreneur. Since the fire, he has begun preparations for an expedition deeper into the Western Forest.

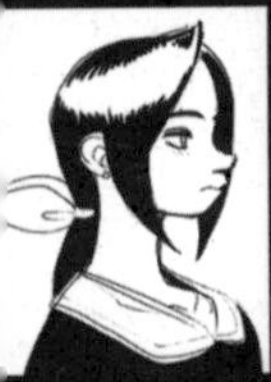

Raynd

Sole survivor of Moore's "Plan B", Raynd's exploitation of Nature's loopholes made Unicorntown thrive. Although technically unable to hunt unicorns, she has convinced Rose to help continue the rare creature trade.

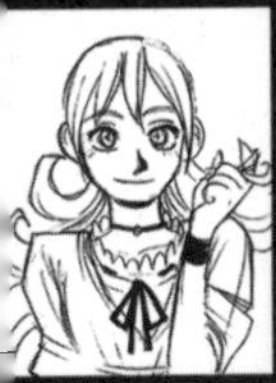

Rose

Moore's dippy, spoiled-brat daughter. Because of her princess complex, she devoted herself to destroying her father's empire. More or less kidnapped, she's now at the mercy of Raynd.

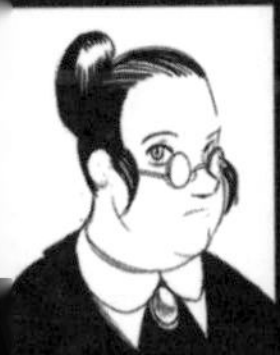

Haley

Nanny to the Moore clan. Almost a mother to Raynd and Rose. Possibly the only stable member of the Moore family.

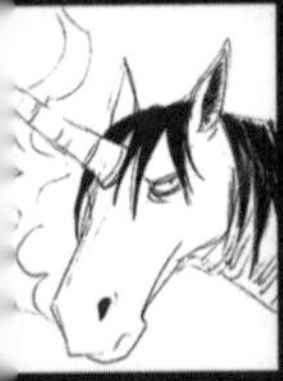

Andrew

Although he traded his soul for revenge on the "human creatures", he never got over his affinity for maidens. As long as Rose is Raynd's hostage, Andrew is her slave.

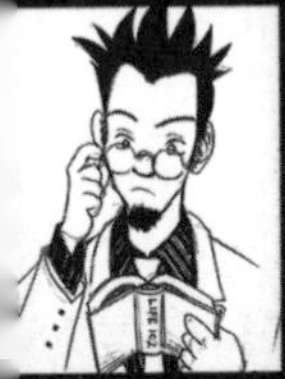

Ira

An intern for Kaldor's most popular food magazine, Ira resents his job. He hopes Moore's journal will result in some journalistic credibility. Currently, he is traveling with the Shanghai Trio.

Shikal

In an effort to bury the "adorable thief" stereotype, Shikal has expanded her areas of expertise to include chemistry, herbalism, and deep-sea fishing.

Des

A freelance adventurer (read: bounty hunter), Des has devoted himself to the study of marksmanship and fashion. Shikal and Amelia are his only known accomplices.

Amelia

Thanks to an astrological mix-up, Amelia was destined to be martyred in "The Neverending War Against Evil." Since escaping from her paladin escorts, Amelia has sworn revenge on the church, her orphanage, and the stars themselves. And become an alcoholic.

Fox

Combat entomology, animal-wrangling, and treasure-hunting come naturally to the spokeswoman of the Shanghai Trio. Although they consider themselves to be lawful monster hunters, their definition of "monster" is constantly rewritten.

Ringtail

The muscle of the Shanghai Trio, Ringtail is known for dispatching enemies with a fifteen-pound hammer. Those who have witnessed the Trio in action suggest this weapon is employed to turn an otherwise gruesome spectacle into a performance art.

Shanghai

One of the last remaining "War Sharpei", Shanghai is as large as a house and capable of speech. In addition to being the mount of the Shanghai Trio, he is also the leader.

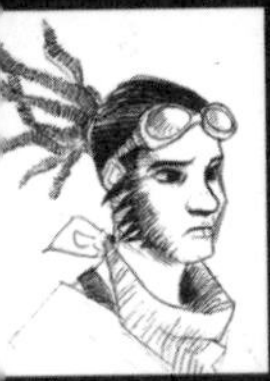

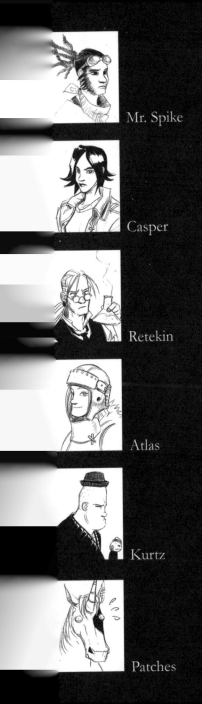

Mr. Spike

This Bay Area troubador was arrested for lewd conduct following a particularly spirited public performance. Since abandoning his music career, Mr. Spike has taken an interest in necromancy.

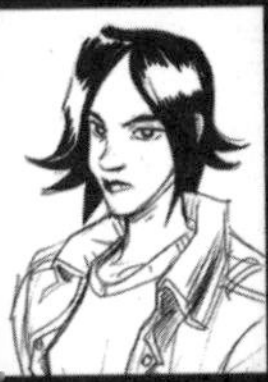

Casper

Former bassist and associate of Mr. Spike, Casper has found herself assisting in Spike's post-music moneymaking schemes. Marginally more levelheaded, her violent streak keeps him in line.

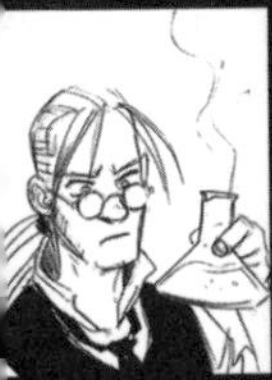

Retekin

The self-proclaimed "Smartest Man Alive," Retekin obsesses over fast vehicles, dangerous chemicals, and women (in that order). Retekin claims to have mastered flight and telepathy, but this has not yet been substantiated.

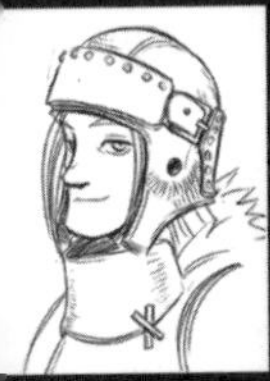

Atlas

A poster boy for the hero community, Atlas left his childhood village to quest for the "Dragon Thing," an item of "great and ancient power." En route, Atlas was killed and eaten. His village was destroyed.

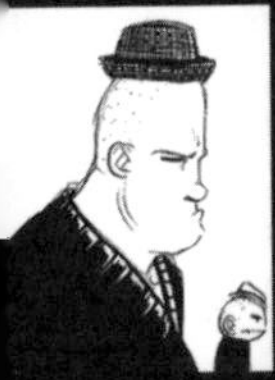

Kurtz

Proprietor of the Old Man With Map Tavern, Kurtz serves drinks to the seedier side of Unicorntown's adventurer population. Lil' Kurtz, his pet/assistant, helps to keep the inkmo customers in check.

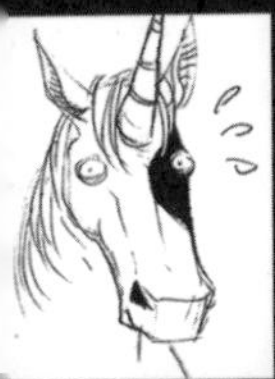

Patches

Patches is the only (surviving) witness to Andrew's infernal dealings. Now afraid of unicorns as well as humans, Patches lives in isolation.

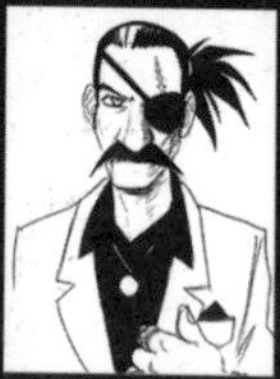

Sr. Espinosa

His art is the knife, and his life is a mystery... A violent, sexy mystery. A member of Moore's expedition, Sr. Espinosa is now the boss of organized crime in Unicorntown.

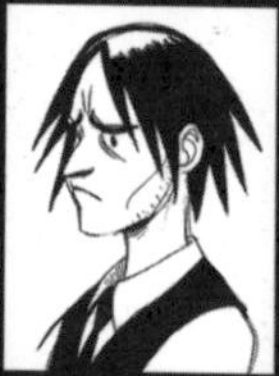

Mr. Exposition

Oral historian or shameless gossip, one thing is clear about Mr. Exposition: Whenever the authors need to set up a frame story, he will be there to dish out the goods.

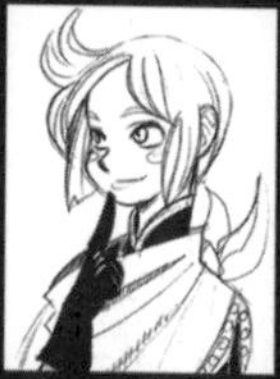

Carbuncle

Some say she's a kleptomaniac. Others think of her as a confused obsessive/compulsive. For whatever reason, nothing shiny or valuable is safe around this accomplished thief girl.

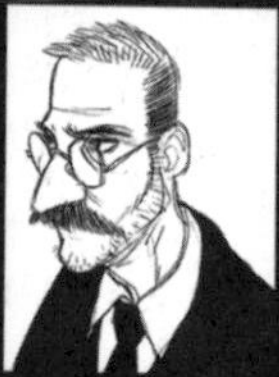

Pollock

Decades ago, Pollock was a celebrated inventor and one of his specialties was firearms. He is most likely the one who crafted Raynd's Rifle. A little older, a little more senile, Pollock is now Carbuncle's partner. No good will ever come of this.

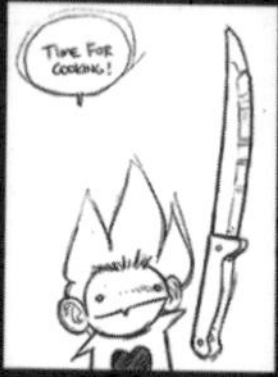
TIME FOR COOKING!

Inkmo

Touted as "the ultimate bait," this bizarre creature was meant to be cast into the sea on the end of a hook. Too greedy and clever to be trusted, this product never caught on. Since multiplying in the wild, inkmos have become the #1 pest in Darkwood.

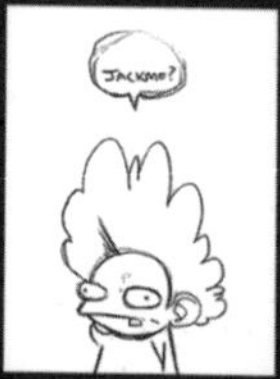
JACKMO?

Jackmo

An inkmo prototype. Though not as quick, they are considered to be dangerous to infants and small pets.

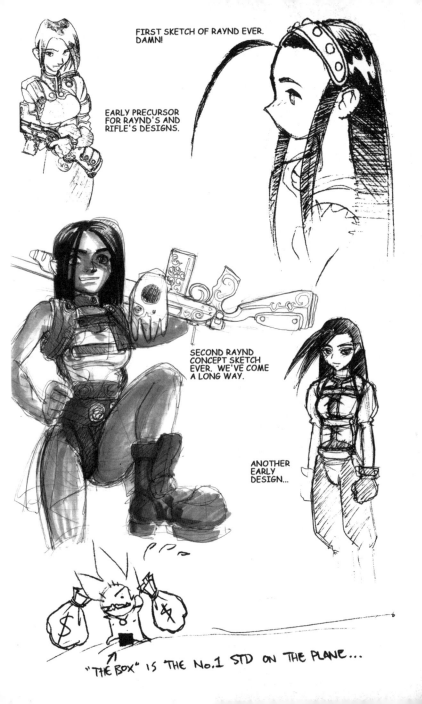

FIRST SKETCH OF RAYND EVER. DAMN!

EARLY PRECURSOR FOR RAYND'S AND RIFLE'S DESIGNS.

SECOND RAYND CONCEPT SKETCH EVER. WE'VE COME A LONG WAY.

ANOTHER EARLY DESIGN...

"THE BOX" IS THE No.1 STD ON THE PLANE...

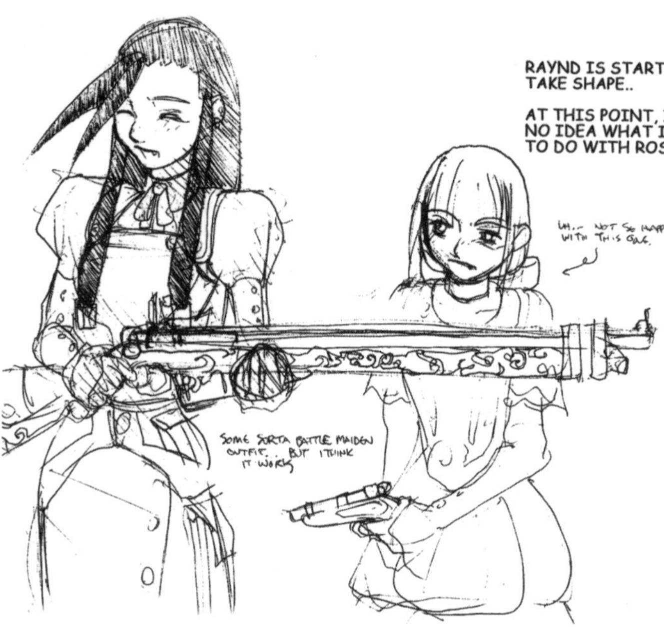
uh.. not so happy with this one.
Some sorta battle maiden outfit. But I think it works

RAYND IS STARTING TO TAKE SHAPE..

AT THIS POINT, I STILL HAVE NO IDEA WHAT I'M GOING TO DO WITH ROSE.

DESIGN FOR HOW ROSE COULD LOOK IN A FEW YEARS. THIS WAS MEANT MORE FOR FUN THAN TO BE A SERIOUS INDICATOR OF HOW WE MIGHT NEXT SEE HER.

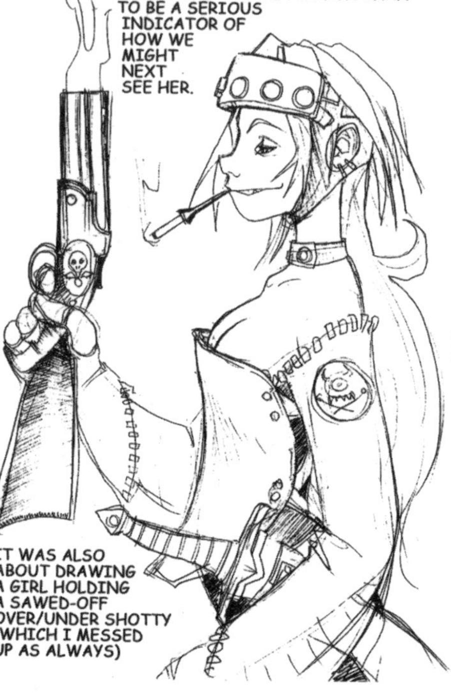

IT WAS ALSO ABOUT DRAWING A GIRL HOLDING A SAWED-OFF OVER/UNDER SHOTTY (WHICH I MESSED UP AS ALWAYS)

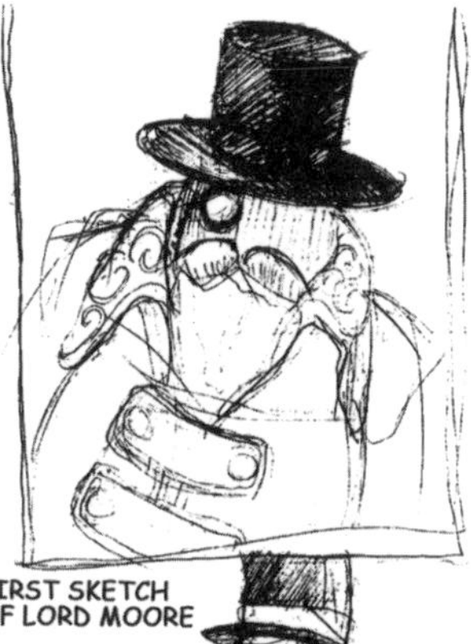

FIRST SKETCH OF LORD MOORE

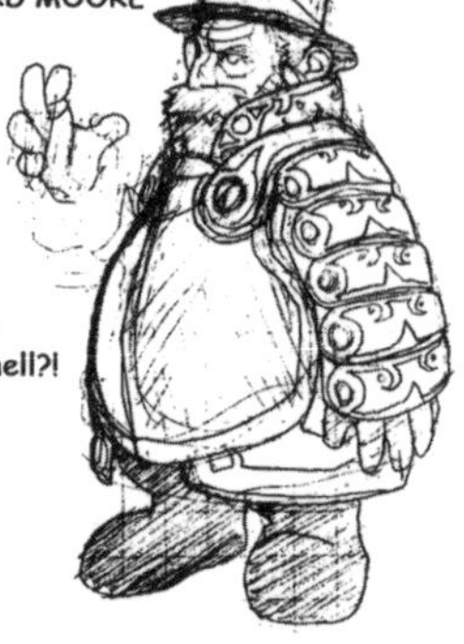

what the hell?!

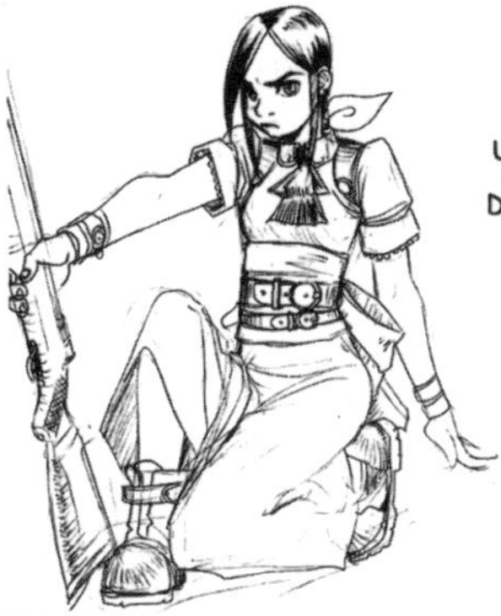

UNUSED
COVER
DESIGNS

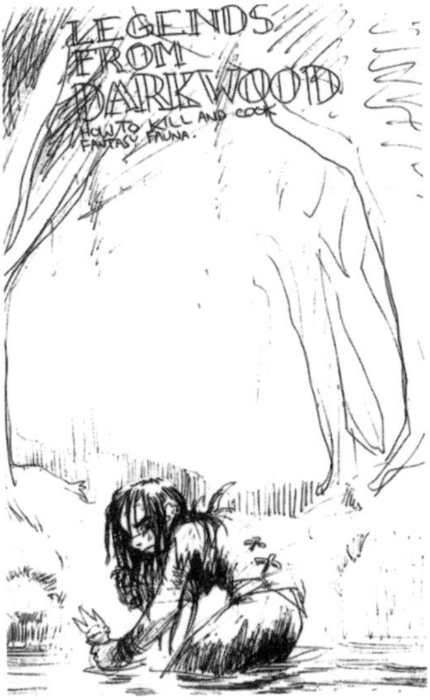
LEGENDS
FROM
DARKWOOD
HOW TO KILL AND COOK
FANTASY FAUNA.

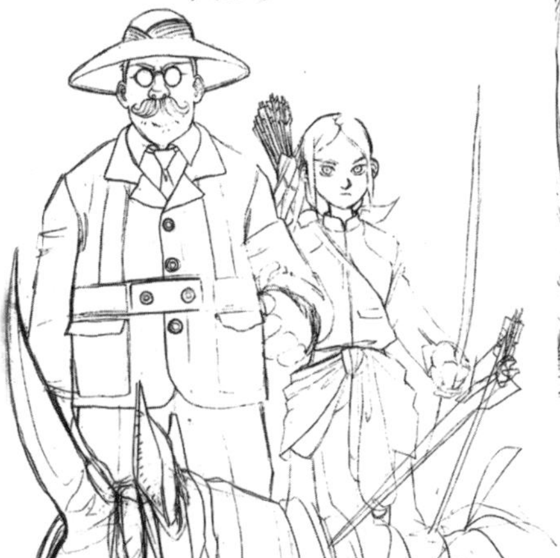

UNUSED PENCILS
FOR THIRD COVER

PENCILS FOR
UNUSED
FOURTH COVER

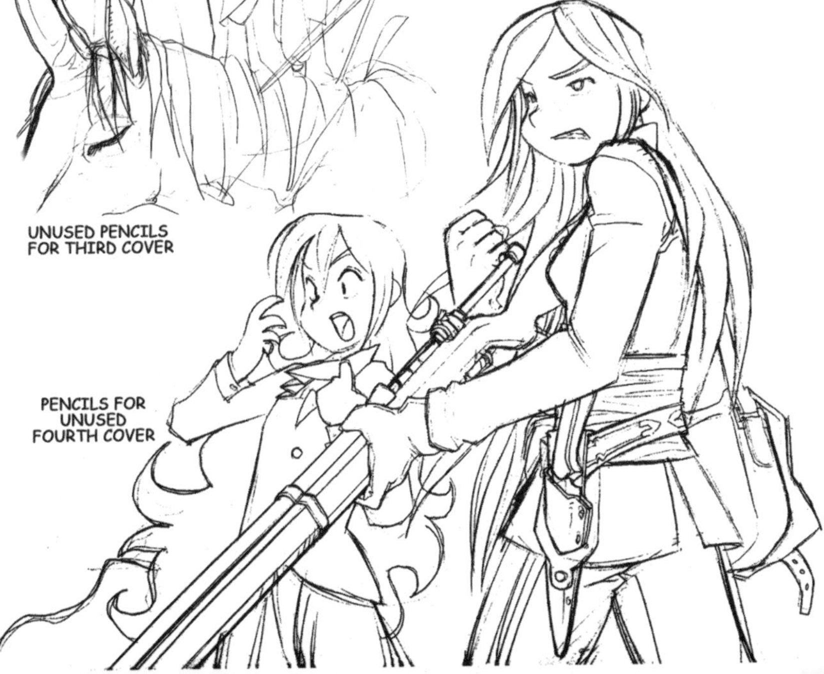

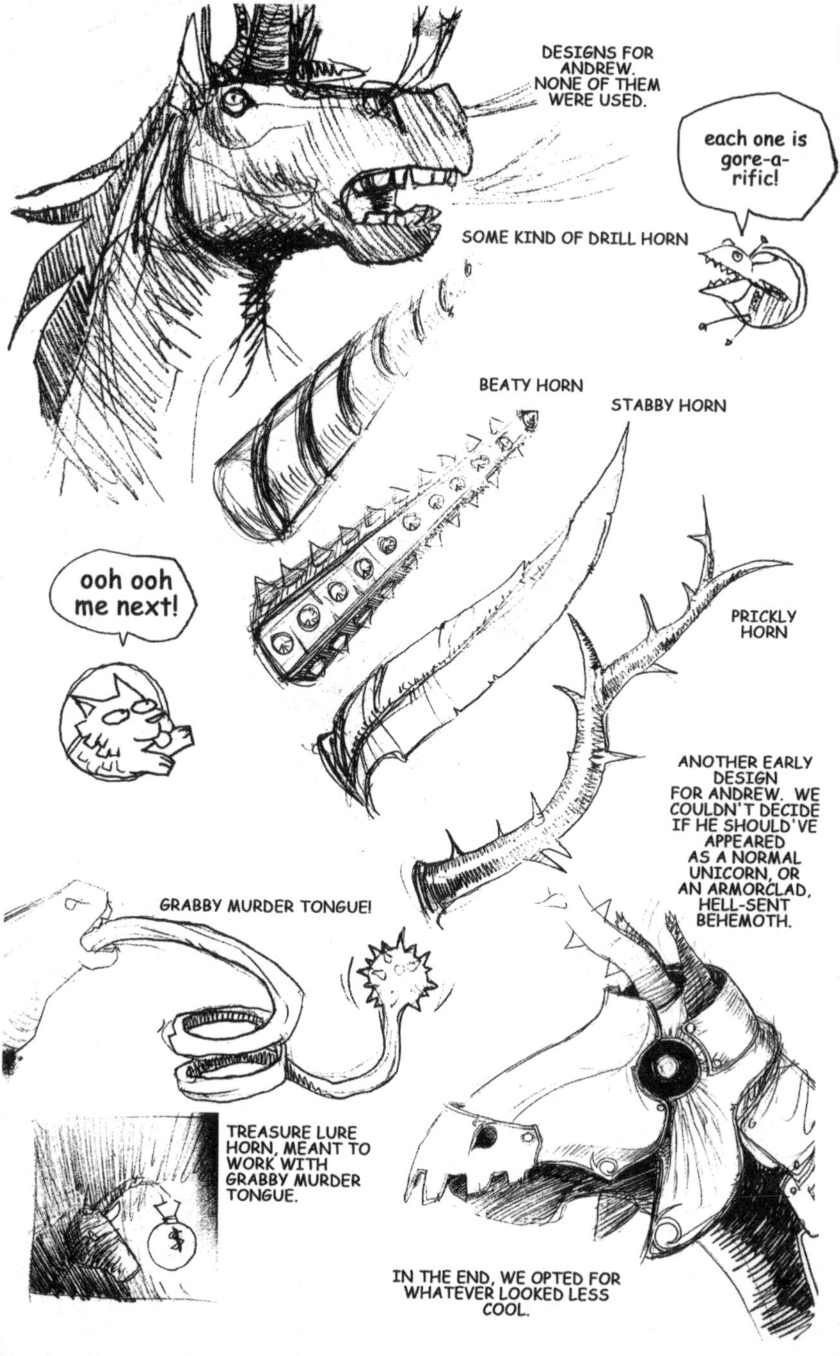
DESIGNS FOR ANDREW. NONE OF THEM WERE USED.
each one is gore-a-rific!
SOME KIND OF DRILL HORN
BEATY HORN
STABBY HORN
ooh ooh me next!
PRICKLY HORN
ANOTHER EARLY DESIGN FOR ANDREW. WE COULDN'T DECIDE IF HE SHOULD'VE APPEARED AS A NORMAL UNICORN, OR AN ARMORCLAD, HELL-SENT BEHEMOTH.
GRABBY MURDER TONGUE!
TREASURE LURE HORN, MEANT TO WORK WITH GRABBY MURDER TONGUE.
IN THE END, WE OPTED FOR WHATEVER LOOKED LESS COOL.

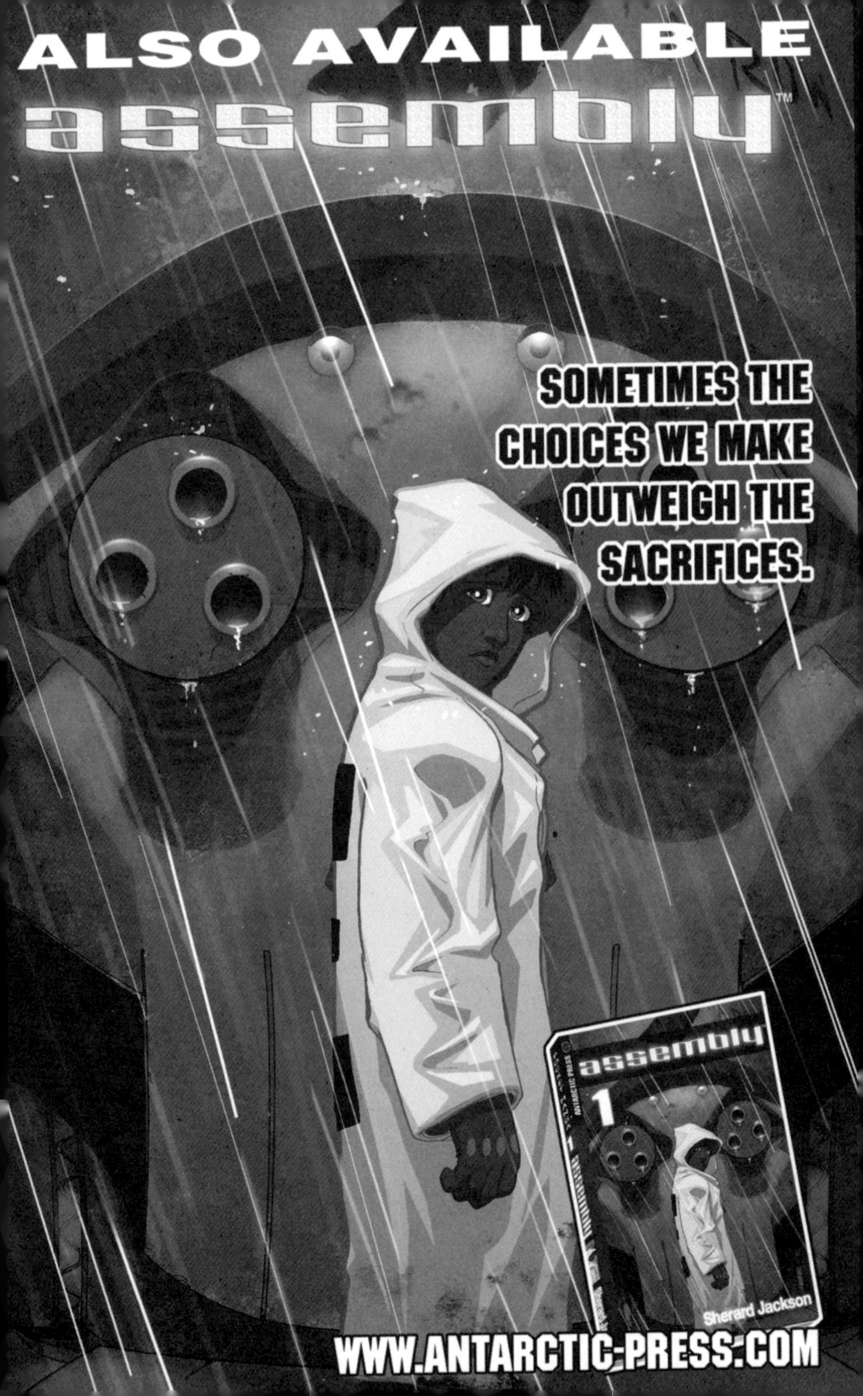
ALSO AVAILABLE
assembly™
SOMETIMES THE CHOICES WE MAKE OUTWEIGH THE SACRIFICES.
assembly
1
ANTARCTIC PRESS
Sherard Jackson
WWW.ANTARCTIC-PRESS.COM

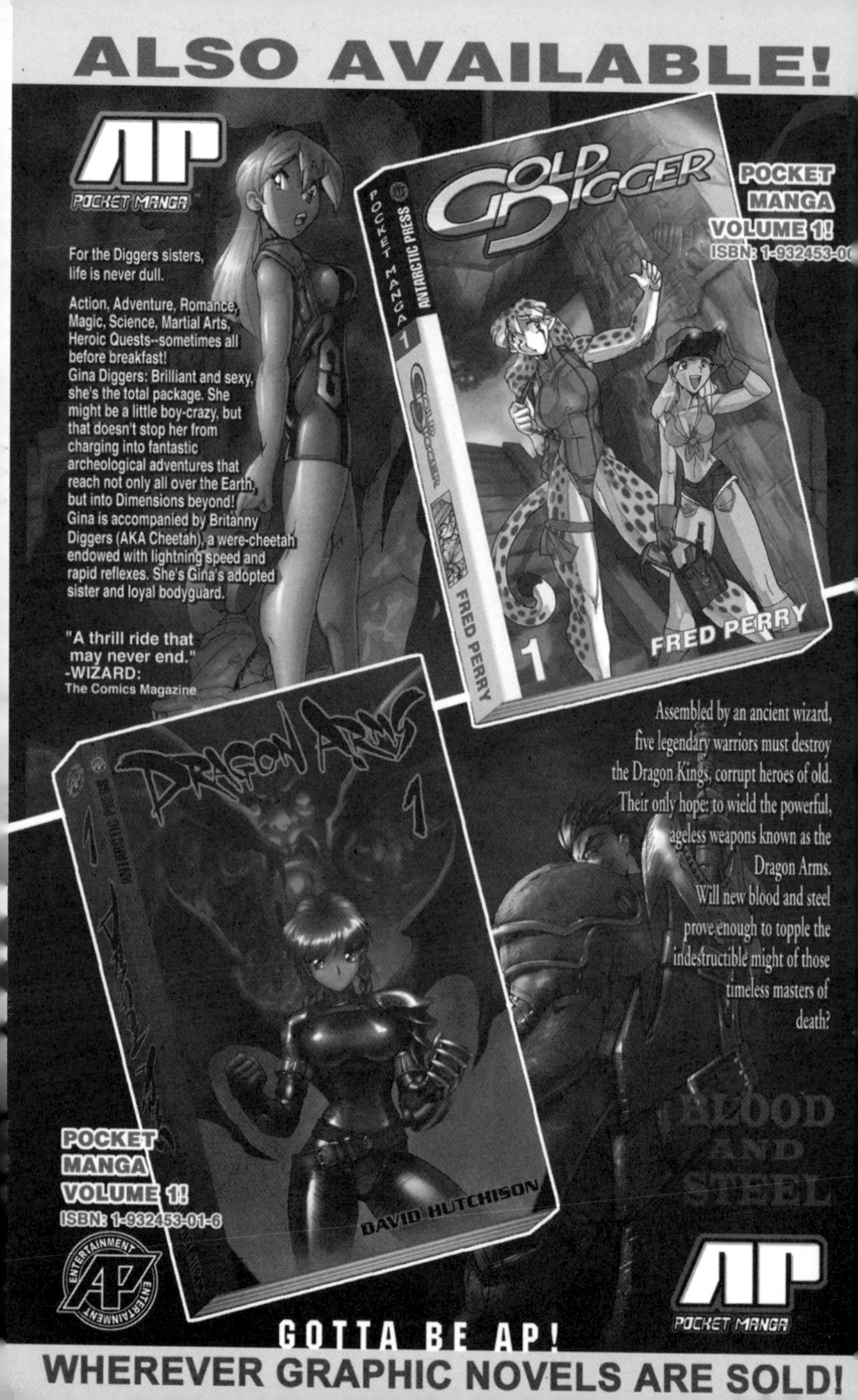
ALSO AVAILABLE!
POCKET MANGA
POCKET MANGA VOLUME 1!
ISBN: 1-932453-0
GOLD DIGGER
POCKET MANGA
ANTARCTIC PRESS
1
FRED PERRY
For the Diggers sisters, life is never dull.
Action, Adventure, Romance, Magic, Science, Martial Arts, Heroic Quests--sometimes all before breakfast!
Gina Diggers: Brilliant and sexy, she's the total package. She might be a little boy-crazy, but that doesn't stop her from charging into fantastic archeological adventures that reach not only all over the Earth, but into Dimensions beyond!
Gina is accompanied by Britanny Diggers (AKA Cheetah), a were-cheetah endowed with lightning speed and rapid reflexes. She's Gina's adopted sister and loyal bodyguard.
"A thrill ride that may never end." -WIZARD: The Comics Magazine
DRAGON ARMS
1
ANTARCTIC PRESS
DAVID HUTCHISON
Assembled by an ancient wizard, five legendary warriors must destroy the Dragon Kings, corrupt heroes of old. Their only hope: to wield the powerful, ageless weapons known as the Dragon Arms.
Will new blood and steel prove enough to topple the indestructible might of those timeless masters of death?
BLOOD AND STEEL
POCKET MANGA VOLUME 1!
ISBN: 1-932453-01-6
ENTERTAINMENT
POCKET MANGA
GOTTA BE AP!
WHEREVER GRAPHIC NOVELS ARE SOLD!

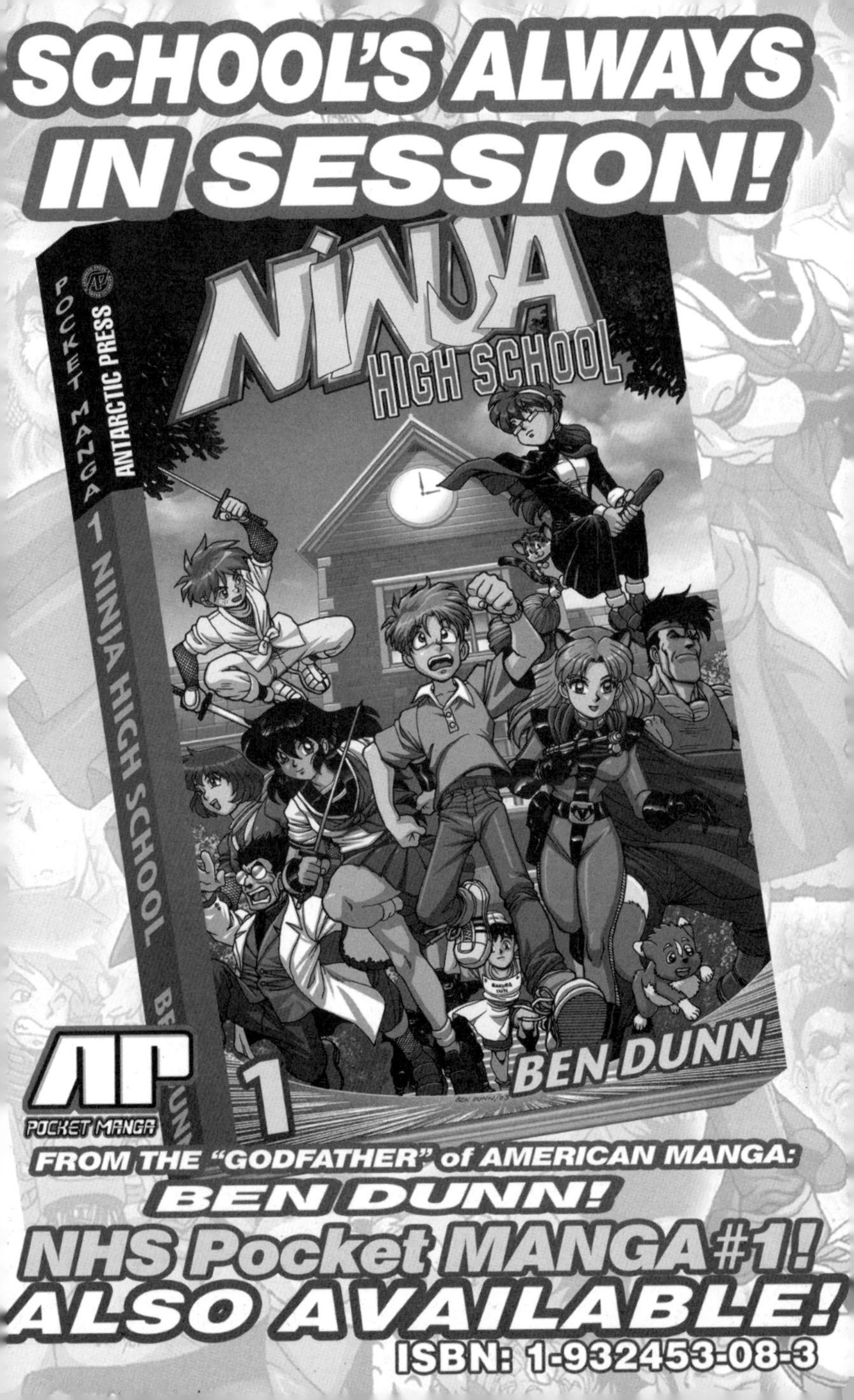

SCHOOL'S ALWAYS IN SESSION!
NINJA HIGH SCHOOL
POCKET MANGA
ANTARCTIC PRESS
1 NINJA HIGH SCHOOL
BEN DUNN
1
BEN DUNN
POCKET MANGA
FROM THE "GODFATHER" of AMERICAN MANGA:
BEN DUNN!
NHS Pocket MANGA #1!
ALSO AVAILABLE!
ISBN: 1-932453-08-3

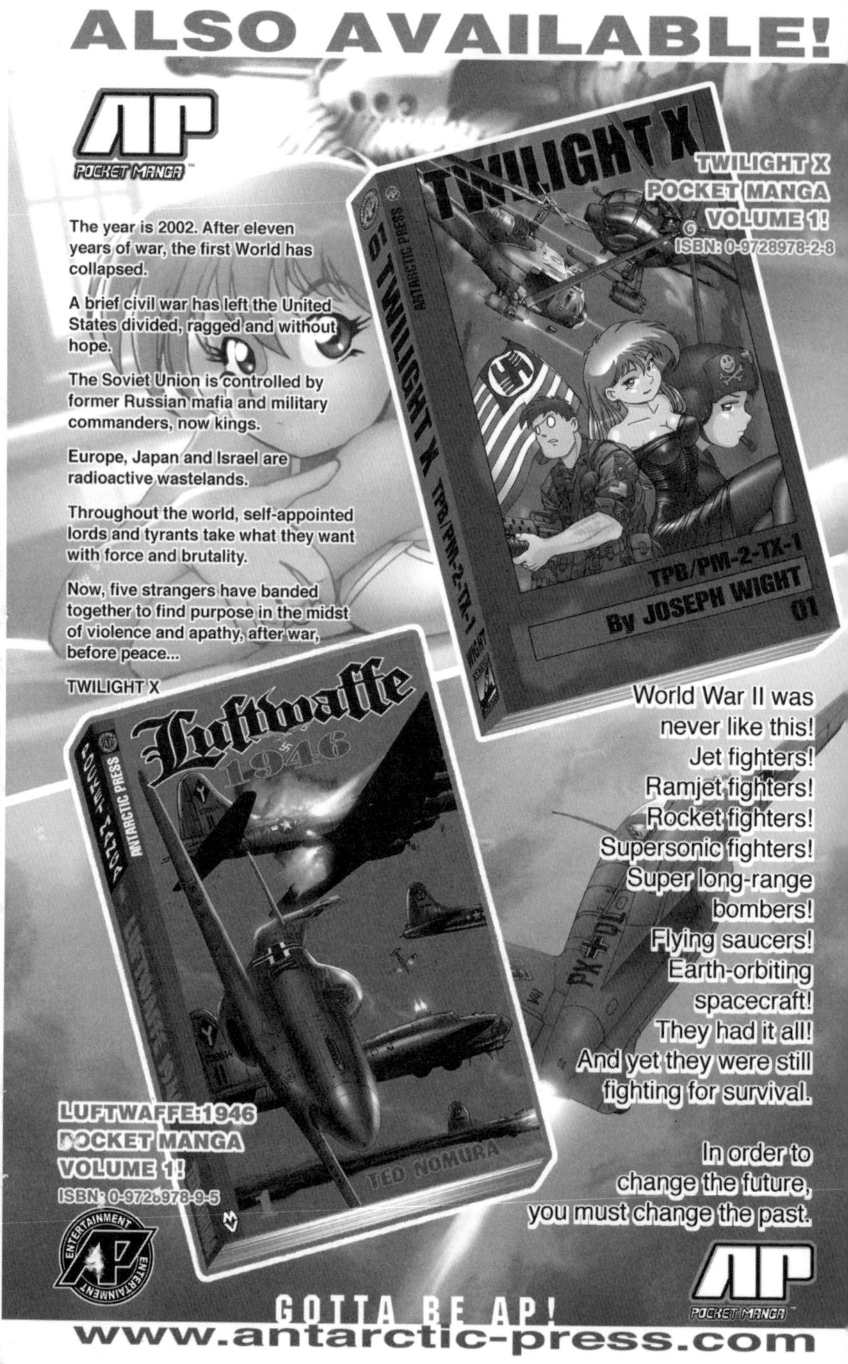
ALSO AVAILABLE!
AP POCKET MANGA
The year is 2002. After eleven years of war, the first World has collapsed.
A brief civil war has left the United States divided, ragged and without hope.
The Soviet Union is controlled by former Russian mafia and military commanders, now kings.
Europe, Japan and Israel are radioactive wastelands.
Throughout the world, self-appointed lords and tyrants take what they want with force and brutality.
Now, five strangers have banded together to find purpose in the midst of violence and apathy, after war, before peace...
TWILIGHT X
TWILIGHT X
POCKET MANGA
VOLUME 1!
ISBN: 0-9728978-2-8
TWILIGHT X
TPB/PM-2-TX-1
By JOSEPH WIGHT
01
ANTARCTIC PRESS
Luftwaffe 1946
ANTARCTIC PRESS
TED NOMURA
World War II was never like this!
Jet fighters!
Ramjet fighters!
Rocket fighters!
Supersonic fighters!
Super long-range bombers!
Flying saucers!
Earth-orbiting spacecraft!
They had it all!
And yet they were still fighting for survival.
In order to change the future, you must change the past.
LUFTWAFFE:1946
POCKET MANGA
VOLUME 1!
ISBN: 0-9728978-9-5
AP ENTERTAINMENT
AP POCKET MANGA
GOTTA BE AP!
www.antarctic-press.com